WRITING FOR THE GREEN LIGHT

Tailor your screenplay to sell. Find out what Hollywood script readers, producers, and studio executives want in a screenplay (and why) from someone who's been there. Discover what it takes to begin a lasting career as a screenwriter.

Peppered with interviews from established professionals, *Writing for the Green Light: How to Make Your Script the One Hollywood Notices* gives you a sharp competitive edge by showcasing dozens of everyday events that go on at the studios but are rarely if ever discussed in most screenwriting books. With his behind-the-scenes perspective, Scott Kirkpatrick shows you why the system works the way it does and how you can use its unwritten rules to your advantage. He answers such questions as:

- Who actually reads your script?
- How do you pique the interest of studios and decision-makers?
- What do agents, producers, and production companies need in a script?
- How much is a script worth?
- What are the best genres for new writers and why?
- What are real steps you can take to 'break in' to television writing?
- How do you best present or pitch a project without looking desperate?
- How do you negotiate a contract without an agent?
- How do you exude confidence and seal your first deal?

These and other insights are sure to give you and your screenplay a leg-up for success in this competitive landscape!

Scott Kirkpatrick is the Director of Distribution for MarVista Entertainment, a Los Angeles-based production and distribution company that produces original Lifetime and Syfy channel films, co-produces TV movies with Disney and Nickelodeon, and has managed international TV deals on major franchises including *Mighty Morphin Power Rangers*, *Digimon*, and *Julius Jr.* Scott has also produced and directed TV series and feature films including *Eye for an Eye*, *Muslims in America*, and *Roadside Massacre*.

WRITING FOR THE GREEN LIGHT

How to Make Your Script *the One* Hollywood Notices

Scott Kirkpatrick

Focal Press
Taylor & Francis Group

NEW YORK AND LONDON

First published 2015

by Focal Press
70 Blanchard Road, Suite 402, Burlington, MA 01803

and by Focal Press
2 Park Square, Milton Park, Abingdon, Oxon OX14 4RN

Focal Press is an imprint of the Taylor & Francis Group, an informa business

Library of Congress Cataloging-in-Publication Data

A catalog record for this book has been requested.

ISBN: 978-1-138-85645-5 (hbk)
ISBN: 978-1-138-01646-0 (pbk)
ISBN: 978-1-315-78100-6 (ebk)

Typeset in Palatino LT Std
By Apex CoVantage, LLC

Certified Sourcing
www.sfiprogram.org
SFI-00453

Printed and bound in the United States of America
by Edwards Brothers Malloy

For my wife, Soha

Bound to Create

You are a creator.

Whatever your form of expression — photography, filmmaking, animation, games, audio, media communication, web design, or theatre — you simply want to create without limitation. Bound by nothing except your own creativity and determination.

Focal Press can help.

For over 75 years Focal has published books that support your creative goals. Our founder, Andor Kraszna-Krausz, established Focal in 1938 so you could have access to leading-edge expert knowledge, techniques, and tools that allow you to create without constraint. We strive to create exceptional, engaging, and practical content that helps you master your passion.

Focal Press and you.

Bound to create.

We'd love to hear how we've helped
you create. Share your experience:
www.focalpress.com/boundtocreate

 Focal Press
Taylor & Francis Group

CONTENTS

ACKNOWLEDGMENTS   ix
INTRODUCTION   1

Chapter One   A CRAZY LITTLE THING CALLED
                 "HOLLYWOOD LOGIC"   5
                 What agents, producers, and development
                 executives at production companies *need* in
                 a script to make it worth spending money on.

Chapter Two   "SO, WHAT'S IT ABOUT?"   23
                 Which genres get produced, which genres
                 don't, and why. . . . Plus, the six best genres
                 for first-time spec scripts.

Chapter Three   WRITING YOUR FEATURE-LENGTH
                 SPEC SCRIPT   55
                 How to transform an idea into a market-ready
                 spec script while including all the points it
                 needs to get past the reader's desk.

Chapter Four   HOW I LEARNED TO STOP WORRYING
                 AND WRITE FOR TELEVISION   75
                 Understanding how to wedge yourself inside
                 Hollywood's TV landscape by building a
                 valuable portfolio of sample TV spec scripts
                 and learning television's real entry points
                 for success.

Chapter Five   CLOSE ENCOUNTERS OF THE L.A. KIND   94
                 Who you need to know and how to contact
                 them; plus, how to fake confidence so you
                 can pitch your script (and yourself) in the
                 way Hollywood needs to hear.

Chapter Six   TO LIVE AND WRITE IN L.A.   114
                 Living the life of a professional Hollywood
                 writer: Protecting your ideas, negotiating
                 your own contracts, and managing
                 your reputation.

Chapter Seven   "GOLD-MINE" GENRES . . . NOW
                 AND *FOREVER*   132
                 Understanding where Hollywood is going
                 and how to get ahead of the curve by
                 following the *principles* of the movie business
                 instead of chasing trends.

APPENDICES   139
Appendix I   Script Coverage   140
Appendix II   The Non-Union Writer-for-Hire Agreement   145
Appendix III   The Non-Union Option / Purchase Agreement   158

GLOSSARY   All the fancy (and confusing) acronyms that get
               tossed around and what they really mean.   175

INDEX   185

ABOUT THE AUTHOR   191

ACKNOWLEDGMENTS

I cannot offer enough thanks to my wife, Soha, for all the support and encouragement she's provided in pushing me forward through each step of this journey. Not only is she my best friend, she's my most trusted professional colleague and confidant (who I'm eternally grateful to have in my life).

To my editors, Dennis McGonagle and Peter Linsley (and to everyone at Focal Press and Taylor & Francis)—thank you for all of your guidance. You have been nothing short of accommodating; I hope this is the first of many!

And a big thanks to all of those who contributed not just directly to this book, but also to many of the professional experiences that led to its creation: Akim Anastopoulo, Nathan Atkins and Amanda Phillips Atkins, Erik Bork, Jason Brubaker, Chad Gervich, Ken Lee at Michael Wiese Productions, everyone at MarVista Entertainment, Donie Nelson, Michael Prince, my mentor Paul Rich, Reem Saleh, and to my parents Joyce and Ralph Kirkpatrick and my sister Jenny for all the years you put up with my endless—and at times *obnoxious*—obsession with the movies.

INTRODUCTION

If you're reading this book, I'm assuming you (or someone close to you) want to be a professional Hollywood screenwriter. Maybe people have told you you're crazy for choosing such a path, but it makes perfect sense to me. Hollywood is a billion-dollar per year industry and someone has to write all those scripts—maybe you've already taken a crack at writing a spec script or two and you're just curious about next steps.

But let's get realistic for a moment: being a great storyteller, rattling off a few ideas to some friends, or even writing a feature-length screenplay cost you nothing but time. . . . Yet, for the studio or production company you're hoping will acquire and adapt your script into a full-on movie, this process costs a ton of money. Unless you intend on producing a film based upon your own script (and funding it out of your own pocket), you're going to need some solid advice on how to get your screenplay in front of the right people and learn how to talk about it with those who have an entirely different motivation than you for telling stories and producing movies: to make money distributing the *finished* version of the movie you've written.

WHO IS THIS GUY?

The first thing you need to know about me is that I am not a screenwriter. The second is that my job is one of the most important during the lifespan of any movie—only you'll never see my name listed in the credits or on the posters of any of the films with which I'm associated.

I'm a film and TV distribution and development executive. . . . Sometimes called a sales agent or a "suit." I sell the rights to movies and TV shows, both here in the United States and throughout the world. I'm the business guy that the producers and financiers of completed films hire in order to make all their money back—with a heavy profit on top, of course. I'm also the guy production companies bring on to advise which films they should produce for their next slate to guarantee the largest margin of profit—and if there weren't people like me with the specific job of knowing exactly how movies make money, there would be few producers out there investing money into making films in the first place.

Ever wonder how a movie gets from picture lock on an editor's hard drive into movie theatres, television, or even onto your smart phone? Or, how a movie gets onto the playlist of an airplane's seat console or broadcast in a foreign language overseas? That's my world. I'm the guy working behind the scenes of the film industry to get the movies I'm hired to distribute from point A to B in the most visible and profitable manner possible.

I go to all the fancy events: Cannes Film Festival, Berlin, American Film Market. . . . I've worked with big-time Hollywood players and been associated with films budgeted in excess of $100 million and those with budgets of less than $10,000. I've aided in financing and preselling films, have served projects during their development and production phases, and have made huge profits for my employers on unknown foreign gems no one else gave a second thought to.

So why would I write a book on screenwriting? Because I can tell you everything about how the business of Hollywood actually works and how you can best position yourself to be taken seriously as a screenwriter by the very people you need to impress the most: managers, producers, and development executives at production companies. I can tell you what kinds of scripts they need, how they work, and how they like to be approached by new writers. Most importantly, I know exactly what the Hollywood system depends upon and how you can best place yourself to be seen as the one most capable in providing it.

I say all this because when I was starting out, following my own big Hollywood dreams, I devoured every book on screenwriting, directing, and producing I could get my hands on. All of them provided fantastic insight into working on set or how things operated in the idealized studio system, but few of them ever gave a glimpse into the steps one actually needed to take to find realistic opportunities to begin their careers. Without real-world guidance, it's nearly impossible for any Hollywood newbie to present their work—or themselves—to anyone who can make a difference in their career paths. Rather than see anyone waste as much time as I did figuring out how the movie business works via trial and error, I'd much rather cut to the chase and simply lay out all the ground rules on navigating your screenwriting career in the most efficient and direct way possible.

In a city where every busboy, auto mechanic, and real estate agent has a script they're secretly writing on the side—each looking for that same big break you are—you're going to need every piece of info you can absorb in order to stand out from a sea of wannabes and be taken seriously by the industry's decision-makers.

HOW TO USE THIS BOOK

Writing for the Green Light is not for those only interested in the craft of screen-writing or for those looking for some easy "get-rich-quick" approach to the business; this book is purely about how to jump-start your career in the actual working world of Hollywood. I'm not asking you to sell out or go against your principles, instead I am asking you to consider the demands of the Hollywood system and what the writer's role is within the day-to-day film business. If it truly is your goal to establish your credibility as a professional screenwriter, then you first need to secure for yourself a reputation as a writer who knows how to deliver a ready-to-go script that meets the needs of the Hollywood system, on time and within an expected budget range.

From there, you'll get interest from agents and managers who will push and promote you to production companies, who will in turn commission your talents, which will eventually provide you with legit writing credits. After that, you can steer your career in any direction you choose—which is what most big-name writers have done. But for now, I'm simply providing you with all the details you'll need in order to cross the career bridge all other resources rarely seem to offer any practical advice on.

All that said, it's important for me to come clean and admit that while on the one hand I am completely guilty of pushing clichéd poster art and encouraging rushed rewrites of scripts for dull TV movies, on the other hand I know what gets a project funded and what gets a completed film sold—and if money isn't coming back into an investor's pockets, then there's zero point for anyone to buy your script (or anyone else's) in the first place.

This "insider info" approach simply does not exist anywhere else in the marketplace, especially not for screenwriters. The vast majority of screen-writing books out there seemingly regurgitate the same old information, focusing on things like screenplay format or on what page Act II should begin. . . . But none of these give you real insight into what to actually do with a script once it's completed, offer qualified advice on how to talk about your script in a professional way, or even what your script is worth in the marketplace. In other words, I won't waste your time with character arcs or genre theory because there are plenty of college professors and textbooks out there that can do that job more effectively than me. I'm much more interested in helping you know practical bits of information, like how much you should be getting paid and how to negotiate your own writing contracts—things that you're somehow just supposed to know yet are shunned for asking.

The information I'm providing in *Writing for the Green Light* won't be given in a vague way, either; I'll be very transparent, blunt, and detailed, not only regarding what works in Hollywood, but also *why*—which is the key component that most other books fail to mention.

Truth is, most novice screenwriters I meet are extremely talented and passionate individuals who more than possess the skills and stamina required to deliver a well-written feature-length screenplay and to build a writing career. The problem is that most writers consistently write the wrong type of script or pitch it in the wrong manner, getting themselves nowhere in the process. Their circles of friends, advisors, and contacts offer well-intentioned yet out-of-date advice, and writers continuously find themselves left clueless, having no idea where (or how) to ever begin.

Not only can *Writing for the Green Light* put any novice head and shoulders above the competition by simply narrowing their focus to what the industry depends upon, it will help them navigate through dozens of everyday events that few screenwriting books ever approach. Things like whether it's actually wise to sign with an agent or union, how to find good connections at film festivals and markets, or even basics like how to get your work in front of the right people.

The title says it all, *Writing for the Green Light: How to Make Your Script the One Hollywood Notices*. If a writer has questions beyond the mechanics and craft of screenplay format, this is where they'll find the answers.

ONE

A CRAZY LITTLE THING CALLED "HOLLYWOOD LOGIC"

In this first chapter we'll lay out the ground rules on why the Hollywood system works the way it does and how distribution and production companies develop their projects from the inside out. From there we'll go into how these companies decide which scripts—or, rather, which writers—make the cut, as well as what steps you'll need to take to get yourself positioned at the top of a development executive's list of writing candidates.

LAST THINGS FIRST

Far too many screenwriting books spend the bulk of their pages yammering on about format and structure and then, at the very end, cram in a shoddily written chapter on what to do with your script after it's completed. This used to bug me to no end. They take the most important aspect of screenwriting (earning money from your efforts by selling your script and seeing your work produced) and skim over it like it's not really relevant to becoming a working professional. Of course, writing a quality script that's well-structured and "fresh" is important, but if it just sits on your desk collecting dust, what's the point? Even more shameful, some of the best "how-to-write-a-screenplay" books out there still attribute selling your script to "pure luck."

Your success being a screenwriter has nothing to do with luck. . . . Your ability to go from a hopeful novice with a great idea knocking around between your ears and transform yourself into a professionally working Hollywood screenwriter has everything to do with only one thing: understanding the *business* of the film industry.

HOLLYWOOD HIERARCHY

When people think "Hollywood," they picture red-carpet premieres, big studio productions, and A-list celebrities. . . . But while all eyes continually stay fixated on this flashy (and closed-off) studio-dominated corner of the industry, few books or resources ever discuss the area of Hollywood that I work in—which happens to be most open and accommodating to new writers: *Independent Hollywood*.

'Indie Hollywood' includes everything outside of the traditional studio system. Although independent theatrical titles (including art-house Sundance dramas) technically classify as Indie Hollywood, they represent only a small fraction of the real commercial bulk. The best examples of *real* Indie Hollywood in action include things like original TV movies (not for premium channels like HBO, but for basic cable feeds like SyFy, Lifetime, or Hallmark) and even "Direct-to" entertainment (such as Direct-to-DVD or Direct-to-VOD level titles).

Despite the fact that Independent Hollywood is often disregarded as a small subset of the industry, it actually supplies the *majority* of Hollywood's overall content—well over 80 percent! Studio Hollywood might get most of the attention for their mega-budgeted reboots, but behind the scenes Indie Hollywood is really the engine that keeps the whole entertainment machine in motion. Want proof? Hop on Netflix. . . . Sure, you'll see a big studio film listed up top, but augmenting those titles are several movies you've probably never heard of—that's Independent Hollywood at work (and you'll notice there are four to five "indie" titles for every one studio film out there). You'll see this same ratio everywhere, whether flipping through channels on TV, skimming available films at a Red Box kiosk, or scrolling through titles on iTunes, Amazon, or Vudu.

For you—as a newbie novice writer—it's not the closed-off studio corner of Hollywood where you'll find your most direct entry point to screenwriting success; it's in the independent zone. And not only is this space the most wide-open to novices in terms of "breaking in" and opportunity, it's also the fastest way of putting together the necessary building blocks you'll need to eventually breach the fortified walls of those big studios later on.

A WALK ON THE INDIE SIDE

Let me first give you a quick overview of what I do within Independent Hollywood—that way I can better explain not just the types of scripts distributors and development executives (like myself) need from writers, but also how we actually look for those scripts and later commission work from newbie writers just like you.

Above I mention Netflix and those four to five "other movies" that augment the one studio title. . . . I'm the guy that gets those "other" movies placed there. What I mean to say is that I have discussions with acquisitions executives at Netflix (employees tasked with finding and buying movies) and I broker deals with them directly. I'm also the guy who secures those same titles a place on TV channels, in Red Box kiosks, or gets them placed as physical DVDs on shelves at retail stores. This doesn't mean I drive around Los Angeles with a trunk full of DVD screeners trying to hawk the actual units; I simply present my available titles to the appropriate buyers at each respective company (in person, over lunch, by phone, or by email), negotiate a few terms, and then enter into a contract with them.

I don't do this work as an individual; I work as a salaried employee for a distribution and production company. And none of these outlet companies (like Netflix, Red Box, or TV channels) pay me anything directly; they pay my employer. After each deal is closed and the money is paid, the outlet companies get to sell our movies and my employer pays me a commission (on top of my salary) for a job well done.

This commission then incentivizes me to go back into the marketplace to find more movies so that I can close more deals and keep the process in motion. Before I list out where I go search for those new other movies, let's first be completely transparent that *none* of these outlet companies are required to buy anything from me. . . . They only buy what they need. So when I'm out in the marketplace looking for new movies to add to our company's catalogue of available films, I use the buying interests and patterns of each of these companies as my filter.

Most consumers out there (meaning the *average* movie-goers who are simply looking for a piece of evening entertainment, not the "movie obsessed," like you and me) simply want easy access to the big studio titles. They want the latest [*Fill-in-the-Blank Hollywood Blockbuster*]. In order for outlet companies to drive consumers to their services, their buying teams will pay top dollar to acquire high-end studio titles so that they can display them front and center. The problem is that only a handful (between six to ten) legit studio films get released to these outlet companies each month. That's far too few to keep the average customer engaged.

And here's the real kicker: Studio movies are so expensive for these companies to acquire and place on their platforms that they'd actually be losing money if they only offered those six to ten rotating titles. So to counter this loss, they expand their offerings by picking up add-on "filler" movies and TV programs from Indie Hollywood; that way each customer has more titles to skim through, screen, and/or transact upon—and this is exactly where a company like the one I work for enters the picture. We help these outlet companies and channels fill in the gaps so that they can continue to acquire those big-time studio movies—which keeps their customers engaged, therefore keeping them in business. . . . As long as they're in business, they'll need people like me to continue supplying them with all those other movies to augment their studio offerings.

But the concept of a filler movie is a bit of a misnomer. As already stated, these outlet companies don't have to buy anything just because I'm selling it. However, if I want to keep my job (and keep earning my commissions), I need to make sure that my employers are making money. In order to do this, I need to ensure I'm able to consistently and reliably present my acquisitions contacts with a steady flow of "other movies" that serve *their* company's needs best (that is, films that are well produced, based on quality scripts, and that meet specific genre conventions). Otherwise, there'd be no deals for me to close. And given my close proximity to each of these companies' acquisitions agents—who tell me in extreme detail what they need—I literally have a recipe mapped out in my head for *exactly* what types of films move the needle.

Most of those outside the distribution business assume we find these "other movies" at film festivals or that they're based on scripts submitted to us from agents—true, but those films only account for about 35 percent of our overall catalogue. Here's the problem in a nutshell: Because the needs of our outlet companies (with whom we're trying to do business) are very specific, it makes our exact content needs very specific—and it's really hard to find available movies or spec scripts that perfectly fit into the mold.

So, rather than spending a great deal of time sifting through endless feature-film submissions looking for that perfect gem or reading the bottomless stacks of spec script submissions, we simply cut out the excess workload and develop what we're on the hunt for ourselves. In other words, we "invent" the content we need on our own (within our company walls), *then* we move forward to develop and produce it.

WHERE YOU FIT IN

So if distribution and development executives (like me) working within the indie space simply invent the movies and TV content we need, why would we schedule pitch meetings with writers and spend time reading your spec script submissions?

Even though we're predetermining and developing the movies we need, very few of us have the required skillsets (or the time) to put these ideas into a quality script. . . . But you do. We might know what sells (and how to sell it), but we need *you* to take those ideas and build a script around them. So when Hollywood's readers and creative executives take time to read your script submissions, they're not actually focused on whether or not they'd buy your script; they're focused on how well you write and what upcoming projects of ours that you might be a good fit for. In other words, your spec scripts are more about showcasing who you are and what talents you can bring to the table.

So the first step towards getting Hollywood to pay attention to you (and your work) is by proving you're a writer that can deliver scripts the system needs and can work with, meaning your scripts will be considered ones that potentially *help* companies make more money and beat out their competition—those are the scripts that move forward in the system. Scripts that don't help distribution companies get rejected and go nowhere. Understanding and embracing this key concept is a crucial first step for a novice writer to fully transform into a professional working Hollywood screenwriter.

Don't take this to mean you have to dumb down your ideas or that our side of the business doesn't fully appreciate the skills required to write a quality script (quite the contrary). . . . We just need to ensure that your creativity and talents are getting applied towards the projects that gain traction with our outlet clients.

A professional screenwriter is not simply dishing out scripts he or she *thinks* are great ideas, and they don't chase the latest big studio trends or fads; instead, they're carefully *crafting* their scripts to meet the real-world supply-and-demand needs of Indie Hollywood. And they are writing them specifically for companies, like the ones I work for, that are open to working with their content—meaning they're purposely writing for mid-level independent producers and production companies, *not studios*.

Therefore, your job as a novice screenwriter is to write spec scripts that show you have the talent *and* the understanding to become a professional. That's the real trick in standing out to managers, producers, and development executives.

THE HOLLYWOOD "HEDGE" EFFECT

As already mentioned, just because we distributors very carefully engineer movies we think would be perfect for our U.S.-based outlet companies doesn't mean they'll buy them. And no matter how great of friends I might become with my acquisitions contacts, none of them will close a deal with me until they can screen the movies I'm selling in full. That means the distribution and production company I work for must fully produce these films *before* I can sell them domestically. This is a major dilemma because that means someone must foot the bill to kick-start the whole project—and despite common belief, it's not us . . . if a project tanks, we *do not* want to be left holding the bag.

So who pays for all this stuff?

I'm going to introduce you to the only fancy finance word you'll ever need to know: "hedge." To hedge something simply means to reduce its level of risk. The phrase "hedge your bets" basically translates into "reduce the amount of damage *losing* those bets will cost you." Therefore, if one were to "hedge his/her investment," he or she would be insuring against a level of loss if the investment turns out to be a poor one.

How does hedging apply to the real world of screenwriting and filmmaking? Producing a movie is a very high-risk investment because all the funds pooled into a film's budget need to be spent (in full) for the film to reach completion. If the film cannot be completed, then it cannot be sold and there's zero potential for profit. That means the closer a film gets toward its own completion, the more money has been spent and the more liability (hot water) the investors are in should the project fall apart.

To add fuel to the fire, movies take a really long time to finish; during that time there's no guarantee that any number of variables won't go wrong, causing the film's budget to run out midway through. Actors get sick, locations change, crews go on strike, and natural disasters can happen anywhere. Without proper management and oversight during each phase of the movie-making process, it's very easy to see how a project could spiral out of control in no time, causing a sinkhole of financial ruin in the process.

If a big studio wants to produce a $100 million film, it's not doing so for the love of cinema or the expectation of making an amazing vision come to life; that studio is producing it because it expects to make that $100 million back plus a major profit margin. But $100 million is a heck of a lot of money to spend solo. So, that studio hedges its investment by basing that film off a book or other proven "audience-grabbing idea," like a franchise or an earlier film (a reboot); they then place money-securing well-known A-list actors in the leading roles (such as Denzel Washington or Angelina Jolie) and hire on a director with a proven track record to manage the production effectively (like Michael Bay or Zack Snyder)—which, in reality, means a director who will follow orders from the producers and executives telling him or her to work harder, faster, and cheaper (far from the film school fantasy of "authorship").

But studios don't just produce and release one film per year; they hedge their overall annual investments by producing a multitude of productions (twenty to thirty annually), each with a very clear and identifiable genre for a predictable audience. That way, if one film bombs, another might soar at the box office, and the difference evens out.

Still, dishing out $100 million on potentially several films at once puts a studio into a major cash deficit—which is why they refuse to do it. Can you blame them? Imagine a life where each January you had to pay your entire year's worth of bills (including car payments, insurance premiums, and rent) all at once. . . . Even for a staunch penny-pinching saver, this would put you in a tough spot at the grocery store come February (and hopefully you wouldn't have any auto-trouble in the near future). Studios don't like that scenario either, so they further hedge their investments by bringing in other studios or outside firms to help share the risk by coproducing/cofinancing films together—meaning they each earn smaller profits if the film is successful but also hold a smaller level of risk if that film tanks.

This is why when some movies begin you'll see the studio logo followed by the logos of three or four other companies, all of whom are collectively "presenting" the title. . . . Each of them "secured" money from their respective sources. But where does all this money come from and how to these companies secure it?

GUARANTEED PLACEMENT: OUTPUT
DEALS AND FOREIGN PRESALES

Just as our U.S.-based outlet companies use big studio movies to garner attention from consumers in order to keep dollars flowing towards their platforms, the same principle holds true globally.

So, if a top TV channel in Australia or DVD distributor in Korea wants to keep ahead of their own respective competition (within their own country's borders), they'd want to find a way to gain "first access" to the content that sells the best—Hollywood studio films. However, contract negotiations on a per-title basis can be horrendously slow and could put the Aussie TV channel or Korean DVD distributor into a price war with their competitors (which is good for the studio, but bad for long term business in the region—as well as their bank accounts). To counter this, both sides have devised a very smart way to simplify the whole process. . . . They enter into an output deal.

An output deal is a long term agreement (ranging anywhere from three to fifteen years) where the buying client agrees to purchase a minimum number of films from the selling client—for a pre-negotiated and fixed price that's fair to the seller, but also reasonable for the buyer. There can be subtle nuances in these agreements (for example, the buyer may get "first look" at the movies just in case one or two of them won't work for his or her clients), but for the most part this is a pretty solid way for a studio to financially guarantee a certain minimum amount of revenue to be received from a given region of the world in a way that doesn't put the buyer in too much risk. This way when a studio executive is attempting to get a project green-lit internally, they have a concrete dollar-amount to apply to that film's bottom line. Multiply this concept across the twenty to thirty pictures the studios release each year by the fact that each studio has several output deals covering the top fifty economically sound countries or regions (U.K., France, Germany, Japan, etc.), and you have a pretty solid system for stable cash flow.

Presales, on the other hand, utilize this same concept of guaranteed placement but generally only for one title at a time. The buying client is either unwilling or uninterested in entering a full-on output deal but does want to have first access to a new title. Distribution executives and sales agents will work alongside their internal production teams to piece together high-concept films that will sell internationally but will *also* meet the needs of domestic outlet companies and that have a high probability of garnering a presale (based on good name cast attachments, solid genre, etc.). Then, they'll head into the international marketplace (during events like Cannes or AFM) and meet with their foreign buyers to pitch their new "in development" slates. If a buyer likes one of the films, he or she will sign a contract to "pre-buy" (or pre-secure) that film's rights. The agreement is set up in a way where that buyer does *not* have to pay anything up-front (or perhaps only a very small amount, such as 10 percent, in "good faith"); they only pay the full amount once the film is finished, which works for the buyer because they're not fronting too much cash in advance, but it also works for the distribution executives and sales agents because if they can secure enough presales, they can essentially go to a bank and present all their presale agreements to have a line of credit extended for that one particular project.

Although any Hollywood hopeful can buy round trip airfare to Cannes, purchase a market badge, and set-up a booth to advertise and promote their project ideas, they'll find that very few buyers will be receptive to pre-buy their pitch. . . . Only those studios and distribution companies with solid infrastructure coupled with a reliable (and proven) ability to deliver the movies that meet their buyers' needs see return business. But nevertheless, from the studio level and across the indie zone, output deals and presales are the real way movies are funded. The buyers must already be lined up, cash in hand, via a secured agreement.

ANALYSIS PARALYSIS

Don't make the mistake of believing that just because studios have intelligently padded themselves against damages that they are suddenly immune to risk or that they "should be" releasing more artsy/diversified content. Studios don't want a flop of any size. . . . They want to make what people want to see and they want every film they release to be in the black. Why? Besides the obvious benefits from earning profits, they need steady and reliable success in order to keep their output clients and cofinancing partners happy, committed, and willing to continue their participation in the investment supply line. As a result, studios and distributors are victims of a syndrome known as "analysis paralysis"—meaning they don't make a move until the dollars make sense. . . . Hard numbers do the talking in boardrooms and executives are completely trapped by imaginary obstacles made up entirely of data. In short, if a project or concept does not have a high likelihood of a financial return—whether by proven target audience, output deal, or secured presales—it simply doesn't get made.

That's why you see so many reboots and remakes. People like to discuss (or complain about) how this is a new phenomenon, but it's not. Cecil B. DeMille made *The Ten Commandments* twice, first as a silent B&W (1923) and then later as a widescreen color epic (1956), and *I Love Lucy* (1951–1957) was a reboot of a radio show called *My Favorite Husband* (1948–1951).

The other fundamental lesson to draw from this is that studio content is heavily vetted long in advance and is almost never pulled from spec scripts or blind submissions. There will always be those occasional stories that Hollywood Hopefuls might quickly pull from their back pockets about "so-and-so, who mailed a treatment to Warner Bros. and received a check for millions." I've never heard of that happening and can safely confirm it never would. Spec scripts simply do *not* go from a novice's apartment to a studio release.

BUT THAT'S THEM, WHAT ABOUT US?

This process is all well and good at the studio level, but studios have access to resources (financial partners, output deals, theatrical structures, etc.) no one else in the business does, right? Not quite.

The independent world actually works the same way. Smaller distribution and production companies (like the ones I work for) might make films direct for home entertainment or Direct-to-TV that cost only a few hundred thousand dollars versus several million, but it's not like you'll see people in the indie zone jumping up and down, ecstatically shoveling out large sums of cash (and thus exposing themselves to large amounts of risk). Even if our companies had the cash, you'll never see us willing to sink it all into just one or two films with nothing but a hope we'll make all our money back. We too spread the risk and work with international presales, output deals, and financial partners.

Just like the studios, independents first map out an approximate value of what the film is worth and where they can secure the funds before they even flirt with a green light. (The ironic part is that outside the United States, the big studios *and* the independents all work with the same international companies.)

Take this concept even further down, all the way to the extremely speculative level—meaning a group of friends who decide to go at it alone and make their own movie. Novice filmmakers also employ the system of hedging by pooling their money into a project so that they all chip in a fair share, and no one bites off more than he or she can chew. Whether by cashing in savings accounts or maxing out credit cards, they share the financial risk by spreading out responsibility. They also, unfortunately, share in the burden of a 100 percent loss more often than not, because unlike the studio system or the indie zone, most speculative filmmakers have no clue what to do with their project *after* it's done—just like most novice screenwriters.

But this last example actually outlines the most crucial point in understanding who's who within the Hollywood landscape. If there's one simple concept that's most vital for you to walk away from this book understanding, it's fully grasping what separates the professionals from the *non*-professionals in the industry: **Professionals have a solid plan for where their content is going *before* they spend a dime making it; *non*-professionals work on spec and can only hope their efforts will be noticed (and compensated for) after completion.** In other words, professionals follow proven data, from which they develop a real-world strategy; *non*-professionals just kinda guess . . .

For a studio to green-light a $100 million film, it knows approximately how much it can charge from foreign clients and financial partners in advance, the market value of the cast, and the current analytics of its target audience. A studio knows who it's making the film for and will go well out of its way to deliver, to the best of its knowledge and ability, what that specific audience wants in the most entertaining way possible. It also knows a great deal on how best to reach that audience, so that it can generate the most buzz possible. Additionally, that studio has a complete system of knowledge on how to exploit every possible line of profit that could ever be generated and perfectly caters its films (products) to the marketplace. This doesn't guarantee success (e.g., Disney's *The Lone Ranger* (2013), which was a studio-level flop), but this certainly puts the studio in a much more likely scenario of, at worst, breaking even.

A non-professional writer or filmmaker, on the other hand, usually spends months (sometimes years) putting together a single project he or she assumes is exactly what the industry wants, only to have their efforts sit on their desk and generate zero opportunities. I see it happen every year at Cannes or AFM. Hopeful screenwriters come in wanting to know "what's selling," meaning which types of films seem to have the most interest. If I say the truth and mention something like "zombie films are really selling this year," that writer might just go and spend the next twelve months writing a zombie film. That doesn't mean his or her zombie script will be any good, nor does it mean companies are (or will be) actively looking into acquiring zombie film scripts once he or she finished. He or she just, unfortunately hears about the trend and attempts to jump on board long after the ship has sailed, without understanding the principle of how his or her spec script fits into the overall picture.

HOLLYWOOD'S BIGGEST SECRET

Now for the big secret that almost never gets told to anyone outside Hollywood's professional walls: Most films are green-lit before a final script exists.

Think this is crazy? It's not; it's absolutely the truth. If a studio or an independent production company knows who their audience is, knows what channels and platforms will showcase their finished film, and understands how much such a project should cost, don't you think they'd also know in advance how the story should be written to best meet the expectations of the clients? And if these professionals can successfully sell movies before they're completed, don't you think they can sell the same film before a script has been written?

The answer is yes, we can. . . . And we do it all the time.

One of my favorite films sums up this process better than any other: Tim Burton's biopic *Ed Wood* (1994). In the early part of the movie, an energetic Ed Wood enters the office of producer George Weiss. Wood is ready to pitch himself as the ultimate writer/director combo; Weiss couldn't care less but is in need of a director for his latest picture. Wood asks, "Is there a script?" to which Weiss replies: "Fuck no, but there's a poster!"

It might sound absurd, but this is how the real business of Hollywood operates. But before you go judging Hollywood execs for being callous or superficial, let's illustrate this in a more down-to-earth way. . . . It's Friday night and you're browsing the shelves of your favorite old-school DVD rental store (or perhaps you're kicking back at home, logged onto one of our outlet companies like Netflix or Hulu Plus). You're scrolling through looking at films, debating which one to watch. How are you making the decision about which film is worth your time to watch? Are you first searching the internet for pirated copies of the scripts for each film one-by-one and reading them to decide? Or are you using signifiers, such as title, artwork, cast/director names, or genre, to make your selection? We're human! We get overwhelmed with too many selections and we like assistance on finding the right type of film that really meets our needs. And if the artwork alone isn't doing it, we're always open to hearing the suggestions of the guy working behind the counter who's made some good recommendations in the past, or simply following what suggestions Netflix and Hulu have algorithmically calculated on our behalf. That artwork/trailer is "pitching" the film to you, selling you that it's the one most worth your time on this particular night. Do you fall for it? We all pick a dud from time to time, but overall I suspect you're quite savvy at seeing through gimmicky artwork.

Distributors (like me) use the same technique when selling (and preselling) films. Unlike studios that have the leverage of A-list talent and mega-franchises to secure guaranteed placement, in the indie zone we have to hustle.

PITCHING THE *MOVIE*, NOT THE SCRIPT

The best way to presell a property is not handing a client or financial partner a 100-page stack of paper to read. . . . It's to show them what the film will look like once it's completed, by presenting the marketing elements such as a one-sheet, poster, or sizzle reel. We're pitching the *finished movie* to them, not the script. This allows the client to see the film in his or her own mind so that he or she can sense the scale, the style, and the look of the production. He or she can quickly assess how much money the company can earn from such a title, and thus how much money is worth investing—and he or she can just as quickly decide such a project is not worth their time and simply ask, "What else do you have?" Once a potential client or financier is intrigued by the idea, then we can give him or her a script—but if no script exists, it's not exactly a deal breaker for us (nor for the movie's future). In fact, some companies prefer working with production companies on "concepts" that they sketch out together. If a company knows what works best for its audience, it's more advantageous to craft a film to their needs versus spending large quantities of time chasing leads and hoping to find something good enough to fill the void.

PRESALES: THE ART OF REVERSE ENGINEERING

INT. HOLLYWOOD PROD. OFFICE — CONF. ROOM — DAY

Two executives, SCOTT KIRKPATRICK, a mid-30s very handsome sales executive (you'd do the same if it were your book) and his BOSS, are reviewing a detailed spreadsheet report titled "Cannes Film Festival — Buyer's List." The list has hundreds of names and contact details neatly categorized. The walls of the conference room are full of framed movie posters with recognizable stars.

                    BOSS
    Oh look, our top pre-buyer from Japan
    is attending. Be sure to schedule a
    meeting with her.

                    ME
    Already done. I have her scheduled to
    meet at our booth on Thursday.

                    BOSS
    Perfect. We need to figure out something
    we're going to sell her though. We
    already secured her with the volcano
    disaster film?

                    ME
    Yes, they pre-bought it.

                    BOSS
    Tell her that we're in development on a
    new one, something with a giant tsunami,
    something simple, like *Mega-Tsunami*.

I scribble a note on a sheet of scrap paper.

                    ME
    If she asks for the script or cast, I'll
    just say it's confidential for now.

                    BOSS
    However you want to handle it. Call
    Michelle in marketing and have her whip
    up a poster. Actually, title it some-
    thing with a number: *9.6 Mega-Tsunami*,
    that way it'll show up at the top of all
    the lists on the digital platforms. Put
    a bunch of fire and a collapsing building
    on the cover.

                    (skimming list)
    Okay, next . . .

The above conversation happened almost word-for-word. . . . And similar conversations happen across Hollywood in conference rooms every day.

Although *9.6 Mega-Tsunami* doesn't actually exist, there was indeed a disaster film our company presold that year and later produced (and broadcast on major U.S. TV networks amongst many other channels worldwide), that was literally created on the fly exactly as stated above.

Why? Well in our case, the Japanese DVD/VOD market had very high demand for disaster films at the moment, and our company had a strong reputation in the business for producing them. To be honest, many territories love disaster films; it just so happened we were reviewing a list of clients from Japan when my boss realized we had a dearth of new disaster films available to sell.

A large foreign-based distribution company—like the one from Japan referred to above—will send their own acquisitions executives to all the major film and TV markets to find new content. Sales agents; distribution executives (like me) will schedule meetings with buyers and present our "line-ups" (or "slates") of new films. As already explained, on strong potential projects—and after some healthy negotiation—the buyers will "pre-buy" the rights to these films for a set cost, usually a standard percentage of the total budget. The sales agent drafts an agreement with clear stages outlined for how the money will be dished out. But agreeing to put down a large sum of money on a project that doesn't yet exist is risky business, so this practice is only done when a buyer is working with a sales agent he or she personally trusts or who represents a company with a strong reputation of delivering films as promised.

When our team secured presales in Japan, Germany, Russia/CIS, and Australia—plus a few smaller countries—the budget of *9.6 Mega-Tsunami* was almost fully funded before a single frame was shot. Again, not anyone can just go into the marketplace blindly and pull a stunt like that; the company I was working for already had a proven track record of being able to produce such films at a certain anticipated quality level *and* we had presold and delivered several films to this client in the past. We already had a name, brand, and secure reputation in the business, which is why our clients were willing to front all the cash—no different than with the major studios.

But let's stop and go back for a moment: After my initial sales meeting, I did exactly as my Boss asked. I walked over to "Michelle" in marketing and explained that I wanted a poster for a new disaster film called *9.6 Mega-Tsunami*. When she asked how I wanted it to look, I shrugged my shoulders and gave a vague answer, akin to "a city scape with fire and crumbling buildings, the usual." She didn't even bat an eye at the concept. . . . That's because drafting posters for films that don't exist is a relatively commonplace procedure.

When Michelle gets to work playing with designs, back drops, and the level of intensity for the destruction elements in her new key art, she's doing a big part of writing the film. She's creating the image of the title, providing a storyline with the visuals—regardless of how indirectly she intends to—and she's actually dictating the level of the film's eventual budget.

After some more back and forth on *9.6 Mega-Tsunami* with Michelle, she had put together a pretty nice poster. The team loved it. In addition to a flood-ravaged city, streets were split apart, buildings were crumbling to the ground, and an airplane was crashing while surrounded by lightning. None of us really had any idea what an airplane had to do with a tsunami, or why the airplane seemed to be getting attacked by lightning—the real reason was that Michelle needed to fill that space in the poster—but it looked great!

And those deals our team secured—the ones that funded the budget of a movie that didn't yet have any actors attached or a director on board, nor even a screenplay—all of those presales were based on Michelle's poster and our pitch to our international buyers. As already stated, our buyers trusted our company's ability to deliver what we were promising them (and what we were promising was a film based on Michelle's poster).

Several weeks after we returned from Cannes, we had successfully closed enough presale deals to green-light two new films into production. Obviously the first was *9.6 Mega-Tsunami*; the other film was a family Christmas movie with a dog. We had a drama, with a very high-end name attached, but that one didn't get any traction, so the film was scrapped. (The rest of the market was spent closing deals on other films, which had already been produced.)

The top executives scheduled our company's official green-light meeting. Occasionally the sales and distribution team would sit in on these, especially if we had put together some presales or if we had to defend "estimates" we made on the value of a film in specific countries. Mostly, green-light meetings were for upper management, pulling in the heads of production to explain to them what films they would be producing. (Notice that it doesn't work the other way—meaning note that production wasn't out finding new material and then bringing it to management requesting money.)

Our CEO began his speech, with the CFO quietly sitting, arms folded, saying nothing. The CEO held up Michelle's poster and congratulated the sales team on securing the money for the film; he then informed the production team that they were going to be "producing *9.6 Mega-Tsunami* as this year's disaster offering." This was the first time the production team had heard about the project. The poster was passed around. A few made comments of "nice" or "that'll be fun." Then the CEO called on one of the development executives on the production side, Sherman, and said: "Sherman, this will be your baby, you're EP [executive producer] on this one; find a writer and get me a script ASAP so I can pitch SyFy." Sherman nodded his head and asked one question, "What's the budget?," to which the CFO spoke next: "450" (meaning $450,000).

Sherman made a quick note, then our CEO went on to the next film.

A QUICK NOTE ON BUDGETS

There's always more than one budget; the dollar amount depends on who's asking. There's the announced budget (which is purposefully made public and is usually somewhat falsified), then there's the actual budget (which is the number we use internally that reflects the legit out-of-pocket expenses incurred).

Four hundred fifty thousand dollars for *9.6 Mega-Tsunami* seems like peanuts in the big scale of Hollywood movies, but this is how much it cost our company to produce and deliver that picture. While friends in indie circles sometimes boast how cheaply they made their first films, that's not necessarily a game we want to play with our clients. Most don't ask. But for those that do, we have different answers for each (for different reasons). Some clients won't acquire or broadcast films under a certain budget level, so we embellish and say the budget's more expensive. For others, if they believe it was a high budget, they might try to siphon off costs against the project or force the film to unionize, which can bankrupt the production making it a total loss—one of those variables that can drain a film's funds midway through.

Also, we used presales to secure the funds for *9.6 Mega-Tsunami*. . . . The way presales work on the financial side is that each country or region has a generalized economic value and is therefore responsible for contributing a certain percentage of the film's anticipated budget. Each regional distributor contributes proportionally to what they are likely to make back based on the currency in which they're working. So for example, India's rupee is weak compared to the dollar. For India to pay us a large amount in dollars, they would have to be able to collect a much greater number of rupees from their clients—even though they have a greater population to sell to than, say, Germany, this is more difficult because of the relative weakness of the rupee. So whereas Germany might have to pay 12–15 percent of the film's budget to acquire the rights, India might only need to pay 2–5 percent.

9.6 Mega-Tsunami cost our company $450,000 in verifiable out-of-pocket expenses. We told our international clients the budget was $1.2 million (so that we had to presell fewer countries to secure the funds), during production we said it was in the $350,000 zone to prevent being taken advantage of by contractors, and later told U.S. broadcasters it was $2.5 million (and that was the number later reported online).

This procedure isn't sneaky or cheap; all parties involved know the game, buyers and sellers alike. And, as a novice screenwriter, so should you. When, in the future, you are commissioned to write a script for a low flat fee and later find out the budget was astronomically high, keep calm. It's much more likely the rate you were paid was in line with the legit out-of-pocket expenses actually spent by the company to make the film.

STRESS RELIEF

A quick comment on Sherman: he was new to our company at that time. *9.6 Mega-Tsunami* was certainly not the first Direct-to-TV movie he'd been EP on, but it was the first he would be producing for us. So you can imagine the stress he probably felt at that moment. When he woke up that morning, he had no clue that before lunch he'd be handed a $450,000 disaster movie with nothing but a poster and the instruction direct from the CEO's mouth of "get me a script ASAP." He knew he had a rushed production before him with very limited money. But before he could make intelligent decisions about how to allocate that money, he first needed to lock down a writer who could deliver a ready-to-go script—and fast.

This is a real world scenario. The clock is ticking and Sherman doesn't have time for games. Simple as that.

Now our company, as with many production/distribution companies in Hollywood, literally had stacks of screenplays lining the walls. The Production team received dozens of blindly submitted spec scripts daily, most of which were neatly filed into a back storage room. I'm certain that many of those scripts, and their authors, showed real promise. . . . But do you think Sherman had time to go in there and start reading? No. Do you think he had time to call several agents and make a request for disaster film spec scripts? No. Instead, Sherman picked up the phone and called a buddy of his in Burbank—a writer he'd worked with before, and who Sherman *trusted*, for a quality script that would be both mindful of budget and quickly turned around.

Sherman didn't care whether this writer's previous scripts had ever won any awards (none of them had). He didn't care whether this writer graduated from film school, or if he'd attended seminars with bigwigs like Robert McKee (he hadn't). Sherman hired the writer he did because it made his job easier. All Sherman cared about was that this writer could deliver what he needed, when he needed it. He could trust this writer to take the pressure off his shoulders so he could get to work on all the other elements required of him to produce the film.

I remember in film school being encouraged to take as much time as needed to perfectly map out the script, scene-by-scene, from beginning to end. Do you think Sherman expressed that to his writer friend? "Take as much time as you need to perfect your vision, we'll wait for you." Nope . . . his writer had six weeks after hanging up the phone to turn in a final draft. That's reality.

UNDERSTANDING THE CATCH-22

Producers and development executives are extremely busy people, generally with multiple projects on their plates in various stages of progression. They know what they need and have little time for anything else. But this "to-the-point" approach they usually use does not in any way imply they are somehow mean or aggressive; most producers and development execs I know are wonderful people (get rid of those *Tropic Thunder* stereotypes, they're few and far between). They truly love what they do and are completely willing to offer help to a young novice looking for a break. . . . But they have limited time. They cannot read ten scripts per day while producing two films back-to-back (and don't forget they have families and personal lives to manage as well).

Just as Hollywood is interested in working with any project that aids its goal in potentially making more money and beating out its competition, producers and development execs are always open to working with writers who can make their job easier by simply delivering what they need when they ask for it (on time, under budget, and requiring little adjustment).

This is why there's that old catch-22. Writers who've already written scripts get hired over newbies because they've already proven they can be trusted to get the job done. When a producer or development executive is in a pinch, they're going to call upon the person they know gets it and can deliver. Before you say this is somehow unfair or frustrating, you do the same thing in your life too. . . . If your car needs maintenance, you'll go to the same old reliable mechanic because you can depend on them to fix your car, without ripping you off, in a timely manner, rather than blindly trusting the new one just around the corner promising he can get it done cheaper. All of us just want the job done correctly and effectively the first time—with as little stress as possible.

This catch-22 of Hollywood is not a defined rule, meaning it's not something that has to be seen as an obstacle. It's just a fact of life (and by accepting this reality, you can use this perspective to help you reach your first green light). A novice will learn to accept and understand why writers with track records have a high chance of getting rehired and will tweak their own writing habits and style to improve their chances. Overcoming this catch-22 is possible. Just as there's a first time for that auto mechanic to prove his or her skills fixing your car on schedule, and there was a first time for me to prove I could effectively close presales of movies, there too is a first time for a newbie screenwriter to be seen as trustworthy and effective.

To get there is as much about personality and reputation as it is about talent and skill. You need both. Not only will you need the right kind of script to prove you understand your role in the Hollywood system, you'll also need to pitch yourself as the writer who can deliver. Think a pitch meeting is just about the screenplay? It's also about proving you're the one to write it!

That's the key to overcoming the catch-22 and to be the kind of writer Sherman calls when in need (and not getting your work filed in the back storage room). It's about being able to deliver the "package" of both talent and understanding of the process that gets writers into the minds of producers and development executives.

HOLLYWOOD BUYS WRITERS, NOT SCRIPTS

The true point for screenwriters regarding the *9.6 Mega-Tsunami* adventure is that the writer who got the job was hired after the film was already presold, funded, and green-lit; he was essentially told what to write and he simply delivered. This writer had written other projects too, ones which he had much more input on the development aspects, but he also understood that sometimes development execs are just in a crunch.

This writer secured this position because he had a strong and proven reputation of delivering what development executives needed on time and worked hard to deliver a script they could work with—meaning one that was mindful of budget and production requirements. (Incidentally, he also came up with a pretty wicked plot structure to explain why the airplane on the poster was getting attacked by lightning . . .)

The spec script he had written years before was never sold, but it did showcase his ability to write what Hollywood needed. It's what secured him his first writing gig (which was actually a rewriting of someone else's script), which eventually secured him with steady work. He was successful with his spec script because he wrote a genre rarely written by non-professionals (meaning he wrote a script that would be seen as potentially helping a Hollywood production company make money). Finishing a halfway decent script was enough to secure him the talent quota, but it was *his choice of genre* and the approach he used when pitching his work—and himself—that proved his business understanding of how to work professionally in Hollywood.

He proved he could write what Hollywood needed and that he could deliver that work in a timely manner. Because of this, his name ended up on the speed-dial of a Hollywood development executive, rather than being just another wannabe stacked amongst the others, in a dusty pile of scripts that would never be read or produced.

Many writers approach their spec scripts in a terrified state, believing that this is their one true shot at Hollywood and that they must write something of such beauty and scope that no producer or development executive could ever look beyond their talents. . . . This approach is doomed to failure because it goes against delivering what Hollywood needs and instead is focused on what the writer assumes Hollywood wants.

No script is ever truly realized as it is, and no film is ever fully faithful to its original script. The script is an outline to principally keep the cast and crew on schedule and the project from going over budget. And the film is the best attempt to match that "blueprint" while allowing for all the craziness that takes place during the entire production and post-production process. Although you should certainly focus on writing your spec script well, the more important point behind writing the spec script is simply showing off the point that you have the talent and the business acumen to feed the Hollywood animal what it needs.

Just as a poster or trailer is more about convincing you to watch the film rather than being true to the film's theme, so too your spec script must be more about convincing producers and development executives to commission your writing talents. Your real challenge is being seen by producers and development executives as a person they can rely on. They're not reading your script to see how well you nailed your formatting or how deeply symbolic your character names are; they want to know that if they call you out of the blue for a TV movie to be written in three weeks that you'll be able to deliver the goods.

HOW TO BE THE WRITER SHERMAN HIRED

Now that you "get" what Hollywood needs to stay afloat, we'll spend the rest of this book explaining in a step-by-step manner how to become the kind of writer development executives call when they're in a *9.6 Mega-Tsunami*-type jam (which is your first step in building a long-term and professional writing career).

No two stories of screenwriter success are the same, but they certainly all involve the same principles, and those are the points we'll be focusing on in *Writing for the Green Light*.

TWO

"SO, WHAT'S IT ABOUT?"

In this chapter we'll go over the most important aspect of your spec script: What it's about (also known as its genre). We'll zero in on which genres grab the attention of producers and development executives, which genres don't, and why. From here, we'll go into the six best genre types for novice screenwriters and what plot points each requires so that you can master the unwritten rules of this system to get your first screenplay green-lit.

THE GENRE YOU CHOOSE SAYS A *LOT* ABOUT YOU

The stereotype about Hollywood is that it's filled to the brim with wannabe writers (and this stereotype is completely true). But contrary to popular belief, most of these wannabes are actually good at writing and the majority of them possess the endurance to deliver a quality 100-page script. The problem is that most screenwriters consistently write the wrong *type* of script—choosing a genre that unintentionally turns away the very professionals they're trying to attract.

The genre of script you choose ultimately showcases what your value is within the Hollywood system. Why? Because the genre is the first, and most clear, indicator as to whether you "get it" or not. To put it bluntly, you either understand what professional producers and development executives need and you deliver scripts they can work with, or you're simply wasting their time and clogging up the system.

So how does one go about choosing the right genre? Or learning the difference between a good genre and a bad one? It sounds absurdly obvious, but if you want to build a writing career in the movie business then you simply need to choose the genres that producers and development executives are looking to develop.

This is where most newbie writers begin making mistakes, simply because they look to the wrong sources for insight into what these Hollywood types truly want. Your friends tell you one thing, an advisor/professor tells you another and endless IMDb research just leaves you feeling more confused than when you began.

But we're trying to help you get your career fast-tracked, so let's jump ahead to which genres work and which don't so that we can bring you one step closer to your first green light.

GENRE: THE GOOD, THE BAD, AND THE UGLY

The Ugly

Let's start first with what does *not* work: It's easy: *Drama*!

There's nothing about a drama's story that doesn't make it work, it's more about the fact that in order for an indie distributor to produce a sellable drama they're required to secure an expensive cast of big names. . . . And that still doesn't account for the risk associated with this genre's limited opportunity for VOD sales and broadcast slots. Dramas are also tough to presell internationally because most of them are dialogue heavy—meaning they're expensive to dub and subtitle.

New writers want to move their audience at the core by writing something of such beauty and vision that their script will be held on a pedestal and admired by all. Truth is, most dramatic script submissions are so awful, poorly written, and filled with such self-absorbed pretentiousness, that the mere indication that you are trying to pitch a story anywhere near a dramatic theme will sink your career before it even gets started!

Even if you have a brilliant dramatic idea, save it! If you start your career on the drama route, you will be buried and pushed aside. Even if your script is fantastic, you will still be forced into going "the long-way around." Wait until you've proven yourself and have a few credits before presenting a drama. Even if you have an agent and are getting consistent work with a production company, they're still fearful of going to their third-party clients with news of an upcoming drama, so you need to get your career to a point where your talent cannot be disputed and those parties are willing and ready to share that risk with you.

Again: Dramas are great; just don't start your career with one.

The Bad

Let's move into the middle zone with a questionable genre: Comedy.

Don't get me wrong, comedy is very high in demand and it's successful throughout the world. . . . But it's very difficult to write comedy, and it carries a very high degree of risk due to all the elements that can go wrong, so it should really be avoided except in very rare instances—especially in your first few scripts. If the old saying is true, that everything that can go wrong will go wrong, keep in mind that comedies have many more variables leaning towards the disaster zone than any other genre.

First, even if your script is laugh-out-loud funny to your reader, there's still the problem of finding a director and cast that can nail the comedic timing elements in your script—they'll also start adding their own ideas and jokes that can make the final production version a far cry from what was originally written—and their bad ideas and failures only fall back on you. Second, with studio-level content dominating the U.S. theatrical space, TV and VOD platforms (like Netflix) are getting more picky and selective by the minute—unfortunately for comedies, unless there's a unique star or run-away sleeper-hit aspect to the film (like *Napoleon Dynamite* (2003)), they just never find the support of U.S. acquisitions agents—for proof, note that the best reference I could think of came from 2003. There's also much more risk around "content sensitivities" in comedy that leave broadcasters and advertisers on edge; one single scene with a "questionable attribute" can keep an otherwise flawless feature-length comedy on the shelf. And third, even if your script is executed by a great production team and some heavy-hitting U.S. platforms are exploited, comedies are very difficult in the rest of the world. They're usually dialogue-heavy (meaning expensive dubbing and subtitling costs) and there's also the very real fact that a majority of cultural and social references aren't clearly understood by most viewers in the world. The very plot of the film might involve something seemingly simple/ordinary to you, but the rest of the world has no idea about it—meaning they'll have no interest in paying to see it. Because of this, comedies that work in one region of the world rarely succeed in the others.

Keep in mind, the above is all assuming your script is top-notch too—comedies are a skill level of writing that can take years (decades even) of trial and error to master. Quality humor is such a very rare talent, that most comedy writers didn't start their career trying to be screenwriters. They were stand-up comedians or performers who later got involved in story development and eventually fell into writing.

Romantic comedies are very successful films, but again all of the above problems occur on these productions as well—and I have seen *many* potentially great romantic comedies fall apart from different variations of the above. Also, as the guy who literally signs deals on movies at the markets, I can tell you from first-hand experience that the prices romantic comedies go for are actually quite low (again, because of the risk and the cost to dub them).

That said, if you're just dying to write some humor, then it's much smarter to focus on one of the below "good" genres and spice them up by adding some appropriately placed comic relief. Believe me, a few witty one-liners cleverly placed into a genre that proves you "get it" will do much more to further your career than a failed attempt at "the next great teenage comedy."

To repeat: Comedies are a very successful genre, but a very risky choice for new writers. Tread with extreme caution.

If you are passionate about writing comedy or drama, don't misinterpret the above advice to mean you can never explore these genres! I'm only suggesting they're not the best "out-of-the-gate" spec scripts to show off your skills; check out Chapter Four for more details.

And the Good

So let's get down to what does work: Basically everything else.

What gains the attention of agents, producers, and development executives are clear, straight-to-the-point entertainment genres. What does that mean exactly? Simple: Thrillers work. So do action films, horror films, and light-hearted family films.

The problem is so very few new writers actually write these genres! That means those that *do* write them have a much higher chance of getting their career into motion because they stand head and shoulders above all the competition out there.

Turn on your TV and scroll through the channels. I bet you'll count six to eight thrillers for every one romantic comedy. I bet you'll find entire channels devoted to horror, action, and dozens dedicated to family. You'll see dramas and comedies too, but you'll also notice these are studio-level movies with major A-list casts (you'll also notice a lot of them are old, except on the pay-per-view channels). This is not the case with thriller, horror, action, or family genres. Click on one. Watch them. Recognize the actors? Maybe one or two, from some TV series you cannot remember the name of. The point is that thriller, horror, action, and family do not require high-level A-list stars to work. . . . The genre itself is enough to give it stature.

What about the international side? What happens when these genres get pitched at the Cannes Film Festival? I have never in my life heard any of my clients ask me for a drama. Not once. When I have had to sell drama, I'll do my best to pitch it, but my client will always end up asking me about the cast in the movie. Unless it's an A-list name, they shake their heads "no." I have been asked for comedy, but it's always a very specific request, like, "Do you have comedies about kick boxing?" or something else out of the blue. Comedy can work if it's slap-stick (because it's understood and doesn't require a dub), but slap-stick humor still needs an internationally known star, such as Rowan Atkinson and his globally recognizable Mr. Bean character. If a comedy is dialogue-based, and most are, then it goes back to who is in the film and any name you provide never seems to meet the clients' expectations. They just cringe their face, shake their heads, and pass.

So what do my clients all over the world ask me for? Here are common requests in my working day: I'll get a phone call from Starz, ION, or Lifetime, "What do you have for family or thriller?" A client from Japan will call me, "I'm looking for action, what do you have?" I go to lunch with Netflix, "Do you have any family or thriller?" I get an email from reps at Chiller, or limitless VOD platforms, "What do you have in thriller or horror?"

See a pattern? Dramas and comedies are dead weight. People don't want them and they clog up the system.

If you want to be taken seriously as a writer, and want to be seen as valuable in the Hollywood system, then hop on the bandwagon and put your effort into what producers and development executives actually want to acquire.

WELL, NO SHIT, SHERLOCK

Okay, perhaps Hollywood wanting entertainment-value genres is far from a shocking revelation. Besides, the word "thriller" or "family" can cover so many different types of stories; it's not exactly a huge puzzle piece I'm providing here. I first wanted to make it clear that dramas and comedies simply need to be removed from your writing lexicon, at least for the time being. Now that they're removed, let's focus on those four top genres: Thriller, action, horror, and family.

Writing a script based on one of these genres will drastically narrow the playing field, but it certainly won't be enough to get you a first green light. You're going to have to dig deeper into these genres and present a script based on what distributors consider absolute "content necessities"—meaning you're going to have to present agents and producers with one of the "gold-mine" scripts.

A gold-mine script is not one based on a certain genre; instead, it's focused on a specific genre *type*. What does that mean? It means not all thrillers or horror films are made equal. Certain trends can define genre types (like zombie horror films), but these are generally fads—meaning that by the time you hear that a genre type is all the craze, the marketplace has already been flooded and your eight months of effort on a great zombie film go nowhere. Rather, a gold-mine script is one that stands the test of time. . . . A film based on a gold-mine script will be of interest to TV channels, DVD/VOD distributors, and content buyers throughout the world, year after year.

Here is the real insight: Not only are the gold-mine genre types the fastest way to get recommended and the most sought-after within the indie marketplace, they are actually the easiest to write! In fact, there are six that are so foolproof and successful that entire companies (and entire individual careers) have grown and blossomed all by remaining true to them. Also, these scripts are so very rare to be received by agents, producers, and production companies that they review these scripts with more acceptance—and forgiveness—than any other (because they know they can sell the hell out of it!) making it much easier for you to edge your way into the top 1 percent of novice screenwriters who truly gain the attention of Hollywood.

THE SIX BEST GENRE TYPES FOR FIRST TIME WRITERS

The following six gold-mine genre types might not be what you expected, but writing one of these films is a sure fire way to grab the attention of Hollywood professionals by delivering what they need.

Gold-Mine Genre Type #1: The Family Christmas Dog Adventure

Next time you're at the grocery store, take an extra moment to check out the Red Box kiosk. Take a look at the bottom two rows. . . . I'll put money down that there's at least one movie with an animal on the front cover, probably a few. Funny enough, they're probably movies you've never heard of with completely unrecognizable actors, yet despite that they're on the front of the machine, alongside major Hollywood movies, taking up very expensive marketing real estate that major studios would love to have.

In Hollywood, "dog films" or "animal films" are equivalent to ATM machines. They're cute, family friendly, and their posters attract both kids and parents alike. Makes sense: Family is one of our top four genres after all. . . . And even the coldest of us can have a soft spot for a puppy.

Another cash-machine storyline involves anything related to Christmas. . . . Holiday specials in general can be very lucrative, but the Christmas holiday itself offers an entire season (thirty to sixty days each year) celebrated by a vast majority of the world—that's almost two months of every calendar year where very specific content is in high demand.

Put these two money-making power houses together and you have the single most slam-dunk gold-mine genre type imaginable: "The family Christmas dog adventure."

By no means are you limited to only using a dog. In general, anything family-safe with some cute animals will be taken seriously—even if it has nothing to do with Christmas. Horse films are very strong, especially stories revolving around a tween-aged girl and her horse; other great animal characters can range from chimps to sea otters—sorry to all cat lovers out there, but cats are pretty lame in narrative live-action films, so don't use them. Just remember, the more exotic the animal, the heftier the cost can be when it comes to production. Not only does the line producer have to budget for the animal, they also need to allocate cash to the trainer(s) and the transportation costs of getting the animals from point A to B. By far, dogs are cheap and pretty easy to handle while remaining extremely effective on the back end (financially).

It's because of these additional costs added to non-dog films (and the added "hedge" of safety offered by the Christmas theme) that makes a family Christmas dog adventure the true gold-mine genre in the family/animal category.

Agents, producers, and distributors seek out these scripts with great interest—they know they can get a nice commission or advance (sometimes even some decent royalties depending on their position) just by having access to such scripts.

Production companies are just as eager to jump on board. They're also relatively easy to produce: They're generally shorter, only eighty-two to ninety minutes, they don't require more than three or four weeks of production, they're usually shot in one central location with tiny crews, and they can be completed for very small budgets. These titles also don't have the added cost of bigger name actors (and the headaches that come from dealing with their agents); instead they use out-of-work yet recognizable TV stars from recently cancelled sitcoms or series.

Once completed, family Christmas dog adventure movies literally have bidding wars (first by us L.A. sales agents and distribution companies, fighting each other to have the right to just sell the movie, then later by all the different channels and home video platforms in each country, including the United States).

The best way to illustrate how in-demand these films are is by offering a real-world example from the office: I'm preparing to attend the Cannes Film Festival next month (with only a few weeks left, I'm starting to see content requests coming in from my clients—sent to me from all over the world). These are the content requests I received just today:

1. This morning, e-mails #2, 7, 9, and 16 in my inbox each came from a different country (one of which was Turkey, a predominantly Muslim country) all requesting advanced notice on what "Dog-Christmas" movies would be available at the film festival.

2. Around 9:45am, the phone rang. The call came from the head acquisitions agent at the #2 channel in Canada (equal to NBC or FOX here in the United States) asking for "Christmas movies, especially ones with dogs or cute animals."

3. After lunch, an email arrives from a long-time buyer in New Zealand (who buys pay-TV rights and DVD/VOD rights for both New Zealand and Australia), "Mate, let me know what doggie Xmas movies you'll have at the film fest next month, I need some for my Q4 slate."

Notice that they're not asking for a pitch or wondering who is starring in the films? The genre type of "family Christmas dog adventure" *is* the selling point.

It sounds like one could write anything and as long as the story takes place around Christmas and there's a dog involved, it's a sure-fire bet! In one sense this is very true, but there are five guidelines and rules for you to keep in mind before you begin plotting out your family Christmas dog adventure:

1. These are family films, but they do *much* better when they attract the whole family (meaning you need to create characters within each generation). A great way to handle this, especially since it's a holiday film, is to involve a family reunion. This way you have an older (wiser/advice-giving) married couple, a late-twenties/early-thirties leading man and woman (both ripe to find a "special someone" who obviously

find each other), then a few "cute kid" characters (who are dealing with elementary school-level crushes on each other). Invent a reason why this family reunion is taking place, but just make sure the leading late-twenties/early-thirties man and woman are both recently single and suddenly "find" one another on this unexpected visit home for the holidays (while dealing with everything else). How you fit the dog in is completely up to you (the dog works best as a bridging character, meaning it helps characters "find" one another).

2. Each of the three generations must experience some kind of love or romance scenario—follow the "boy-gets-girl, boy-loses-girl, boy-gets-girl-back" model, even if they're not lovers and instead just friends. Also, women are the main audience in these films, so be sure to give the female characters that last witty (biting) "told-ya-so" type comment once the "boy-gets-the-girl-back." (A Christmas Eve party is a great setting for this third act moment, especially with the obvious mistletoe references.)

3. Do not write a "talking dog" movie. The dog can have special talents (like playing a sport such as the hugely successful *Air Bud* franchise), but it should not be able to speak. The Hollywood (and international) marketplace only likes talking animal movies if the animal's mouths are animated as they talk. . . . And to animate at the quality-level required is extremely expensive—the *Mister Ed* trick doesn't cut it anymore, and cheap animated mouths devalue the film. And don't try that voice-over "thinking" or "telepathic" animal trick, that only works if you have an A-lister providing the voice. The producers and production companies behind these films don't have A-lister budgets and will pass not just on your script, but possibly even you as a writer.

4. The *whole* story must take place before Christmas. It must focus on all the shenanigans leading up to the big day. These movies must end as everyone settles in on Christmas Eve, able to enjoy the full holiday with all of the drama and chaos settled and resolved. Also, Christmas Eve offers a great excuse to get all your characters into the same location at the same time.

5. The dog must mirror the story arc of the humans. . . . Since we have so many great loves finding one another, it only makes sense that our hero dog (also a female) is introduced to a very attractive male dog. This happens at the end, usually at the Christmas Eve party, once all problems are wrapped up—one of our character's friends comes over, bringing his/her dog, which is the male canine of our hero dog's dreams. It's perfectly acceptable to push this to the next level, adding a "SEVERAL MONTHS LATER" chunk where our hero dog is resting with a litter of adorable puppies.

Aside from the above guidelines, the storyline and character details of the family Christmas dog adventure are purely up to you. I didn't add this in the rules, but it goes without saying that you should steer clear of heavy subjects or themes, such as abuse, alcoholism, and so forth—keep things light and fluffy.

This genre type might be a bit more mainstream than some of you had hoped, but it is a guaranteed one-way ticket to being taken seriously by the Hollywood machine. Most agents, producers, and production companies have a radar scanning the Los Angeles basin, looking for these exact types of screenplays.

To get a sense of the style and tone of these films, check out these real-world examples: *3 Holiday Tails* (2011) or *Scoot & Kassie's Christmas Adventure* (2013). For a non-dog version of this gold-mine genre, check out *The Christmas Colt* (2013). And to see a "family dog" film applied to a different holiday, check out the family Valentine's Day dog adventure *Gabe the Cupid Dog* (2012).

Gold-Mine Genre Type #2: The Woman-in-Peril Thriller

This genre type is actually a win-win on both the business side as well as the creative. On the business end, there are dozens of slots open for these films across a wide variety of platforms (these are fantastic for TV with heavy cross-over into theatrical distribution and DVD/VOD throughout the world). There's usually one playing each weekend at the movie theatre and you can find countless examples at any time of day on TV (look at the Life-time Movie Network or A&E, both of which have built empires off them).

For screenwriters, a woman-in-peril thriller can offer a lot of innovative plot twists and unique character development, granting much more latitude for creativity in a way that's fun and satisfying, while still providing Holly-wood a script it's on the hunt for.

Distributors and production companies see woman-in-peril thrillers as very sound investments and take their submissions very seriously. They're always eager to expand their catalogues with these films, but they do expect them to meet certain Hollywood standards.

The drawback for new writers is that woman-in-peril thrillers are not nearly as easy to write as a family Christmas dog adventure and they will be judged much more critically than "fluff" genres. But there are definitely ways to approach this genre type in a manner that positions you, and your screenplay, on solid ground to nail your first green light!

Let's first review the three best-selling types of woman-in-peril thrillers, the ones agents, producers, and development executives are in search of:

1. *The Stalker Ex*—The storyline is very straight and simple, also the most obvious. A young woman is completely loving and devoted to her perfect husband/boyfriend. But it's soon revealed that he is abusive. With little money and no one to turn to, she finds the courage to escape and is forced to create a new life for herself elsewhere. She finds a new man, a truly kind and wonderful sweetheart, but their relationship is strained because of her past. . . . It's also discovered that the ex is now stalking her. Act III starts when our leading lady and her new man

have an argument: He feels hurt that she won't commit, and she hasn't yet been able to express her emotional conflict stemming from her past. The film climaxes when our heroine is in a vulnerable situation (alone, naked, and helpless work best, think *Sleeping with the Enemy*'s (1991) poster with Julia Roberts in the bathtub, realizing she's not alone in the house) and she must face her stalker ex head on. The new sweetheart comes to her rescue at the perfect moment and all order is restored.

2. *The Vigilante*—The exact circumstances can vary drastically in these films, but they do follow the theme of our leading lady taking justice into her own hands. These stories begin with a young woman who seems to have it all together. Then, someone in her life changes that—this incident must always be an act of violence against her that steals part of her innocence, one that is usually very dark, generally a sex crime. Hurt and vulnerable, she gathers herself and reports the crime to officials. But something goes wrong. Either the officials are corrupt and they pardon the bad guy, or there is some legal loophole and the criminal is set free without punishment. Our leading lady has a choice: She can do nothing (and continue to be victimized), or she can take action and destroy her assaulter. Again, these films don't always have to be physically violent; for example, *Notes on a Scandal* (2006) was absolutely a vigilante woman-in-peril thriller (even though our "hero" was the twisted one). But *Double Jeopardy* (1999) is probably that most cut-and-dry take.

3. *Don't Take My Baby*—Generally more of a TV Movie-of-the-Week, this is still a highly successful plot that offers a surprising number of storylines. Films in this category can cover a wide range, from exposing adoption loopholes to courtroom custody battles. The point here is that *all* characters in the film actually want what's best for the baby, they just have drastically different views on what "the best for the baby" actually means. Incidentally, the baby can be any age; infants are just easier because of the limited time crews can work with child actors on set. These are the films where you will find a young teenage mother down on her luck reluctantly leaving her baby on the steps of a rich person's home. Darker versions can show a court custody battle go awry when an abusive parent is wrongly granted victory and our lead must fight the system to get her child back. They must end warmly though, with the child reunited only with the character most fit to be its parent (who should always be our leading lady). These stories also work well with themes of extreme optimism, sometimes faith (but only lightly), where a mother's persistent love is a force to truly be reckoned with.

All three of the best-selling types of woman-in-peril thrillers are secure choices; no one type is better than another. You should aim your script to fit into TV standards since that is most likely where it will be placed, even though your script format will still be for a feature film. It is best to think out your storyline in a way that follows the standard three-act structure but that also allows for a climactic turn or plot reveal every seven to eight minutes (perfect for that commercial break).

As with the family Christmas dog adventure, successful woman-in-peril thrillers also have their own set of guidelines for you to keep in mind. Regardless of which of the best-selling types of thrillers you choose to write, they're all governed by these five rules:

1. Your main character *must* be a woman! Sounds so simple, but a great deal of supposed woman-in-peril thriller scripts have male lead characters. She also must be a very good person, someone every female audience member can relate to while also hoping to aspire to be like (meaning, she seems in control of her life, is effortlessly talented, and seems to just have it all going for her). But this character shouldn't be completely perfect; she is far from being a picture-perfect model, and so on. . . . She's very pretty, but in a way that's natural and simple (think of the "Girl-Next-Door" type). She also needs to be human (meaning she needs realistic faults).

2. Our main character has two enemies: First is the antagonist directly responsible for violently taking a part of our heroine's innocence; the second is the system in her world that allows this antagonist to walk free or continue victimizing her. The main character must fight against both of these enemies before completing her journey—how that happens is up to you.

3. Our main character is the living definition of a moral compass. She's certainly not a boring Miss Goody-Two-Shoes, but she's comfortable with who she is and seems to have never felt the temptation to do the wrong thing. This view of life has served her very well, until the violent inciting incident throws her moral compass out of whack and pulls the rug out from under her feet. She now realizes her morals cannot prevent the wrong people from entering her life. She must confront a new understanding of what is right or wrong, realizing sometimes we must commit acts we swore we never would in order to maintain the only thing any of us are able to uphold: our integrity. (This means she must do a full 180 before our eyes in order to restore order to her world.)

4. A kind, wise, and balanced character is what propels her towards the transition listed in rule #3. This can be a "new man" she meets, or it can be a close confidant (a parent figure even). When she is at her darkest moment, when her moral compass has been pushed so far out of whack that she is giving up hope, the very fact that this character has entered (or reentered) her life is the ignition switch to find the courage to complete that 180 degree transition.

5. Kids are always innocent. Any character under the age of eighteen can only be presented in a way that upholds morality. Even if it is a troubled teenage character who is committing crimes or violent acts, he or she is misguided because of external factors. Infants, toddlers, or any minor, can only be—at their worst—a byproduct or victim of a

broken system. They are always symbolic of hope for the future, and the optimism of a better generation ahead.

That's pretty much it; the woman-in-peril thriller offers a very large playing field with *tons* of possibilities for screenwriters. Keep the content TV safe (meaning don't get to excessive on the graphic content and avoid non-TV-friendly language). At the end of the day, these films are really all about the character (both their development and their journey forward). Develop a very dynamic and strong leading lady, avoid clichés, and really connect with the theme of doing whatever it takes (even going against what you once believed) in order to regain your integrity.

Get a feel for the high-stakes emotional drama from these real Indie Hollywood woman-in-peril thriller examples: *The Nightmare Nanny* (2013), *Accused at 17* (2009), *Stolen Child* (2012), or *Sexting in Suburbia* (2012). . . . You can always just switch on the Lifetime Movie Network or other similar basic cable TV station and find a movie in this genre playing.

Gold-Mine Genre Type #3: The Family-Safe Tween Romance

This is a very underrated genre that offers writers a lot of creative opportunities. Just like the woman-in-peril thrillers, these require strong character development and innovative plot structures; however, as with the family Christmas dog adventure, the family-safe tween romance is a much more relaxed in its requirements. It's kind of the best of both worlds; it offers writers creative challenges within a format that won't be too heavily scrutinized by its readers.

Family-safe tween romances are an absolute delight for agents and distributors alike. . . . These might not sell as fast or easily as the family Christmas dog adventure, but when they do sell they sell big. These do very well in the TV space and home entertainment world of DVD and VOD. There are definitely theatricals of this genre type as well, but television and VOD is what really makes this a powerhouse for the industry.

Nearly every major communications company on the planet holds two or three channels aimed at kids' content. Schedulers for these channels always have a dilemma on their hands because they need a certain number of hours of "tween"-aged content that is less expensive than the studio titles (and there's very little of that out there). This is where indie distribution companies come in for the save: They offer these channels packages of Family-Safe (meaning TV-safe) Tween Romances. It's the family-safe/TV-safe aspect that gets the channels interested, however it's actually the romance aspect that keeps tweens and teens (regardless of gender) glued to their screens—meaning big boosts in ratings, which increase the ad dollars.

Don't forget, this tween-to-teen demographic is the number one purchaser of Transaction VOD content. . . . Today's tweens are very comfortable buying (or renting) digital copies of movies via TVOD platforms (e.g., Hulu, Amazon, and iTunes) even if presented with very limited information about the film in advance.

Family-safe tween romance films are also excellent in the marketing world; producers and production companies are provided with fantastic opportunities to cross-promote with record labels, clothing companies, and merchandising brands. Outside of the studio world, family-safe tween romances are one of the few genres still capable of garnering product placement deals.

But business aside, the family-safe tween romance is a very fun and engaging genre that should be taken very seriously by new writers. It's relatively easy to approach (meaning the basic story structure is quite simple), but the opportunities to make it something unique and moving are really an open playing field.

These films always follow a young girl (age thirteen to sixteen) dealing with her first major problem: She's the good girl, the one *not* noticed by the cute boys and *not* accepted by the popular girls—she's also realizing being "the good girl" isn't working for her. She's average, but with the potential of being something amazing. She has a slate of problems, some from family and some from school (safe problems—avoid the temptation to go into anything crazy here like abuse). But her real problem is that "missing" element in her life that she longs for. . . . Then she sees *him*, that amazing boy who makes her weak at the knees. He's so perfect—he's also taken by some stuck-up mean girl and part of a completely different social group. (*Like, what-ever!*)

We know the story from here: She ends up in some awkward embarrassing situation and that's the first time she actually talks to him (by force, and out of her comfort zone). She feels like she's blown it, but he seems to like the fact that she's different. Then this boy has a problem that he cannot trust his normal social group with, so he depends on our hero girl for support. She agrees to help him, but she's now reluctant because she must become something she's not in order to do so.

Finally, she gets straight about who she is and finds a way to help the boy of her dreams overcome his problem on her own terms (by doing things the right way). The day is saved and she ends up with that amazing guy she never thought she had a chance with (all just by being exactly who she always was—an amazing young woman in the making).

Add some character names and a goofy best friend and you're one step closer to a first draft (and your first green light).

We've all been in this girl's shoes because all of us felt insecure as teenagers! Adolescence is a terrible time: Acne, body-image problems, gym class, and on top of that we all have had that secret crush that would never be. . . . But this is where you as the writer get to ask the best of all storytelling questions: What if things in your own life had been different? Pull from your experiences; we all have a thousand embarrassing moments from those awkward years that everyone on the planet can identify with.

The rules on this one are much more specific. There are five of them, and once added to the above general story arc you pretty much have all you need to get a thumbs-up from the readers:

1. No sex. These are kids. Assume all are virgins and that the big kiss at the end is the home run they're all hoping for.

2. She has a close circle of three friends, each very eccentric and goofy—this is great for comic relief scenes; the circle must be coed. They are her counsel when she is obsessed with this new guy, but she will turn on them in order to help him. These friends call her out on what she's turned into, and it hurts to hear the truth. She must go back to them and apologize, but she needs their help to set things right again. This circle of friends is a key component. Spend time—and have fun—developing them. The more eclectic, the better (as long as it seems realistic that they'd all actually hang out together).

3. Our hero girl has a special talent that can be used as a secret weapon. She at first is embarrassed by it, seeing it as one of the traits which holds her back, but later realizes it's the tool she can use to help her big crush out while also regaining trust with her circle of friends. This special talent is something simple: She's really good at math, she is an amazing public speaker, she has an awesome singing voice, that sort of thing. It's something tangible (meaning real audiences can identify with it) that is her fallback when everything else is going haywire. But don't limit yourself; if you feel like pushing the envelope and having your hero possess a secret magic power, go for it! We all pretend and fantasize silly things, these are what make film fun and entertaining. Remember Nickelodeon's TV series *The Secret World of Alex Mack* (1994–1998)? A totally fun idea.

4. Our hero girl must have an advisor, one that is not her parents nor a part of her clique. . . . This can be achieved in a variety of ways, but this advisor must appear a minimum of three times conversationally (and must make a fourth non-verbal appearance at the very end—when this advisor sees how our hero girl has made the world right by trusting in herself and fixing things her way—this is when they see each other from across a room and have a personal non-verbal acknowledgement, like a wink or a nodding smile). Teacher characters are great for this, but so is an elderly character from a nearby nursing home, or the spirit or ghost of a lost friend or relative. The more creative the better.

5. If any kind of spell or magic can take place to propel the story, the better. This is where your script really takes a leap from "good" to "green light". . . . For example, think of a high-concept idea like having a birthday where wishes really could come true, or having the advisor offering a charm bracelet that can make one relive the same day in order to fix past mistakes and finally make it right. This is a really fun concept that we all think about—really ask yourself the "what if" questions here. . . . What if you could re-live your high school years, what if you had gone for that kiss you'd always wished you had, what if you could have "done it all better." This "magic" element really makes the film click, both for the audience, and for the agents, producers and development execs who will be reading it.

And, in a nutshell, that's a family-safe tween romance film. The most obvious storylines involve high school scenarios—just avoid giant "stadium scenes" (for money reasons)—but don't forget summer breaks or "forced relocation" scenarios like a family moving from the big city to a small town, which can offer extremely good story opportunities while forcing the script to have a more limited number of characters and settings. And, as briefly described in the Family Dog Christmas Adventure section, these tween films do very well with horses. If the great coming-of-age young boy story focuses on "a boy and his dog," then the female version would be a "girl and her horse." Just remember, horses are expensive, so keep their role in check. In addition to equestrian themes, you can also push the sports route with gymnastics, tennis, or ice skating.

Have fun with this genre; not only is the family-safe tween romance genre a gold mine for a spec script, they're much more entertaining to write—and read—than you might think. Here are a few real-world examples: *3 Times a Charm* (2011), *Pop Star* (2013), or *Jinxed* (2013).

Gold-Mine Genre Type #4: The Creature Feature

Creature features are not horror films (but they can be); they're not science fiction (but, again, they can be). . . . They are a very specific *type* of film that can be played out and used in a variety of ways—all while striking a chord with audiences worldwide. They're visual, easily understandable, and most importantly, entertaining.

Jaws (1975) is considered a horror film, but it's actually a creature feature. *Alien* (1979) is classified as a science fiction film by some, horror by others, and action by a few. . . . But, again, it's a creature feature. Know what else is a creature feature? *Outbreak* (1995). . . . Even though our heroes are fighting a virus, that virus is representative of a living (and adapting) entity that *must* be destroyed.

The reason creature features work is because of a simple thing we like to call "subtext." Subtext is a fancy word describing that idea we pull from a film (or a book) that isn't actually there on the screen or page. Sure, it seems like the underlying theme or storyline is so blatantly obvious, but if you actually watch the film (or read the dialogue) you realize everything is simply suggestive and you, as the audience member, put together the subtext in your mind. It's like watching *District 9* (2009), a film about aliens forced to live on Earth in slum-like conditions. Although *District 9* is a very well-made (well-adapted) science fiction film (not a creature feature), it's actually very honest to how humans treat one another. So while making no real direct comparisons, people from all over the world read into the film different subtextual themes. For some, they were convinced it was all about Apartheid in South Africa. For others, it was clearly about the Israeli-Palestinian crisis. And still for others, it was purely a film about racism in modern society. Nowhere in the film were any of these mentioned, but viewers walked away convinced of what they just saw, based solely upon their background insights and personal experiences. The more interesting phenomenon is that despite which opinion they actually held onto about any of the above hot-button political issues, the film seemed to support their views.

But before you get tempted with the idea of being "smart" and hiding a secret theme inside a creature feature, think again: The way quality creature features work is by *not* writing with a political or ideological agenda of any kind (avoiding any intentional subtext). Going in with that approach is a one-way ticket to rejection. Anytime you consciously (or "cleverly") place themes or ideas into *any* script, people can smell what you're doing a mile away and it becomes forced (which reflects very negatively on you). Instead, you're simply going to take a giant step back, and focus only on a simple storyline and making sure your *characters* reflect what true human reactions and/or behaviors would be. That is how your reader or audience member will see what they want in the film—and that is when the creature feature becomes a force to be reckoned with.

So as long as you stay true to human nature, you pretty much have a free ticket to conceive of the biggest monster or most horrifying science experiment going awry, right? Not so fast. . . . Although this genre allows you a great deal of creative freedom, there are a few restrictions we'll need to apply to your spec script for it to gain traction. Here are the tips on making your creature feature spec script stand out amongst all the others already littering the Hollywood system:

1. Make your hero a heroine. . . . That's right, make your main character a woman. If this is simply impossible for you to do, then at bare minimum your female lead needs to be just as sharp and gutsy as her male counter-part (which means, you'll need to give her plenty of great "told-ya-so" one liners to her male partner throughout). Let's stick with our example of *Alien*: Sigourney Weaver's character Ripley could just as easily have been a male, but it makes the film stand out more that the gender assumption is breached and the secondary officer (a female, meaning the secondary gender) was the one who ultimately defeats the creature and survives. If you use a male lead as the hero, then the male/female dynamic needs to work throughout the film, meaning they must be partners and fully work together and depend upon one another to defeat their creature and survive. For a fun example, look at *Tremors* (1990): Kevin Bacon's character Valentine is a very linear, blue collar male character, but his female counterpart Rhonda, played by Finn Carter, (the brains) is the one who brings all the valuable data to the table. . . . They both survived because they worked together, sharing information and depending upon one another, but it was the female character that made it happen. If your hero is a female, there are no constraints on relationships. . . . If your hero is a male, then there must be some kind of sexual tension/attraction each has for one another. In *Outbreak*, the male/female leads were a divorced couple forced to work together again; in *Tremors*, they were

polar-opposite characters, but each embodied exactly what the other truly needed in the opposite sex. (Need I remind you that both *Alien* and *Tremors* spawned countless sequels, spin-offs, and rip-offs?)

2. Isolate your characters. This doesn't mean your film cannot take place aboard a space station or on some distant moon (ideally it shouldn't, both sound as if they might require expensive set design or effects), but you should limit the scope of the film by isolating its characters in an out-of-the-way location. In short, don't make your creature attack New York City, requiring hundreds of thousands of people to be running amok; instead, limit it to a mountainside or some other locked-away place. In *Tremors*, the film takes place in a dinky Nevada town with a population of seven. Getting your characters off the grid keeps things centralized in terms of location, making it easier to shoot; it keeps the characters limited (fewer actors means less money); *and* it affords you as a writer more opportunities to keep conflict and tension high. In a city, your cell phone always works and there's always a gas station nearby. When you're out in the middle of nowhere, signals drop and a low tank of gas suddenly becomes a crisis. It's an old trick that still works today. It saves money, time, and offers you simpler options to keep your characters in constant jeopardy. Everybody wins. (Great locations include the woods, a lakeside, a small mountain town, swamps, the desert. . . . Any place you wouldn't want your car to breakdown in.)

3. Keep the creature primal. The creature can really be anything your imagination can come up with—the crazier the better—but you need to keep them biologically possible—meaning reasonable that they could logically exist. Even though I've referenced *Outbreak* above, for the purposes of your spec script, avoid viruses or other bacteria. Instead, go with something like the giant worms from *Tremors*, an undiscovered lake monster, a massive man-eating killer snake that has developed claws while evolving for centuries in the Louisiana swamps—whatever you can think of, and again, the crazier the better. Don't make it a swarm of bees or school of killer fish . . . limit the numbers to an individual creature, or at most two or three. Also, keeping your creature natural and primal, makes the creature's instinct to hunt and kill much more plausible; since our creature is some undiscovered species, it places our hero(es) into more conflict, since no one will believe their stories (forcing them to act alone). Although the creature could be alien in nature, it's best to keep it an organic creature from mother earth. You could stick to basics, like a bear or a lion, but generally these read as pretty boring. . . . Even though *The Grey* (2011) starring Liam Neeson was a very solid wolf "creature feature," it's not as imaginative as the types of creature features Indie Hollywood is on the hunt for. Push the envelope to crank up the fun with an undiscovered man-eating [fill-in-the-blank]. (No zombies!)

4. The first ten pages of the script must show the creature attacking innocent static characters. . . . We need to know this creature is out there and witness the deadly power it can inflict upon humans. And we need an inciting incident that lets our readers, and our viewing audience, know what type of film we're in for—and to keep them hooked through the boring exposition that must inevitably follow as we introduce our main characters and so on. We'll have tips on how to make these exposition style chunks more entertaining for readers and viewers in Chapter Three.

5. Keep it PG-13! If you want to impress people with your spec script, then show Hollywood you're capable of delivering what it needs. If a studio or production team wants to make your film an "R," they can easily drop a few extra f-bombs on set and add some nudity. . . . But it's much harder to take an R-rated script and tone it down to PG-13, which is the real target for creature features: These films perform best with the teenaged audience or as TV movies . . . PG-13 scripts allow this to feel possible, R-rated scripts make it seem like too much work. You don't have to skimp on the blood and guts . . . they can be adjusted as needed, but avoid profane language and cut the sex scenes (for now).

6. The real enemy is *"The Man"*. . . . Whether police, military, or any other organized group existing to protect us, they actually represent enemies of our hero(es) in the creature feature. These films are about acting alone to accomplish the goal of survival. When our hero(es) first goes to the authorities, seeking help, he or she is generally laughed out of the room. Even if they offer limited evidence, they are rejected assistance and forced on their own. (Or, in other circumstance, a police or military force is aware of the danger and purposely quarantines our hero(es) into a situation to destroy the creature, or to even protect the creature, even if it means endangering innocents). In order to successfully defeat this creature, our hero(es) must act completely solo (with their partner if required), after having exhausted the option of going to the normal protective routes. You do not have to introduce a police or military force, but you must have our hero(es) going after this thing on their own terms. (You can always have a "good" sheriff or similar who's on the side of your hero, but they too must encounter conflict with other enforcement elements.)

7. If possible, add a family dynamic. Who's to say we only have to focus on adults with this one? It could be a brother/sister team that discover a creature and their parents are the ones not believing them. . . . Or perhaps our film is about a dysfunctional family on a camping trip attempting to reunite, only to see their plans go through the ringer when they find themselves stalked by the creature. They now must work together to defeat this thing, in turn repairing all those broken bonds. The family dynamic is a tool rarely seen in spec scripts, but it's one that really piques the interest of agents, producers, and

development executives because they can be marketed so well on the back end. Companies I've worked for have done great business on family-centric creature features (note, these should still be PG-13 films; just because a family is involved doesn't mean it has to be suitable for younger audiences).

8. Our hero(es) get the recognition at the end, only by now they don't want it. Perhaps our hero is a hopeful college professor seeking full tenure, but his or her belief in the mythic (fill-in-the-blank) creature has held them back as the laughingstock. . . . Until they discover and fully defeat it. The protective forces (police/military) give their subtle apologies, and our hero(es) are granted full recognition from parties they previously sought it from, only now they don't care. They have changed and move on. If the creature attack and defeat happened without the awareness of others, then our hero(es) keep it to themselves, as something they'll never share with outsiders. In short, our hero(es) learned something very amazing about their own individual abilities when the going got tough. . . . But they also learned something very ugly about society in the process. They walk away, better off on their own.

Creature features are simply fun movies. They're easy to watch and simple to understand. These are true man-versus-nature conflict films at their heart and our heroes' battle is one we wish we could embark upon. The only trick is to fully immerse yourself into this magical world and completely flesh out each character into living, breathing people. As long as all your characters are well-created and three-dimensional (we'll have tricks on how to do this in Chapter Three) and their actions/behaviors make logical sense, the introduction of the creature will simply ignite everything you need.

Here are some real creature features to have a look at (and possibly a laugh): *Xtinction: Predator X* (2010), *Sharknado* (2013), *Arachnoquake* (2012), and *Dragon Wasps* (2012). . . . But don't disregard classics like *The Blob* (1958) or *It Came From Outer Space* (1953), both of which were indies.

Gold-Mine Genre Type #5: The Aging Name-Actor Comeback Action Film

When people first think of action films, they're thinking major studio productions with ridiculous budgets (such as Jerry Bruckheimer/Michael Bay films). But what's often overlooked is the humungous straight-to-home-entertainment division of the action genre—and that's what we'll focus on here.

Studios release only a handful of action titles each year, yet the home entertainment market releases hundreds (if not thousands)—and they're in constant need of a very specified type of action film, one that affords them the opportunity to use an aged yet known name-actor as the lead (which allows them to create a great looking poster and presell all while offering a role to a name-actor who would be inclined to taking the part even for limited money), and that offers high-intensity action that can be delivered on a budget. Thus, the aged name-actor comeback action film is our fifth gold-mine genre type.

Let's consider Chuck Norris for a moment. What probably first comes to mind are all the recent "Chuck Norris Facts" you may have heard, of which I have many favorites (e.g. "Chuck Norris does not sleep, he waits"). But the reason all these manlier-than-man jokes exist about Norris are because of the string of straight-to-video titles he starred in during the 1980s and 1990s. He even had a guest cameo in *The Expendables 2* (2012) cracking fun of these old films. He was the ultimate homegrown, salt of the earth, action hero. A typical Chuck Norris film would begin with a terrorist attack or some kidnapping. . . . It would be quickly surmised that America's most elite soldiers (Delta Force and Navy Seals) would be unable to accomplish the mission (owing to high end politics, or some other issue), so top brass military officials would call their best man, who would conveniently be played by Chuck Norris. He would drop whatever he was doing and go suit up. Twenty-four hours later he'd be dropped into some hot zone in the world, ready to kick some ass and save America. Regardless of whether you've seen them, quickly consider the imagery each of the following Chuck Norris titles put into your head: *Forced Vengeance* (1982), *Invasion U.S.A.* (1985), or *Delta Force 2: The Colombian Connection* (1990). . . . That's the style and tone we're going for here.

A good example of a recent aged name-actor who has proven very successful in this category is Dolph Lundgren. . . . But also (still) holding strong worldwide is Jean Claude Van Damme. (Not that you should write your spec script assuming either of these actors would be the lead, but definitely check out their more recent films to give yourself a good sense of genre direction.)

Just as with the woman-in-peril thriller, this male-skewed action film has three particular storylines that work best when received as a spec script. No one storyline is better than the other, so again, it's really more about what clicks with you and keeps the innovative and creative juices flowing:

1. *Terrorism*—The subject of terrorism offers a great opportunity for a "bad guy" character(s) who has an unswerving goal of inflicting harm and death upon innocent people. But get off the stereotype couch and don't go for Muslim extremism. Make the terrorist—and their motivation—unique. If you go for the current hot-button terror topic, you risk way too much (and really limit your scope). Lay off the politics and religion. Make it a terrorist attack for revenge or simply selfish reasons. . . . A madman threatens to blow up a grounded plane because he wants money and he'll execute one passenger each hour the money isn't delivered. . . . Or perhaps that madman is using the same grounded plane only he's seeking asylum. It's an open playing field.
2. *Kidnapping/Hostage-Taking*—This is always a classic scenario; a high-ranking official (or other high value target) is kidnapped. This

isn't always done for money—sometimes it's for revenge, or just to gain some leverage. The victim you choose plays a major role in how the rest of the film will play out; if your victim is the ambassador to a foreign country, that's one set of rules . . . if your victim is the daughter or child of the same ambassador, that's another altogether. Not to push the gender stereotype here, but a damsel in distress (especially a young girl) generally adds more tension, but a high-ranking male can add an extra edge depending on what he represents in the world.

3. *Everyday Hero*—This is a real gem of this genre because it offers the greatest level of fantasy for its audience. Take *Black Dog* (1998), where Patrick Swayze, an ex-con gone straight, takes a trucking job only to find out he's been misled and he's driving a truckload of illegal weapons and must fend off some rough characters in order to do the right thing; or *Walking Tall* (2004), where a U.S. soldier returns home only to find his town overrun by drugs and corruption. Both films offer high-stakes action, but our hero is an everyday man who simply went to work that particular morning having no idea what would happen upon his arrival. They're good-natured yet flawed characters, with real world problems. . . . But they've got a job to do—and with the love of their family deep in their hearts, they're willing to go that extra step to put their world back into order.

All of these are great choices; many of these films use elements from all three types within the same movie—but one "type" is always the driver over the others. Whichever scenario you choose, your first task is to unbalance the storyline. What this means is that the bad guys must initiate the first move (meaning the bad guys should be in control and hold all the leverage) within the first act of the movie. . . . Ideally, within the first ten to fifteen minutes if possible.

This unbalancing can (and probably should, for certain storylines) happen before we've even been introduced to our main character, who will be our comeback star. However, once the bad guys are in control, we're led to your next major writing challenge: you need to make sure there's a reason *why* your hero is the best suited for the job (meaning you need to really think through why any other option wouldn't be a better alternative). If your hero is a police officer, why does he need to go solo and not with a force? If your hero is a former Delta sniper, why must he go and not a newer (fresher) individual? What is it about this particular situation that calls upon the unique traits of your aged and worn character?

Let's use an example, and for fun we'll go with a classic . . . *Escape from New York* (1981), a wonderful example of a kidnapping/hostage-taking name-actor comeback action film (that was a mouthful). Yes, I know Kurt Russell wasn't coming back from anything in his career when he starred in this, but the *script* on which this film was based would absolutely classify in this genre type, including budget level.

The film takes place way in the future (1997), at a time when the crime rate has risen to such a staggering rate that the U.S. government has simply sectioned off the entire island of Manhattan and transformed it into a max-imum security prison. The film is quickly unbalanced after terrorists (from a worker's party, not a Muslim extremist group) hijack Air Force One; with the president on board, they purposely crash the plane into a building in lower Manhattan. The president survives the crash via an escape pod, but is now being held by New York inmates, who will use the president's life in exchange for their freedom. To make a bad situation worse, the president has with him a tape-recorded speech about ending a high-stakes nuclear sit-uation with foreign nations. . . . To protect the United States, the president must be saved and the tape recording must be delivered to an international peacekeeping summit within twenty-four hours. That is an extremely unique high stakes situation!

Why must a different kind of hero move in for the objective? Upon first notification of the president's location, a military dispatch is sent into the city to recover him, at which point they're met by one of the inmates, holding a bloodied rag with the president's severed finger (presidential ring and all) wrapped up in it; the inmate presents a stern warning: if they don't leave immediately or if they attempt to come back, the president dies. Our team needs someone on the inside to accomplish the objective. Enter Kurt Russell, as "Snake" Pliskin. He's former Delta Force but has turned his back on the country he once swore to defend; after unsuccessfully committing a bank robbery, he's been issued a life sentence in Manhattan's prison. He's per-fect. He can covertly enter the prison and save the president without raising eyebrows.

The world the film takes place in is quickly defined. The bad guys have the upper hand early on. The good guys respond by initiating a status quo first move (conventional police or military action), but the situation is much too delicate and the first approach fails. They need something different, some-thing unexpected and unique. . . . They must call upon our hero and commis-sion his talents for the job.

As with all of our gold-mine genre types, there are some rules you must follow to effectively pull this one off:

1. Our hero doesn't want to be in the movie. What I mean is that when we are first introduced to our hero, he has moved on from his life in the CIA, Special Forces, or whatever mysterious background he might have, and just wants to be left alone (similar to Stallone in *Rambo* (2008) where he's isolated himself in Thailand, or Mark Wahlberg in *Shooter* (2007)). He's seen too much, lost too many friends, or perhaps he's lost faith and turned his back on the ideals for which he was previously fighting. If he's an everyday-man hero, then he's struggled with personal matters and just wants to focus on his work and his family. His past must remain in the shadows, but we can see a glimpse of it here or there, usually in the scene where he's being sought after for the help. "We know what happened in Somalia, but we have no one else we can go to . . ." The biggest leap you'll need to make is in

figuring out how to get this aged hero off the couch and back in the saddle. Here are a few reasons to help cure the writer's block:

    a.   *Family*—An old enemy of our hero has kidnapped his daughter (or grand-daughter . . . or some other family member) to seek revenge, or to purposely get our hero in a face-to-face situation.

    b.   *Revenge*—Turns out an arch nemesis, "the one that got away," is now the culprit behind the current hijinks. . . . Rather than see this scumbag get away with it, our hero will take the risk.

    c.   *America*—Let's be honest, the United States is a very conservative country and many an action fan loves a hero who's willing to risk it all for the better ideals of the good ol' U.S. of A.

    d.   *Woman and Children*—If an evildoer is causing harm to a group of adult males elsewhere, it's easy to dismiss. . . . But if this menace is purposely targeting women and children, it will send a hero like ours off the deep end (he could have some past demon haunting him, this mission might help put that bad memory to rest).

    e.   *Freedom*—Just as in *Escape from New York*, our hero (or anti-hero, in this case) is entering prison but will be granted immunity if he can safely get the president out of harm's way and complete the objective. He doesn't care about the who or the why, he cares about himself. . . . But offers a wink of humility at the very end.

2. The second major hurdle your hero (and your script) must endure is the double cross portion of the film. Your hero must learn that the objective they're undertaking has some additional element or that they've been somehow misled into accepting the mission (or discover an element that puts them, or their family, at risk that was never previously explained). In *Shooter*, Mark Wahlberg realizes he's been set up to be the fall-guy. In *Escape From New York*, Kurt Russell learns that two small explosives have been placed into his arteries that will burst in twenty-four hours if he attempts escape. You can play these events in a variety of ways, but it's important to have some kind of double cross to separate your hero from the establishment who hired him, confirming his status as a maverick. . . . That always puts him more into a position of going after the mission in his own way and on his own terms (which allows for a nice transition into Act III).

3. Our hero and our bad guy(s) have more in common than either would like to admit. And for you as the writer, you must also realize that these characters are completely related in terms of storytelling techniques. Consider the *Star Wars* saga: There is one unifying "Force," however some parties chose the good side while others chose the dark side. Perhaps our hero and his nemesis were both highly trained operatives for their individual countries, so in many ways they have a great deal in common. . . . While their loyalty toward their nations makes them enemies, their training allows them each to know the other's strengths and weaknesses. Your bad guy will define traits in your hero (and vice versa). This is not a yin and yang concept, where every attribute is a polar opposite. . . . In reality, they're very similar, only our hero is utilizing his skills to fight for the needs of others, while our bad guy is using others to serve himself. Our hero can do bad things, but he will change his ways for the better, our bad guy is incapable of change and will forever be evil.

4. Our hero must always be outnumbered yet always manages to cleverly get out alive. Remember, he has a mysterious past, training, and experiences that no one outside of him possess. This puts him in a unique situation when it comes to fighting (whether gunplay or hand-to-hand). Use these skills, make the stakes impossible and allow your hero a clever way out. What's most important is that you provide logical and grounded reason why he has these abilities. (On the character of the everyday hero, it's not out of the question to make this character a former criminal or hoodlum, who's now gone straight. . . . The events that have been thrust upon him require a few tricks and traits from his old ways, but all are acceptable because now he's using them for good.)

5. Your hero isn't a sexual being, at least not while on duty. He has a mission and won't be deterred by sins of the flesh. If he's a recovering alcoholic, his mission gives him strength to resist. If he has a sexy partner, they don't engage in the deed on screen (perhaps she makes a move and he pushes her away). The bad guys, on the other hand, are very much influenced by sins of the flesh (because they put the needs of themselves before others). They are the ones likely to have meetings in strip clubs or alongside prostitutes.

6. The bargain. After your hero agrees to take on the mission, then later learns he has in some way been misled about the objective, he goes rogue. Maverick moves are made and the objective is complete. But at the tail end of the movie, especially for an anti-hero character, there is a bargain he must secure from the forces whom have employed him. For Kurt Russell, the explosives in his neck are neutralized and he's not put into prison. For Rambo (in the 2008 version), he is granted emotional freedom and returns to the United States. Perhaps your character's record is being expunged, or he's granted immunity for his deeds, he's again offered a position on the force. . . . Whatever the

scenario, he only accepts in his own way, or just wants the offer made so that he can reject it.

Obviously we have some constraints regarding budget, but these films will usually have a bit more cash allocated to them than, say, a tween romance or Christmas dog adventure. However, that's not to say we can start crashing helicopters or blowing up stadiums. What we need instead is a very specialized world of more covert-style action. Characters follow one another on a city street, then have the big fight in an isolated warehouse or alleyway. Shoot-outs will certainly take place, but they work better if located in interiors where elements can be broken down and controlled during production. Blood, guts, and gunplay are absolutely welcomed, as are some witty one-liners. I won't go into any regulations on location—if you feel your story works best in East Asia or deep in the jungle, I'd say go for it. . . . But you need to limit the scope (and make sure the content is accessible to viewers). You cannot have major action taking place on the streets of Hanoi, but you can have it taking place in a lush jungle or forested area. (Just cut the helicopters and make them jeeps.) If you want to keep things close to home, and use a drug cartel as the opposing element, then have the bulk of the film take place in the desert.

When writing or visualizing this genre type, remember that if the film is ever produced, it will most likely be presold, so make sure you can easily picture your hero on the cover of a poster, gun in hand, somehow taking on more than he can chew. Presell the story to yourself first. . . . Does it offer a high level of interesting action, a character an aged name-actor would be interested in playing, while offering audiences enough bang for their buck that it won't put a producer at financial risk?

Have fun with the title, keep it simple and focused, but consider the imagery the Chuck Norris titles placed in your head. . . . It was easy to see a muscled badass toting a machine gun while saving the day. When in doubt, go for visual, descriptive and "sudden impact" extremes (e.g., *Kill Shot, Maximum Force, In the Crosshairs*).

This is the only gold-mine genre that we will permit as an R-rated film, but keep the language to a minimum. We're not here to set a record with f-bombs, instead keep the R rating potentially related only to violence or light sexual situations. The occasional f-word here or there is fine, but limit them to no more than five to ten throughout the whole script.

The important component is to keep the stakes high, create a logical reason as to why your hero is the only possible person to handle the job, and take us on a journey that adult male truck drivers and cubicle workers can picture themselves in to escape for a little while. Keep asking yourself the "What if?" questions and get to work.

To see real examples of these aged name-actor comeback action films, check out *Blood of Redemption* (2013) featuring Dolph Lundgren, *6 Bullets* (2012) with Jean Claude Van Damme, or *Puncture Wounds* (2014), starring Cung Lee. . . . If you want to see this gold-mine genre with a female twist, have a look at *Border Run* (2012) with Sharon Stone.

Gold-Mine Genre Type #6: The Young Boy's Action/Adventure Film

This genre type is sort of the male version of the family-safe tween romance (and the family/kid-friendly version of the aged name-actor comeback action film); in a similar way, it too fills a much-needed family/tween demand many channels and VOD outlets have, meaning agents, producers, and development executives are always very ecstatic to come across these gems to fill the supply line.

Young boys (ages seven to eleven) are a very imaginative and active bunch. And it's not just sports they're interested in playing—they go off into the woods and invent all kinds of creative scenarios. Whether they're pretending to be top-secret spies, detectives, war heroes, or are searching the neighborhoods high and wide for buried treasure, boys are always up to something. . . . And it usually involves a great deal of mud.

The best combo for these films is a group of three friends. It works if all three are boys, but it can also work as two boys and one girl (for me, coed is always best). A gem of an addition is a dog or an animal, though this is not advisable if the film involves a lot of movement, action, and so on (since having a dog on site during all those production days would be very difficult). However you want to structure this trio is purely up to you, so just see what feels right as you start toying around with ideas. The only rule is the hero must be a boy.

The problem for readers and development executives is that most of the spec scripts claiming to be young boy's action/adventure films are more in the vein of coming-of-age stories—a wannabe move. Occasionally, a few of these come along and do excellent, but they're few and far between. The *Writing for the Green Light* move is to draft a spec script catered to the needs of Hollywood, which means designing a film that will attract the interest and imagination of a young boy while gaining his parent/guardian's approval.

Regarding budget constraints, there are three storylines that that work best—and guarantee the strongest placement on TV and home entertainment venues here in the United States and worldwide. I'm giving examples, but there are a multitude of directions you can take these storylines. The real goal, as with the family-safe tween romance, is to take yourself back to this age in your life and really think about the fantastic ideas you had, and roll with them! What adventures did you get into during those long summers? Did your neighborhood have a creepy old house you were dared to sneak into? Ever have to spend a long summer at camp or with relatives in a different state? What fantasies did you imagine where you played the hero? This is your time to live them out:

1. *Top Secret Spy Adventure*—Spies are cool, and most young boys wish they could be one (perhaps that's actually a secret most men never fully shake off even in adulthood). If you want proof on the validity of this genre, check out the hugely successful Robert Rodriguez departure of *Spy Kids* (2001) and its many spin-offs. Imagine a fifth-grade

boy, perhaps not the most popular kid in school, who's somehow swept up into a large-scale spy adventure. . . . Brilliant. He can't tell anyone, not even his parents, but the CIA or some other organization needs his help. Whatever the reason (and it has to be a family-safe one), our hero has witnessed something and the CIA/FBI are forced to utilize him—either he's related to the bad guys, has some unique trait or skill that grants him access where CIA/FBI technology cannot reach, etc. . . . After all, who would suspect a kid? Eventually he must confide in a few close friends in order to accomplish the objective(s) (which are safe ones, but ones that put our hero into some precarious situations). Obviously we're in a zone where there's no gunplay or explosions, but plenty of following, sneaking, and walkie-talkie action (with close calls of being caught). The stakes are very high, and some very important organizations are fully depending on our hero to accomplish his objectives—and he's only able to do so with the help of his friends. In the end, all is secured. Imagine a conclusion where all order is restored and our kids go back to school. They're still not the most popular and no one would ever believe their story. . . . That is until a very special visitor arrives: Picture something ridiculous like the president of the United States pulling up to your school in a limo, entering your math or science class, and shaking your hand, giving you public recognition and bragging rights of a job well done. That's the kind of stuff a young boy would be ecstatic for, and those are the kinds of scenarios you can live out here.

2. *Crime Stoppers*—This version is much more open-ended and can cover a great deal of plot lines. (Ideally, this is the plot where a dog or an animal sidekick works best.) Essentially, a series of local crimes are taking place (someone is stealing equipment from the school, someone is taking very specific objects from houses or shops in the neighborhood, that sort of thing). The police are baffled and so are the residents. That is until our hero, his friends, and their trusty sidekick (if an animal is used) come to the rescue. Usually what happens is that one of the characters has the crime directly affect them (or their parents, grandparent, etc.). After the police have left, they do some investigating of their own. They find a clue the police missed. They try to do the right thing and turn it in, but the police give them a "Thanks, we'll take it from here," and dismiss the significance of their discovery. But the kids decide to go at it alone. The plot really takes off when the kids realize it's someone they know (an adult) who's guilty of the crimes, someone the police and their parents are overlooking—and of course, no one will believe our young heroes. If you use an animal here, make it really fun and interactive (the dog has a great nose and links this adult to the crimes, or a puzzle-solving chimp whom the kids refer to as "Detective Banks" when in a jam, puts the pieces together and finds an identity of the crook). In the end, the kids are able to solve the crime; they accuse the wrongdoer, and just as the wrongdoer is about

to inflict harm or threaten our heroes, the real police come in and save the day. That first "Thanks, but no thanks" cop reaches down to apologize and admits that he later followed up on the lead and realized the kids were onto something, so he had been following them just to make sure they were safe. Alternatively, if we're following a group of wrongdoers, one of them is in fact an undercover police officer. In the end, crime does not pay, and our heroes are given all the credit they rightfully deserve.

3. *Treasure Hunters*—By far, *The Goonies* (1985) is the classic version of this tale, but I've seen it at much smaller levels too. Essentially, a young group of boys (or a small coed team) witness their parents in some kind of financial hardship. Unable to help, they go kicking around town until they decide to investigate the local legend of a buried treasure. Whether by doing some research at the library, or stumbling around old attics, they find a map or other clues and begin their journey. But, as fate would have it (i.e., good plot structure) it just so happens a couple of thieves are after the same goods. Our young heroes must get to the treasure first and defend it from the bad guys. In the end, of course, the young kids save the day—but their parents' recognition (and helping out their family when they're in need) is the real climax. The treasure doesn't always need to be a legit buried treasure either. . . . The kids could have a chimp friend who just happens to be amazingly talented at surfing, so the kids cleverly sneak the chimp into a surf competition in order to beat out the snotty prep-school kids and win prize money for their parents.

The most important thing to remember when writing a young boy's action/adventure film is to simply have fun. You can have the film center around a downhill go-cart race, secret passages from the sewers, or any other childhood daydreams. Take the crime stoppers character of "Detective Banks" (a chimp character I invented for example purposes only). The phone rings, Detective Banks (a chimp) answers, on the other line is our bad guy, who starts asking questions not realizing Det. Banks is a chimp! "What can I give you to call this whole thing off, Detective?" Our chimp puts his lips together and makes a fart sound. The bad guy gets angry and loses his cool, "Detective Banks" just laughs or makes other potty sounds. (Potty humor obviously goes over great with this crowd, bad guys getting knocked over in port-o-potties, or their skin getting dyed blue with toilet bowl cleaner, etc.) The more fun, the more goofy (and the more dumb/easily tricked the bad guys are), the better.

But as with all our gold-mine genres, here are the ground rules:

1. No guns. Drop the shoot-'em-up concepts and focus on the storyline. If you need violence, then keep it slapsticky. Think *Home Alone* (1991) levels of violence. A good hit to the balls or knock to the head is much more effective in this group than a gunshot. Only our police or

military personnel are allowed to have guns, in that it's part of their uniform.

2. Our hero has two nemeses: Our "B-story bully" (someone who makes fun or causes trouble in our hero's day-to-day life) and our "A-story bad guy" (the real nemesis within the true plot of the film). Ideally, our hero's ability to overcome the A-story bad guy is able to make the B-story bully a joke and our hero can overtake him without hesitation (in a nonviolent, outsmarting way . . . one that promotes good values). Perhaps our hero defeats our B-story bully by inviting him into the Crime Stoppers' or Treasure Hunters' Club?

3. Our hero must have a love interest—it could be the girl in the trio, or it could just be a cute neighbor down the street, but there is someone whom he longs for, who certainly pays attention to him at the end of the film after our young hero saves the day. It could be fun if she's been interested the whole time, only our leading young man didn't know how to respond, but at the end he's developed the confidence to show her what he's made of. . . . But again, just like the tween romance, the most action these youths are going to get is at most a quick peck on the lips.

4. Our hero boy's interest in the beginning of the film is what he'll end up living out as his adventure. Meaning, for our crime stoppers storyline, our young hero already has an interest in detectives or police officers from the beginning. . . . That way, when he sees an opportunity to live out his fantasies in real life, he's already prepared. In our treasure hunters surfing-chimp example, our young boy would already have a huge interest in surfing, that way he'd be up to speed about the local competition long in advance. . . . Perhaps he's even been training for it, but got injured (and using the chimp is the maverick move to secure the treasure).

5. Remember logistics! These kids cannot drive, so you're going to need to think through how our characters are logically getting from point A to B; whether they sneak off during a class field trip, or they're able to get to their destination on foot or by bike, how they arrived has to make sense. . . . Otherwise, one of them needs to be able to convince his mother to drive them, for which any mother would ask way too many questions.

6. The theme is a valuable lesson. Whether we're focused on crime not paying, respecting authority, or being kind to those different than ourselves, you need to treat the playing rules of this genre type as if they're the principles of Cub Scouts or some other youth organization. The idea that if we work hard and follow the rules, we'll succeed is very appealing to this demographic (and to their parents, who will be buying/renting this content for them).

You can see that there's a great deal of latitude within this genre type. Again, the idea here is to fully immerse yourself into a youthful state of mind and start asking yourself about all those imaginative fantasies you had. . . . The ones in which you were asked by the fire department to assist in a dangerous rescue, or where the CIA landed a helicopter on your playground and needed your help. Take *The Adventures of Tintin* (1991–1992), breed it with *The Young Indian Jones Chronicles* (1992–1993) and make the hero your young fifth-grade self, living out those crazy adventures for real. The most important rule is keep it safe and logical. . . . After that, have fun!

For real examples, check out: *Junior High Spy* (2011), *Monster Mutt* (2011), or *Sam Steele and the Junior Detective Agency* (2009).

WHY NOT HORROR?

Horror is a very underrated and popular genre for films, but that doesn't make it a wise choice for your spec script.

This is the one commercial genre that most newbies feel semi-comfortable attempting—because they feel as if they're allowing themselves to write commercially while not becoming a sellout. As a result, there's a huge surplus of horror scripts, most of them following gimmicks or trends (such as the zombie films mentioned earlier). . . . Whenever there's a surplus, all candidates in the same category get judged more harshly.

Horror scripts do hold strong value; if you have a great idea for one, it's definitely worth pursuing—just don't use horror as your out-of-the-gate spec script. Hold onto your idea, wait until you have a little clout or some trusted contacts before pulling a horror film out of the woodwork.

BUT YOU PRESOLD A DISASTER FILM. . . .

9.6 Mega-Tsunami was a disaster film, that's true. But our company had our disaster films streamlined from beginning to end. We were never speculative with these films; we only produced them if they were commissioned from us (meaning there were clients out there willing to pre-buy the rights).

At that same company, we attempted to sell numerous disaster films (probably three times the number we actually produced) that never got traction in the marketplace. When disaster films work, they work really well. . . . But they're volatile, and far from being considered a stable or reliable standard.

The gold-mine genres are your real ticket in; they have worked consistently for decades as a proven need in Hollywood. Stick to those.

I'VE BEEN TOLD TO WRITE "HIGH CONCEPT"

The phrase "high concept" gets thrown about constantly and it seems to be the "in" thing everyone in Hollywood is looking for—so what is it?

At first glance, most people apply the term "high concept" to big-budget summertime blockbusters, the ones with superheroes or epic space battles. More recently, the phrase became a generic way of instructing screenwriters to write bigger-budgeted ideas, but in a way that can be shot for cheap.

The truth is that a "high concept" movie is nothing more than a very simple idea that can be explained in a clear, concise way. Go back to our classic creature feature *Alien*: The title is clear, so is the poster. Even better, so is the pitch: "*Jaws* in Space." Brilliant. All the information you need to know about the film is laid out in front of you.

The idea of high-concept films isn't new; Hollywood has always had an intense appetite for them. . . . But it's becoming more common for pretentious types to use this phrase in all the wrong ways, saying things like "I'm trying to write more high-concept scripts" or "You should be writing more high-concept ideas if you want to get an agent."

So what does it really mean? And if Hollywood is looking for these high-concept ideas, shouldn't that be what a novice writer turns in rather than these gimmicky gold-mine genre types?

Truth is, these gold-mine genre types *are* high-concept films. Again, a high-concept idea is a movie based on a very simple premise that is clearly summarized by its poster and its pitch. Yes, big-budget films meet these demands, but a family Christmas dog adventure does as well. Picture it: A poster with two good-looking people, a Christmas tree, and a golden retriever wearing a Santa Claus hat is extremely clear. . . . You know exactly what you're getting. Add a title as simple—and adorable—as *Santa Paws* (a real movie) and you're set. Same holds true for all the gold-mine genres.

A high-concept movie is a *sellable* movie, one that is straightforward and has a secured audience out there ready to watch it. It's a film that is instantly identifiable by its poster and offers audiences exactly what they're expecting from it. It has nothing to do with its budget or theme. If a film has a concise concept targeted towards a secured audience, then it's hedged against risk—meaning producers and distributors feel more comfortable investing money to make it.

High concept does not mean bigger and bolder; it means simple, clear and sellable.

WRITING FOR UNIVERSAL APPEAL

The most important thing to remember, regardless of which of the gold-mine genres you pursue, is to keep the story, the characters, and the theme you're presenting as honest to your experiences as possible. Agents, producers, and production companies are not just evaluating your script for the U.S. market, they are thinking global! They are very excited to find scripts based on the above genres, but they're even more apt to green-light you if your script can be understood universally, so keep that perspective in mind as you draft out your ideas.

Not everyone on the planet understands Thanksgiving, but everyone celebrates New Year's. If your story involves sports, try to avoid highly regionalized sports like baseball or American football and instead use a sport that's popular worldwide, like basketball or soccer. Remember Clint Eastwood's Nelson Mandela/rugby film *Invictus* (2009)? They got away with it since it was a studio film based on a true story. . . . But I certainly had no idea what was happening during the climax of the final game. And since you're not being commissioned by Eastwood to draft a script, you need to appeal to the entities looking to evaluate your talents.

Despite the simplicity of each gold-mine genre type (and how visually they put a poster image into your mind), they also hit at very approachable themes, understood by everyone. The family Christmas dog adventure is really about connecting with family and finding new love (very warm and fuzzy emotions, and adding the dog just makes it even more heart-warming). The woman-in-peril thriller explores deeply rooted fears, not just how frightening it is to feel vulnerable and victimized, but how emotionally shattering it is to realize the very system that's supposed to help you is also protecting the enemy. The family-safe tween romance explores all those early and exciting rushes of first love that helped shape the adults we would all grow up to become. The creature feature is all in the subtext. And both the aged name-actor comeback action film and the young boy's action/adventure film explore a male's desire to do the right thing while living out a fantasy of saving the day.

Everyone, regardless of gender or nationality, understands these feelings and emotions. We've all felt them one way or another. Take a look into your own life and experiences, ask yourself when you've felt any of the above, then ask yourself "What if?" What if you'd made a different choice? What if you could go back and stop yourself from making the decision you did? What if things had been different?

Asking these questions and using your personal experiences will allow you to find which of the six genres best works for you as a writer. Also, by asking these questions of yourself, you will avoid many pitfalls found in first-time scripts, such as clichés, forced resolutions, and illogical character progression. In addition, getting real about yourself and your own past experiences will create those magic movie moments that truly do strike a chord in both script readers and audience members alike.

THREE

WRITING YOUR FEATURE-LENGTH SPEC SCRIPT

In this chapter, we'll outline how to transform an idea into a market-ready spec script—one that showcases your talents while also proving you're a writer who "gets" what Hollywood needs. We'll lay off heavy emphasis on formatting and instead discuss how to write a spec script that will stand out to those tasked with reading it.

THE HARDEST PART ABOUT SCREENWRITING

You would think the hardest part about screenwriting would be getting someone to see your talent, believe in your potential *and* give you that first professional break. . . . But in truth, the hardest part about screenwriting is just getting someone to actually read your script from beginning to end.

The good news is that the very people who have the power and means to give you that first big break are actively looking for quality scripts from talented writers. (They want to find you; their jobs depend on it!) The bad news, however, is that in order to find those quality scripts and writers, they must accept unsolicited material—which means their offices get bombarded with dozens (if not hundreds) of scripts from wannabes every single week!

With that kind of volume rushing in, agents, producers, and development executives have all learned they can save a *lot* of time searching for that next great script by first weeding out all the bad ones. But take a moment to understand what this really means: In order to weed out bad spec scripts, those tasked with reading all those submissions are much more focused on finding mistakes rather than discovering potential. The faster an individual reading a script can find something they *don't like* about it, the faster they can put it down and move onto the next one.

We all know the first ten to twelve pages of a spec script are crucial, but your work is being judged before it is even opened. . . . But have no fear, because getting someone to read your script from cover to cover is not a matter of luck; it's a matter of strategy.

GETTING PAST THE *READER'S* DESK

No executives in Hollywood want to read scripts. . . . Again, it's nothing personal; they simply don't have the time! Besides, there are so many *non*-gold-mine genre type scripts to sift through—which simply clog up the system—that agents, producers, and development execs are completely burnt out.

So, they delegate this task by hiring staff members to read all the submissions and filter out the good from the bad. Once these "readers," as they're known, are finished with each script they write-up a three to four page synopsis and sum the whole thing up with a one-word ranking: "Pass," "consider," or "recommend." This process is called "writing coverage," or simply "covering" a script. (I've provided a sample of this Coverage in Appendix I.)

Studios generally employ card-carrying unionized readers to cover their scripts (who are full-time, salaried employees with benefits packages); however, for an unknown writer submitting an unsolicited "foot-in-the door" spec script (like you), your work will not get to the studios. . . . It will instead enter the topsy-turvy world of the independents. Unlike the studios, independent talent agencies and production companies have much tighter budgets and prefer free labor (or, at best, *extremely* cheap labor). . . . So, they hire interns to be their readers and train them on what to look for.

Interns are generally nineteen to twenty-five-year-olds with very limited professional experience who are trying to gain their own first break in the business. Despite the fact that most of these interns are unpaid, still in school, and have zero experience in any professional sense, these are the individuals who have been granted exclusive permission to decide whether your script should be "considered" or "recommended" to those with the power and means to professionally represent or produce it—meaning, by default, interns hold the power to rank your worth in Hollywood.

But coverage doesn't just "pass," "consider," or "recommend" the script; there's also a section where the reader must evaluate the strengths and weaknesses of the writer. If a reader decides to reject your script, they still have the ability to "recommend" *you* as a potential future writing candidate—which would certainly give your name more clout the next time a producer or development exec is in need of a writer to commission.

Don't falsely assume that this "fact-of-Hollywood" is just for the newbies. Even if you have a few legit contacts in the business, having your script vetted by a reader first is almost unavoidable. And if a spec script comes in that's highly "recommended" (even written by someone an agent, producer, or development executive knows well and trusts), there's still a high probability they'll hand off the burden of reading it and wait for the coverage. They don't do this because they are self-righteous or callous; they do this because they are busy!

So for you and your spec script, there's really no way around the reader's desk. *Readers* are the ones for whom you are really writing. . . . Avoiding this reality does not make it go away, but accepting it (and working with it) does get you one step closer to your first green light.

TAKING BACK CONTROL

Intern-level readers are usually either aspiring screenwriters or producers—generally in film school working for class credit while attempting to make a few professional connections on the side. The great part about these readers is that they're very eager to experience and contribute to the real working world of Hollywood. . . . And for you there is an added silver lining; readers truly do want to be the one to have discovered that next great script—which means they will attempt to read your entire screenplay (because it is their job to do so).

The downfall is readers are human. I see them arrive in our offices every day, dressed to impress, ready to take on a new stack of scripts and hammer out their coverage to "wow" their bosses. But the hours drag by, their energy gets low, and as the day comes to a close they've lost that good posture and their eyes grow red and distant from sheer exhaustion. Reading five or ten scripts a day (500 to 1,000 pages) is a heck of a lot of work by itself, but remember they have to write three to four pages of coverage for each script on top of that!

Personally, I would like to believe that if I were in their shoes I could maintain the composure (and decency) to evaluate each new spec script with an open mind and an attentive focus. . . . But I know I wouldn't be able to. If I'm really honest with myself, I know that after a few hours, I'd stop reading each script word-for-word and simply start skimming the pages. After a few days, I too would start looking for mistakes in each script just so I could put it down and move onto the next one. After a few weeks, I think I'd start to feel madness at just the sight of the words "FADE IN." (And readers have *stacks* of scripts to go through each day . . .)

You as a writer have no control over where your script will fall in that stack or what time of the day your reader will pull yours from the pile. (You also can't control whether your reader has just been dumped by their college fling, is suffering a hangover, or is more interested in flirting with the cute intern next to them—all of which I've seen.) I wish your spec script would simply get the respect it deserves. . . . It won't.

Don't get huffy about the cruelty of the system (a wannabe move), because there is a way to take back control from this unfortunate reality and proactively shape your spec script with a "reader-conscious" contingency built in. How? It's actually quite simple: **Write a spec script that makes the reader's job easier.** In short: Readers want a very clear-cut script, in a style that's easy on their eyes, one they can follow even if distracted or tired, which allows them the ability to write coverage in a relatively easy way—and that's precisely what you're going to write for them.

But making the reader's job easier doesn't guarantee you or your script a ranking of "consider" or "recommend"; it's only the first step. The second important factor is ensuring your script stands out from all the others while also representing something Hollywood is actively in need of. . . . We covered this in detail in Chapter Two. Writing a gold-mine genre type is a very rare decision for a newbie writer, and these genres are very much in demand at the indie production and development level (meaning readers will have been briefed by development execs in advance to keep an open eye for such genres).

So, now that you know what genres work, you just need a breakdown of how to make your script easy on your reader's eye, right? Unfortunately no. There is one other unspoken factor about readers you need to be aware of—they are overly sensitive and extremely picky. After reading script after script for weeks on end, readers develop a very finely-tuned set of observations about spec scripts that they use as their "pass-or-consider" barometer. We can consider these pet peeves, but in reality, it's a list of occurrences readers have grown to absolutely *hate* when reading a new script, regardless of its genre, style, or story.

As already stated, readers are first looking for a reason to "pass" on your script. . . . Having a detailed list of what readers *hate most* in spec scripts is a pretty good way to know how to get your work past their desk.

TEN THINGS READERS *HATE* ABOUT SPEC SCRIPTS

In preparing for this chapter, I went directly to the source and interviewed several actively working readers. Sure, I wanted to get a real sense of what it is they looked for when reading scripts, but more importantly I wanted to learn what it was that triggered them to close a script midway through and rank it with a "pass."

I found if I asked what they wanted to see in each script they picked up, I'd get the same old answers: "Good characters," "good story," and so on. But to get the juice, I asked each of them point blank: "What do you hate most about the scripts you read?"

That question alone got each interview into a very productive zone, which is exactly where I wanted them to be. (Oddly enough, each reader described almost the exact same list.) If a reader was on the fence about a script, or its writer, the following observations were the factors that would push a reader into the "pass" zone, which is exactly where we *don't* want your script to be. . . . So, let's go over each of the top ten things readers hate about new spec scripts:

#10: Scripts that are too long or too short—Readers are judging your script before they've even opened it. If they pick one up that's too thick or too thin, their judgments about your writing capabilities are already in motion. With the "1 script page = 1 minute on screen" rule of thumb, your script needs to be in the zone of an average film's running time. However, movies are get-

ting shorter, not longer. The old parameters surrounding the 120-page target (with your Act II commencing on page 30, and Act III on page 90) are gone. Now, a 90-minute movie is passable all by itself—sometimes a bit shorter is fine. In the sales and distribution contracts I negotiate, narrative feature films are usually defined as having a minimum running time of 86 minutes (with credits). So for safety, your script needs to be in the mid-90s to be acceptable to a reader. The ideal minimum number of pages is 95—this allows a reader to feel it's a shorter (and faster-reading) script, while also giving them the confidence that it has enough content that, even with a few cuts, it will still meet minimum running times. On the length side, 120 pages today is way too long. If your script is going to break 100 pages, then keep it at a maximum of 109 pages tops. Once you break that 110 number, you have psychologically scared your reader before they've even opened your script. They'll look extra hard for reasons early on to say no just so they don't have to read that behemoth. Aim for a range of 95 to 109 pages—no more, no less.

#9: *Scripts with confusing character names*—There are generally three problems for readers when it comes to character names: Names that are overly "deep," multiple names starting with the same letter (or that look the same), and names that are just too difficult to quickly read. It's fun when there's a bit of thought put behind the names you give your characters, but there's no need to create some overly elaborate concept in the process. At the end of the day, simplicity always trumps complexity, so the names you give your characters should be no different. Think about the people you know in your daily life, the bulk of them have pretty common names. The differences are usually more subtle nuances (such as Character A comes from Texas while Character B comes from New York); it's generally the backstory of a character that dictates their name rather than their role within the story. And when you consider many of the films you watch, we barely know the actual names of our characters (unless there's a reason for us to know). If you really fall in love with your own creativity about a deep-meaning character name, and then force another character to speak that name, this falls into the realm of forced dialogue and reads awkwardly. This doesn't mean the names you give your characters can't have some subtle context or meaning to them, but don't hammer us over the head. And regarding character names that begin with the same letter, this principle doesn't mean you have to choose a different letter for each character you introduce—just make sure each name is easily differentiated when glanced a). . . . Good example: Using JOE and JIM on the same page of dialogue can be confusing to the tired eyes of a reader, but JOE and JOHNATHAN are easily differentiated by length.

#8: *Scripts that can't keep their facts straight*—This one is a bit more challenging and open-ended, yet it covers a wide variety of annoyances that readers mentioned. One example would be a writer's misrepresentation of history—not just textbook historical information, but simple historical elements related to the story (using incorrect dates, lacking an understanding of chronology, or confusing how one story event leads to the next). You'd be shocked how many scripts present a character one way, then 180 everything last minute (there's few real-world examples to pull from since they never make it to production). Take time to truly map out not only your story, but how each sequence of events shapes then next. If your story involves references to the past, make sure you have a clear list of dates when each of the events supposedly took place. A second example would be a lack of continuity within a story's framework (which can range from time-lags, like when teenagers can clearly outrun the "walking" Jason Voorhees from the *Friday the 13th* movies, yet he's always able to get ahead of them, or the full understanding of how one event truly dictates the direction of the story while eliminating other options or opportunities, for example by forcing a character to make a decision because it's right for the plot, but doesn't make sense for their character). Think of it like this: If a character injures his or her hand early in the script, that hand must stay injured (until enough time has passed for it to heal)! If a character picks up a gun and is carrying it, then that character must be carrying that gun until her or she puts it down (or uses it). And if a character makes a major decision, make sure it's the right decision for the character, not just the plot. As one reader pointed out, "If you don't care enough about your own script to keep the facts within it straight, how can you expect others to?"

#7: *Scripts with mixed genres*—Readers voiced very negative opinions about writers attempting to mix genres instead of just picking one and sticking to it. A large number of newbie writers try to stand out (or show off) by taking two unrelated genres and forcing them to work together. Writing a story that blends multiple genres is a very difficult skill to master, even for a veteran screenwriter. Without a great deal of expertise, most mixed-genre spec scripts read as choppy, sporadically shifting gears between genres from one scene to the next (or even worse, within the *same scene*). But even for those newbie writers who do choose only one genre for their script, they still commonly come up short because they don't fully adhere to their genre's expectations—they try to invigorate the genre by adding unexpected elements which they falsely believe is showcasing a unique twist without realizing it makes their work appear weak. The gold-mine genre types are a great way to stay focused and keep your story filtered with one clear-cut genre—each outlined in Chapter Two, including character and theme. Don't be tempted to bend the rules or step outside of the box on this front. Your genre keeps you grounded and establishes the rules you need to play by; there are plenty of other ways to make your story and characters stand out—mixing genres just adds too many variables toward disaster. "It's okay if there's a touch of this or that to spice it up," said one of my readers, "just as long as there's one clear genre we're using as our foundation." Pick a genre (ideally a gold-mine genre type), embrace it and marry yourself to it!

#6: *Scripts that don't get to the point!*—Readers approached this irritant in a variety of ways, but their end message was the same: They couldn't stand thumb-twiddling (or casual page filler) of any kind. Watch any TV program or film you respect (meaning one you believe is well-written) and you'll notice that characters drop many of our real-world formalities: They rarely say "goodbye" when hanging up a phone, there's rarely any "how's the family?" chit-chat upon entering a room. They cut these "fills" and simply jump right into what's important. Film editors call this "cutting on action" and you can do the same with your spec script. From page one, every word of your script must only serve the purpose of propelling your story forward, toward its natural resolution (*not* just toward its appropriate page count). But there's more than just making sure your scenes are starting on action and resolving when the important plot points have been covered, you as a writer also need to ensure you're getting to the point with your descriptions. Some books refer to this as keeping as much white space on the page as possible (especially since readers cringe when they see dense blocks of descriptive language). You'd be surprised how many 100-word paragraphs of text can be cut down to fewer than 15 words. Your job as a writer is not to dictate things like camera angles (cut out the "CUs" and "POVs"—you're not the director, you're the *writer*), nor actor directions (such as 'sighs' or 'pauses,' those decisions don't belong to you). Stick to what's important: Where the scene is taking place, which cast members are in the scene, and what props or elements are absolutely necessary to progress your story forward. Keep cutting and cutting (and cutting) until losing one more word would make the story fall apart. Not only will the large amount of white space make a reader appreciate your to-the-point writing style, it will also make your script read much faster (which will keep a reader reading your script). Too many words slows them down and makes your story drag, causing your reader to lose focus. Make sure you cut out, condense, and combine as many words as possible so that your script *feels* like a fast and effortless read. (This point is also your best way to gain more traction in the "consider" or "recommend" column on your writing talent, even if you script is passed upon.)

#5: *Scripts with no hook*—There's no magic or hidden meaning to the classic Hollywood phrase: "Give me the same thing, only different." Agents, producers, and development execs will always claim they want something new and original, but in reality, they're looking for these six gold-mine genre types, only redelivered with a twist. The common word is "fresh" (e.g., "Make it fresh," or "Bring something fresh to the table"). But a better way to explain what readers and their employers are really looking for is what we call a "hook." Although readers are trained to seek out gold-mine genre types (and are therefore more forgiving of their clichés), there are still limitations to boredom and predictability—especially if yours happens to be the last script of the day. A "hook," by contrast, is that special "it" factor. . . . That element that leaps from the page as that perfect add-on or twist. It makes a boring carbon-copy spec script submission suddenly exciting or interesting (and it makes a reader accept minor clichés and continue reading). Good example: *Snakes on a Plane* (2006). . . . Rumor has it Samuel L. Jackson agreed to star in *Snakes* based on the title alone. *Snakes on a Plane* is by no means a good film. . . . But it has a very simple hook. It's a creature feature (about snakes) in an isolated environment (on a plane). That's it. . . . Gold-mine genre type #4 with a hook. It's the same old creature feature, but delivered in a fresh and compelling way. Going back to *Alien*, it too is a creature feature (about an alien) in an isolated environment (on a distant space ship). *Alien* is "*Jaws* in Space" and for its time, it too was the same thing, only different. You don't have to reinvent the wheel here (and you certainly shouldn't try!), but do understand that if your script is going toe-to-toe with nine other family Christmas dog adventures, they're all going to blur together in the mind of a tired reader. . . . What little twist can you add that makes yours stand out? It can be as simple as placing your setting somewhere unexpected (Christmas in Miami Beach). Or performing a role reversal, as was done in a secret favorite film of mine, *Bring It On* (2000). . . . It's gold-mine genre type #3, the family-safe tween romance, only our confused and uncertain heroine already is the most popular girl in school (which, as it turns out, doesn't actually make her high school experience any better). The mistake most newbie writers make when trying to add a hook or an edge to their spec script is to first attempt to poorly blend genres (which is why the seventh most common thing readers hate in spec scripts is forced-together genres). Take the extra time when plotting out your story, consider the common trends and patterns you find in the competition, then find one aspect that you can pluck out and add your own personal spin to. . . . Even just a small amount of effort goes a long way with those tired, bored readers.

#4:   *Scripts that lack a consistent point of view*—All of my readers mentioned that the majority of spec scripts they read had a main character—who was clearly the focus—but that the story wasn't experienced *through* them. (This I found very interesting and unexpected). The audience must experience your story through one consistent lens. . . . This is usually from the perspective of the main character, but that doesn't mean your protagonist needs to be present in every scene. I'll pull a fun example from a studio-level movie we've all seen just to illustrate: *Ferris Bueller's Day Off* (1986)—even though many scenes and sequences of the film take place without the character of Ferris Bueller (Matthew Broderick) present, the events are still filtered through *our* experience of *his* day off. . . . Picture all the scenes with the two garage flunkies taking the Ferrari for a joyride (even though Ferris is unaware of this action, it will be a problem he must later deal with), or the ruthless determination of Principal Rooney (Jeffery Jones) to catch Ferris (again, all build up to Ferris's overall story and experience). "I need to know whose point of view I'm supposed to experience this journey through," said one of my readers. "I don't have to necessarily identify with them, but I need to understand their perspective to grasp the overall context." Regardless of which gold-mine genre you choose or however you shape its main character, the world your reader needs to experience must be the world according to the perspective of your main character. Again, scenes (and sequences) can take place without the presence of your protagonist, but you must ensure we're only experiencing such moments because of *how* they will affect your hero later on.

#3:   *Scripts with poor structure*—To my surprise, most readers admitted that a script's structure was slightly more important than its story—keyword: *slightly*! The story is critically important, no question about that; but the story's structure of events—and the decisions your characters make as a result (commonly referred to as "beats") that make one event logically flow to the next—is really the glue that keeps it all together. For my readers, a strong story delivered through a poorly structured script was just too distracting for most of them to overlook. Remember, readers are conditioned to use superficial mistakes as a way of judging a writer's experience. . . . An artistic decision from your perspective might not *read* that way on the other side. From the reader's perspective, writers that followed the strict guidelines of their genre's structure came off as writers in control of their craft—leading readers to evaluate them in the coverage as more professional and more talented. A development executive also weighed in on this point, explaining that by the time a script is delivered to a production company, it's simply seen by everyone in an "as is" kind of way. Therefore, any changes or edits suggested by the team tend to be ones based on what's already written on the pages before them (meaning suggestions are mostly about dialogue, description, or other surface-level changes). A strongly structured script with clichéd dialogue is just a polish job, easy to fix in one or two rounds. But taking apart a poorly structured script and reassembling it from scratch is much more labor intensive, and there's no guarantee the time investment is even worth the effort. So, even for upper-echelon members of the production team, a solid structure was much more telling of a writer's talents and abilities than just story alone. This plays heavily into the way Hollywood hedges itself against risk; people like to boast how they want to be a part of something groundbreaking and unique, but at the end of the day, they're completely dependent upon proven structures for guidance. . . . If you show them your mastery over structure, they're much more likely to consider your work. The three best books I've found that offer strong (and applicable) insight into how to structure your script are: Blake Snyder's *Save the Cat: The Last Screenwriting Book You'll Ever Need* (2005), Syd Field's groundbreaking *Screenplay: The Foundations of Screenwriting* (1979), and Raymond G. Frensham's *Teach Yourself Screenwriting* (1997).

#2: *Scripts with* idiot *dialogue*—There's bad dialogue and then there's idiot dialogue. . . . Bad dialogue includes things like overly long dialogue blocks, run-on sentences, or multiple characters speaking with similar phrases or styles. Idiot dialogue, on the other hand, is the screenwriting equivalent to fixing a jet engine with chewing gum; it's used by weak writers to fill-in plot holes, explain irrational character behaviors, or to simply fill space and reach the correct number of pages. If a script has a solid structure, which follows the rules of its gold-mine genre, and has a fun hook to spice things up, bad dialogue is a relatively easy cleanup job (it's certainly not advised, but it's not a death wish). Idiot dialogue is a clear and incurable symptom of a script (and a writer) with nothing to offer. So what is it, exactly? Idiot dialogue is the literal and verbal explanation of events, actions, thoughts, or intentions—this has also been referred to as "As you know, Bob" dialogue, because the phrase "As you know, . . ." typically precedes a character recapping something that happened in order to bring the audience up to speed. Do we as humans speak of our feelings or thoughts openly or literally? Absolutely not. . . . We say we're happy even when we're miserable. We refuse help when we're desperate for it. We say we're in love when we're not and we say we're not when we are! People don't speak literally; in fact our words are quite meaningless. It's only our *actions* that prove our strengths. If a character is lonely or hurting, a great deal of spec scripts will contain long passages with that character explaining their thoughts or feelings. . . . This is idiot dialogue. First, people rarely just openly pour out their hearts to others—and honestly, few people want to listen to it (which is why therapists cost so much money); second, if your goal as a writer is to convey the level of hurt and loneliness your character is going through, it would actually be much more effective for your character to lie and say "no, I'm fine" when they're in need. People generally say the opposite of what they mean, so characters in your script must follow suit. And if we're not lying about our thoughts or feelings, then we're explaining them through analogies. . . . People only pony-up and speak bluntly when they have something to gain. (Use this observation to build real character interaction that not only strengthens your conflict, but makes it more interesting—and fun—to read.) But it's not just thoughts and feelings that read as "idiotic" on the page; characters explaining plot points or motivations are forms of idiot dialogue as well. . . . For example: Two spies running through a corridor, explaining to each other why it's so important they stop the bad guy. We already know stopping the bad guy is important—not only that, they're spies and it's their *job* to stop the bad guy (so they would already know stopping the bad guy is really important)! If you're writing your rough draft and you fill it to the brim with idiot dialogue, that's totally fine (because it's a draft, it's not your final submitted version). We all write junk to initially get our ideas on the page and flesh out where we want things to go. But as you fine tune your script's structure, tighten its plot points, and develop its characters, make sure you're using dialogue to *progress* the themes and meaning of your story, not to explain them or to lazily fill in the gaps.

#1: *Scripts with typos or grammatical errors*—Sad that each reader actually mentioned typos and grammatical errors, but even more so as the number one reason most of them put a script down after ten to fifteen pages. You don't have to be perfect; you can use loose or free-flowing language to get your points across. Readers will even forgive a typo here and there; but when a reader picks up your script and comes across blatant typos or poorly constructed grammar, it gives the appearance that you didn't really take much time to revise your work. And if you as the writer didn't have time to value your work, why should a reader? Remember, readers have the ability to "pass" on your script while still recommending your writing abilities. . . . But they have to be completely confident in your writing in order to ever recommend your script. (It doesn't work the other way around.) Do you think a script full of typos is going to get a writer recommended? It won't. One reader told a story of picking up his first script of the day, opening to page one and reading this as the first scene:

```
FADE IN:

INT. CITY STREET — ALLEYWAY — EVENIG
CAM turns into an alley.
```

The reader closed the script right then (after only twelve words, including the standard "FADE IN:") and tossed it into the reject pile. What time of day or night is "Evenig," exactly? Perhaps slang? And this character, "CAM," can certainly *enter* the alleyway, but how exactly does a person transform on screen and literally become an alley? The story might have been decent, but the writer absolutely lacked the ability to convey his or her ideas in a clear or professional manner, so they got the boot. (Incidentally, at the end of the day, the reader did give the script a second chance, as he'd suspected, the poorly constructed grammar persisted and his gut instinct had not let him down.) As you've read this list of the things readers hate most about spec scripts, nothing is more within your ability to perfect than the spelling and grammar of your own writing. Handing in a professional sample of your writing with typos and grammar is absolutely inexcusable.

To quote the great Stanley Kubrick: "I never know what I want, but I know exactly what I *don't* want." There's no shortage of spec scripts coming through the door of agencies or production companies; the faster readers can get through their pile of scripts, the faster they can go home. Sometimes the strategy to best convey your writing talents to Hollywood and move up its ranks isn't just writing the best script, but rather, writing the script with the *fewest mistakes*.

HOMEWORK ASSIGNMENT

Hop onto iTunes, Netflix, or your cable provider's pay-per-view service (or any other outlet platform you frequent). Skim the artwork of the available independent movies. . . . Without focusing on the titles, try to guess which gold-mine genre type each "non-studio" movie offering represents. (Also, pay close attention to which indie titles reside directly next to major studio releases.)

For extra credit (and valuable screenwriter skillset development), rent or purchase a movie (or two) you identify as falling into a clear gold-mine genre type. As you watch them, consciously think about the list of ten things readers hate and really focus on your selection's structure. Whether you ascribe to Blake Snyder's *Save the Cat* "Beat Sheet" philosophy or Syd Field's act breakdowns from *Screenplay* (or any other valuable screenwriter formatting theories), apply them to the gold-mine genre type you're watching. Literally map out each movie's structure, from beginning to end (act by act, beat by beat) . . .

What you'll notice is that they're formulaic as hell and easily approachable. . . . More importantly, you'll realize there is absolutely no reason you cannot write a spec script that's just as good—if not better—than any of these other indie gold-mine genre types already in the marketplace.

Get to work!

MOST IMPORTANT RULE: HAVE FUN

Just because you're writing a spec script that exists within the boundaries of a specific genre type doesn't mean you can't go all out with your ideas. . . . You should totally have fun with your script!

Make it entertaining, break clichés, and push the envelope wherever possible. As long as you're keeping the focus of your screenplay filtered through the *principles* of each gold-mine genre type, you can absolutely experiment and juggle unique ideas. Don't feel as if you're working on an assembly line regurgitating the same old thing—you get to add whatever spin you choose to your spec script as long as it fits within your genre type. Make the villains the baddest, make the creature feature monster the creepiest . . .

Writing gold-mine genre type scripts doesn't make you a "sellout". . . . It makes you more likely to get your work noticed so you can build a professional career as a Hollywood screenwriter.

FINALIZING YOUR SPEC SCRIPT FOR THE READER

After you plow through your first draft (or two), I do recommend two great books for advice on revising your spec script: William M. Akers's *Your Script Sucks!: 100 Ways to Make it Better* (2008) and Denny Martin Flinn's *How Not To Write A Screenplay: 101 Common Mistakes Most Screenwriters Make* (1999).

In addition to the advice presented in both of these books, I'd like to include a few *Writing for the Green Light* tips my reader contacts clued me in on:

Drop the "Ums"

It's not uncommon for readers to skim the descriptive blocks and only read a script's dialogue. . . . Therefore, how your dialogue appears on the page (and how it reads) is very important for how your faithful reader will evaluate your writing abilities. Look at each dialogue block in your script and start cutting any occurrences of "um," "so," or "but" you find.

```
          CHARACTER
     Um, I think you're lying to me.
```

Cut the "um" and get to the point.

```
          CHARACTER
     So, do you want to go to the movies?
```

Cut the "so"; it doesn't matter if it sounds natural in your head, it will always read awkwardly.

```
          CHARACTER
     But, she told me she wasn't
     interested.
```

Again, cut the "but" and move on.

This accomplishes two things: First, it is a fast way to clean up *all* the dialogue in your script so that any of the dialogue that is to remain from this draft is essentially ready to go, but second, it makes it much more obvious if the dialogue being spoken is simply overly wordy or unnecessary.

An interesting challenge one writer told me about is that he first removes the "ums" and "sos," but then goes back through the dialogue and tries to see how many dialogue blocks he can condense down to five words or fewer. . . . Sounds crazy, but using the three simple suggestions above, we can immediately see improvement in the quickness to read and the ability to see direct conflict from the language used (all vital to a spec script's presentation). Let's cut these examples down to five words or fewer:

```
                    CHARACTER
          You're lying.

                    CHARACTER
          The movies?

                    CHARACTER
          . . . Said she wasn't interested.
```

Already there's a marked difference in tone, but also in the level of concentration required of your reader while taking in your script. They have a stack of ten more to read after yours, so readers appreciate your assistance in getting them through the important stuff quickly and easily. (There will obviously be portions of dialogue that need to extend beyond five words; this "rule" is more about cutting down as much as possible.)

Scenes Begin with Dilemmas but End with Decisions

Scenes always begin when things are going as planned until an action or event disrupts the flow. . . . A guy walks into his office, only now there's someone already in there waiting for him. His anticipated flow of events has now been disrupted. The scene exists because your character needs to hear information or experience something that forces him or her to move things forward. . . . But where to end?

Scenes don't end just because characters are saying goodbye to one another. Scenes end when our protagonist has been in a dilemma, but finally reaches the decision he or she must make.

This doesn't mean you need to verbalize or tell us what decision is being made, sometimes it's when a character is all alone (staring at themselves in a mirror), they're making a decision while looking at themselves—it's not until we cut to the next shot that it's revealed what decision has been made.

Make sure each scene of your script is beginning with a disrupting dilemma and concluding once a decision has been reached. Everything before and after can simply be cut out. And if there's no real dilemma that affects your main character (and will not force a decision from your main character) you can scrap the whole scene!

Parallel Lines

I'm sure there's an actual storytelling term for this, but I call it "parallel lining" your script. This is the phenomenon used when your A-story and your B-story sync together, when the rise and flow of events from both storylines seem to mimic one another (and it's something that masterful screenwriters do constantly).

As the events in your A-story are taking off, so too should the events in your B-story. An even better example, when your protagonist in your A-story has a falling out with a friend, your B-story must also be going through some type of loss or hardship. When your hero encounters a setback in your A-story, they must also be getting pushback in B as well. See the pattern?

The real reason this works is because the decisions your protagonist is making will certainly affect his or her direct situation (the A-story), but every action or decision also has consequences elsewhere in our lives, or the lives of those close to us (B-story). So when things in our lives are going well, we tend to approach all aspects of our routine with positivity, but when things are hectic and stressful, it's easy to feel all aspects of our lives are wearing down on us.

This flow of events is universal, so it's best to skim through your script and ensure that your A-story and B-story plot lines are syncing up. This is a great time to experiment if a cut away from A to B should take place in a different place in the story, or if there's a better way to transition.

PUTTING YOUR LINE-PRODUCER "BLINDERS" ON

There's lots of producers on a movie. . . . There's the producer-producers (the ones who carry the project from beginning to end, who hustle and grind, hire and fire, and manage the project from concept to completion), there's executive producers (who effectively represent the money or the financial interests behind the film, or are sometimes directly financing it themselves, either out-of-pocket or through their company), and there are associate producers (individuals who contribute something relatively small in scale yet absolutely vital to the overall production; they might work for one day, or sometimes make one phone call, but that one action connects the production with the people who can finance it or otherwise saves the day).

But there's a producer out there who rarely gets the credit they deserve: The line producer. They're hired on productions, sometimes very early on, and their job is to (1) review the script and come up with a real-world budget, then (2) manage the money throughout the production process (including pre- and post-) to ensure that budget is properly followed.

A line producer generally doesn't care about the content of the script; they principally read it for informational purposes only. They get the name "line" producer because they skim every single page of the written script (line-by-line) and look for indications of cost and expenses. They are keeping track of things like: how many characters are in the script, how many locations, what props are used in this scene, how many extras are in that scene, does a particular sequence take place at night (if so, will it require additional lighting or a generator), how involved is that fight scene and will it require a stunt double or additional trainer on set.

They also map out matrixes of information like which characters are in which scenes and which scenes can be shot in the same location (meaning are there characters that need to be at a location for an entire day or for only one or two shots). They also calculate details like the age of certain actors, if there are there minors on set (and if so, how many hours they're working, which can require an on-set educator to be present).

It's an extremely meticulous job, one that you can never fully appreciate until you've actually stood in their shoes (and I can safely tell you from afar I have zero interest in trying those shoes on!).

However, bringing that mindset to your now polished and revised reader-ready spec script is a very useful way to get your work market-ready.

This process not only makes it much easier on the readers (round number one), when it gets to the hands of development execs (who use a methodical thinking style similar to that line producers use), they will take note of your carefully structured script, it's attention to clear detail, and its logical breakdown of locations and chronology of events.

Every word you write costs money. That's fine, the project is going to have a budget and investments will be made to produce it. . . . But the more money conscious you can be during your rewrites, the better. Not only does taking two characters and combining them into one reduce your cast (which saves money), you also need to think this way regarding props, locations, sequences, and actions.

I have a challenge for you: Hop on Google and search for production software or film scheduling breakdowns. . . . Get a real-world sense of how scripts are actually broken down into day-by-day shooting schedules. Give it a try; actually schedule your script as a legit production. Number the scenes, enter the data of each scene (location, time of day, props, cast, etc.), and actually start thinking about how you would structure a shooting schedule. Assume you have an eighteen-day shoot, how would you arrange locations? How many (and which) characters need to be on set each day (and do they all need to be there for the whole day)? How many props are needed and can they be cut down?

You will see your script in a completely different way! If your script has a scene with two characters speaking while cruising together in a car, this comes across as extremely time consuming and difficult to shoot. Now you need car mounts, possible street permits, and so on. Can that conversation happen elsewhere? Could you even take the "new" location and combine it with another scene?

As your spec script is passed around a production company, these are the kinds of questions and concerns that working development executives voice when reading your work. . . . Scheduling out your own spec script will truly open your eyes to how much more complex seemingly easy ideas can become for a production crew to break down.

Fix those mistakes and rework your script with your line producer blinders on. It is tedious and frustrating, but it will have a huge payoff when readers and development executives can see the ease of shooting it (which will show them *you* are a writer who gets how difficult their jobs are).

GETTING FEEDBACK

I think one of the toughest things for a novice writer is getting someone to read their script and provide them solid feedback. It's actually a pretty big favor to ask. And for those of us working professionally in the movie/TV business, we have many acquaintances that have put this burden onto our shoulders. A good friend of mine, a producer, summed it up for me pretty well: "I hate scripts; these writers ask you to read them, so you spend ninety minutes reading it, then another hour writing notes, and the writer only scoffs at your opinions and they apply nothing to their efforts." That's a pretty raw deal, wouldn't you say?

It's hard to hear criticism, but it's also quite hard for those reading your script to relay it. The emails I've written where I must criticize something always take me two to three times longer to write than others. . . . Mostly because I keep rereading my statements to make sure I'm not saying anything that's coming off as too harsh or could be misunderstood.

The other problem with getting feedback is knowing who to ask. If you have professional friends, maybe those are favors you're not ready to cash in. . . . But you can't just give it to close friends who know nothing about the movie business, you need real criticism and advice—but you also need to make sure the person giving it to you knows what they're talking about. This sounds absurd, but the truth is most screenwriters hand their scripts to the wrong friends for advice or guidance. It's all well-intentioned of course, but those unfamiliar with the industry might not fully understand what it is you're going for and thus might steer you in a direction that takes you away from your goal of selling your work (and yourself).

Here are a few vetted ideas where you can get some real advice on how to improve your script:

1. Pay a professional. As a guy who will advise you against paying unnecessarily for anything you absolutely do not have to, this is one of the few times I'll advocate spending cash for someone's professional advice. There are numerous qualified script consultants working, each of whom has years of credible experience they can use to not only improve your script, but also help you pitch it and professionally discuss it. They'll also be able to point out your overall strengths and weaknesses as a writer—so that you learn where you can improve, but also point out which genre type you excel in (which can help you hone in on a genre type that will get your work noticed more quickly).

There are two script consultants whom I recommend that handle this job very well (both of whom offer their services for very modest and reasonable prices).

Erik Bork—Erik is a professional screenwriter and two-time Emmy winner for his writing work on the HBO miniseries *From the Earth to the Moon* (1998) and *Band of Brothers* (2001); he's also worked on the writing staff of two primetime dramas and written feature screenplays, pilots, and other miniseries scripts for many of the major Hollywood studios, networks and top tier producers. From the outside, Erik leads the kind of life most newbie writers would dream of—including having been a trusted writer/producer on many projects with players like Tom Hanks and some with Steven Spielberg. But Erik doesn't come from some well-connected "Hollywood family," he comes from a modest background in Ohio—which is also where he earned his film degree (meaning he did *not* attend the big L.A.- or New York-based film schools). I say this because Erik is proof that you can come from far outside Hollywood's fortified walls and truly "break in" and climb up to the studio level by writing what Hollywood needs and presenting yourself (and your work) in the way professionals need you to. He's fantastic at fixing structure and helping you logically work out your script's overall flow. What I personally respect about Erik is his modesty and true attention to getting *your* script in its best shape (regardless of your experience level). His rates are very reasonable (and clearly posted on his website), which you can also use to reach out to him: www.flyingwrestler.com. Bookmark his website; it's a very valuable resource for writers, which he updates all the time.

Donie Nelson—Donie is a true Hollywood legend who started her professional career in the story department of the big studios. Although she's not a pen-to-paper writer, she's had more scripts pass through her hands (and had more lunches with persons who went on to be leading voices on the subject of screenwriting, e.g., Linda Seger, Lew Hunter, Syd Field, Skip Press), than anyone else I've ever met—meaning she's seen firsthand what truly works and what doesn't in the world of professional screenwriting. What she can offer you is real-world perspective and advice on how to pitch your work (and yourself) to Hollywood's gate-keepers, so that you can get your script into the right people's hands. . . . She's also a fantastic script doctor who can give you excellent guidance on how to improve your script specifically so it reads well for the readers who will be judging your work later on. Think of her not just as a resource for one-off script advice; use her as a career coach during many of the early aspects of your professional journey. Her consultation prices are very reasonable and her advice is top notch. You can reach out to Donie directly by email at: wrtrconsult@earthlink.net

2. Writers' Groups are great places to get legit feedback, but you need to ensure you're with the right one. There's always a few pretentious ones that are a little too focused on overly criticizing each other's works; then there are others that are a bit more about social networking versus quality feedback. There are writers' groups in all cities, but here in Los Angeles, there's dozens focused on quality feedback for the real working world of Hollywood. Audition them; it's okay to experiment and see which one makes you feel comfortable. Like any social group, you want to make sure you feel confident presenting your ideas and that you like the way others provide appropriate feedback. You can also attend classes at The Writer's Store or take UCLA Extension programs; both offer instructors who are actual working writers and can give you wonderful advice on your work. And don't forget that these programs will be full of other like-minded screenwriters whom you could stay in contact with and exchange scripts.

3. Shoot your script! Of course, you don't have to go produce it solo (though that's certainly an option if you're up for the challenge), but you can pull in some friends, order some pizzas, and have a read-through together (where you record the entire thing on camera so you can play it back and watch it later). Maybe you have your friends stand and semi-block out scenes. . . . Nothing too involved, but just enough to give you a sense of things. You know what you'll quickly realize? How little of your script is logically choreographed or that there are actually several holes in its narrative or its logic. You'll hear any of the idiot dialogue and feel where sections just drag. It's okay, better for you to find out about these problems now in the company of friends (with some good pizza) before a reader picks up on them and gives your work a "pass" on their coverage report.

KNOWING WHEN IT'S READY

There will never be a perfect script; you can edit and revise for years and it will never please everyone. Eventually you have to make the executive decision for yourself that your script has been written to the best of your abilities and that it showcases your talents in their best light.

    But how can you judge when you've actually reached this point? It's a tough one, because there is no formula, it's a gut instinct you (and only you) can really know. You can read (and reread) your script over and over again, and probably find a word here or there you'll change, but that's very surface level and you're probably just apprehensive to call it complete. If there's a nagging feeling that a sequence should be changed or a series of events tightened, that's definitely something that requires some more work. . . . But if you find yourself simply nit-picking on a few word changes, you're probably quite close to the end.

The best way to tell is by maybe giving it to one last person to read and getting their feedback. You don't need them to give you thoughts on how to improve anything—in fact, ask them not to tell you their ideas—just ask for a general overview on their impressions. Did it make sense? Was it clear? And more importantly, did the writing seem to flow? Were they genuinely curious to turn the pages? You don't need them to lie and exclaim it was a page turner and they couldn't put it down, just as long as it felt like it read fast and clear. You're not asking this individual to help you make changes or offer suggestions, you just want their general impressions on how it felt to read it.

If you pay a third person for this job, just remember that they're going to feel obligated to make comments and suggestions. . . . Listen to them, are their suggestions things that must be changed? Or are they personal requests?

The best answer is simply to put the script away for a while. . . . Try to keep it out of sight (out of mind) for a month. Remove yourself from it a bit. Work on other projects. When the time is right, pull it back out and read from page one and don't stop. Don't make notes, don't make corrections, read it completely in the mindset of a reader (a person who will not mark a word change or offer suggestions, they will simply read what's before them and report on the results).

Ask yourself the same questions. Did it read easy? Quickly? Were there sections that dragged?

If you need to make adjustments, make them. There's no "correct" amount of time to finish a script. But eventually, you will have to pull the plug and call your work on this script complete. It will be easier for you to do this in time, but you've got a career ahead of you (one full of many writing opportunities) so you will need to fine tune your own gut instinct of when your work reaches a point of completion.

CONCLUSION

Writing a quality spec script is much more than just drafting a screenplay. . . . Your script is a billboard advertising your talent and ability to deliver quality writing in a time crunch for production and distribution companies.

However, there's no need to feel unnecessary pressure that you're somehow competing with all the other novice screenwriters out there—because most of them are writing the wrong types of scripts. . . . As long as you find a gold-mine genre type you like, let yourself have fun. Be creative and original. Use *your* unique voice when you write. You're here to deliver Hollywood what it needs (that's what gets your script noticed), but don't think that doesn't allow you the chance to add your own spin to make your work fresh and exciting. I'm not here to tell you that you cannot express who you are with your writing (you totally should!), I'm only suggesting you filter your talents through the gold-mine genre types and present your work in a way that makes the jobs of Hollywood professionals easier.

Those are the attributes that get Hollywood to notice you and your work.

FOUR

HOW I LEARNED TO STOP WORRYING AND WRITE FOR TELEVISION

In this chapter, we'll outline the basics of writing for Hollywood's small screen—not just the tricks for presenting your ideas and getting your work seen, but also *how* the TV side operates (and differs) from the movie end of the spectrum.

TELEVISION WRITERS: HOLLYWOOD'S NAVY SEALS

Television writers hold some of the most coveted writing positions in the industry—and earn some of its highest paychecks. But little has been explained about how such writing positions are ever reached or how a newbie should best guide themselves toward attaining that goal. Perhaps referring to staff TV writers as Hollywood's own "SEAL Team Six" is a bit of a stretch. . . . But for any novice writer starting out, those TV writers who are already inside the system—who've earned "staff writer" status on a major network or cable series—certainly seem pretty elite. And unlike the film side of the business, where a great number of books have been written on the subject of "how to write a feature," the television side consistently remains cloaked in a fortified veil of mystery.

The real reason breaking in to television writing is so difficult is because the TV side offers no direct path to follow—which means there's no industry-vetted (or "right") way to approach it. It sometimes feels that way on the movie side, but when it comes to feature-length spec scripts—although challenging—there is a method behind the madness. A major factor for this ambiguity lies in the fact that on the film side, a feature-length spec script can exist all by itself, as a "stand alone" property. When a feature-length script works, it requires no other elements (not even from the writer) to make it shine—and even if a great feature script comes along, its writer may never deliver another quality script for the rest of their lives. . . . Meaning, on the film side, a writer has the potential to be a "one-hit wonder."

On the TV side, however, a writer must be a creative machine! They must be capable of constantly churning out great ideas on a moment's notice and be able to add a fresh spin to even the most exhausted of ongoing storylines. In addition, to join a *staff* of writers, they must be a team player, willing to work with (and fit into) a core group of people with the collective task of out-putting great scripts for a single long-running program. And for a writer to show they have what it takes, they must prove they're not only talented but *consistently and reliably talented*—which takes a great deal of hustle, strategic schmoozing, and a steady output of quality writing.

All that said, even though the television side does have a rigid system in place—one that's designed to only admit those select few who are lean, mean, and sharp enough to navigate themselves toward the end zone—that certainly doesn't mean there aren't dozens of entry points wide-open to you—along with several ways to fast-track yourself towards TV's inner circle.

And, to your great advantage, you are entering the writing game at a very unique time in Hollywood's history. . . . Where there were once only a select few TV channels available, there are now hundreds. And as interactive VOD platforms (e.g., Netflix, Amazon, and Hulu) make a gradual shift toward producing original series content, the constantly widening land-scape of opportunity within the TV market has never tipped the odds more in your favor.

WHERE TO BEGIN?

Not all TV writing is one-size-fits-all; it ranges from TV movies, miniseries, one-hour dramas, and long-running multi-episode sitcoms (just to name a few). These examples also leave out the endless array of non-scripted real-ity shows, one-off (one-episode) documentary programs, and even lifestyle series (e.g., cooking shows or DIY programming).

To break this down into a simple division, agents I work with like to refer to anything based upon scripted material as "television" and anything tradi-tionally viewed as *non*-scripted content as *"alternative* television" (I wouldn't consider these terms to be "industry norms" quite yet, it's just a trend I've recently seen). . . . That's not to say non-scripted TV programs don't involve a fair amount of writing (e.g., narration, title cards, and "paper" edits of interviews), but generally "alternative TV" (non-scripted TV) just isn't as appealing to novice writers as the scripted side. (Incidentally, many of these "alternative" television programs may never list their staff writers as "writers"—they might be classified as "segment producers" or some other stealthy name to dodge the fact that most "reality" TV content is completely staged. Great example, when I produced the "reality" daytime courtroom series *Eye for an Eye*, the cases were based on "real incidents," but we had a team of writers (including myself) who adapted these ridiculous stories into a TV format—none of us received writing credit, we were called "case interns" or "case coaches.")

But if you want to truly break in to the world of scripted television writing, there's one very clear principle you must adopt and accept fully: **Most television is *non-scripted*!**

Whether it's reality dating programs like *The Bachelor*, talent and singing competitions such as *The Voice*, or game-show/competition genres, including anything from *Wheel of Fortune* to *The Amazing Race* down to *Wipe Out!*; all are highly rated and internationally popular series (with numerous seasons to boot) that dominate prime time yet don't require a traditional script.

Novice writers are generally taught that this reality-check about television is somehow their greatest obstacle. . . . Quite the opposite! TV's non-scripted side is literally a wide-open doorway to its scripted end. Think about it: As you read this, there are literally thousands of non-scripted content hours currently airing or streaming across hundreds of cable/satellite channels and VOD platforms. Most hopeful screenwriters bypass those and only focus on that small sliver of scripted programs, without realizing that many of the scripted and non-scripted programs are being produced on the same studio lots, sometimes by teams sharing the same production offices.

To "break in" to scripted television writing, you'll use its *non*-scripted side for entry. But you'll need a few tools in your arsenal before you begin. . . .

BACK TO THE SPEC-WRITING BOARD . . .

Same as with the feature world, if you want to build a career as a television writer you first need to prove you know *how* to write. . . . That means you'll need to write a few sample spec scripts (a minimum of two, ideally three) that not only showcase your abilities, but also indicate your overall focus and direction.

Already have your feature-length movie gold-mine genre type spec scripts dusted off and ready to go? Sorry, that won't cut it. . . . If you want to write specifically for the small screen then you'll need to offer television's decision-makers TV-focused samples of your writing—meaning in order to prove you've got the chops, you're going to have to write sample TV spec scripts.

A sample TV spec script is exactly what it sounds like: it's an invented episode—written on spec—purely for the purpose of proving you understand how to write for a particular series (or ones very similar to it).

In the past, a newbie TV writer was expected to draft a sample TV spec script based on a long running and current TV series, like *That 70's Show* or *How I Met Your Mother* when those programs were still at their peaks. There are still writers who choose this route, but they are now far in the minority. Today, it has become the norm to come up with your own original series idea and write a pilot screenplay for it—which you can use as your sample TV spec script.

Keep in mind *selling* an original series idea or a TV spec script (if based off a current series) is damn near impossible. . . . Full-on television series (scripted and non) almost always come from within the system (either from executives, veteran writers, or well-connected showrunners). Your sample TV spec scripts are being circulated only to showcase your writing strengths within the TV space.

What Type of Writer Are You?

Before you go open your laptop and start hammering away at the keys, you first need to figure out what kind of TV writing your personal style best lends itself to. . . . You don't need to get all deep and philosophical here (no need for a long walk in the park to contemplate), just ask yourself a very simple question: Would you rather write comedy or drama? There is no gray zone in this question; it truly is a "one or the other" answer.

This is a huge contradiction with the world of feature-length screenwriting. . . . Not that dramas and comedies are polar opposites, but that they represent "the bad" and "the ugly" of the spec script world. . . . In the land of *feature*-length spec scripts, attempting to submit a drama or a comedy is a one-way ticket to the reject pile, but in television these two genres are the lifeblood of Hollywood! And if you want to prove your worth amongst Hollywood's TV writers, you have to be willing to take on the two most challenging genres, something you should avoid if breaking in on the indie feature side.

If you want to be a comic writer, then you will need to focus on the world of shorter form (half-hour) sitcoms; if you're a dramatic writer, then you'll need to focus on the longer form (hour plus) dramas. Want to really show off and blend these two together and hit Hollywood with a sitcom episode with heavy dramatic undertones or a one-hour drama with great one-liners? Don't do it! Pick one route or the other and *stick to it* all the way.

If you choose comedy, you will need to complete a minimum of two sample TV spec scripts (each from different original sitcom ideas), and if you choose drama, you will also need a minimum of two samples (also from different—and original—one-hour dramatic series).

And, no, you shouldn't write one half hour comedic sitcom and one hour-long drama and keep the image alive that you can "do it all"; you need to show consistency, so go comedic *or* dramatic only.

Developing Your Own Series

When crafting your own series idea (and its eventual pilot episode), it's important *not* to focus on creating one giant story, but rather to design a framework capable of endless story possibilities. . . . A great series idea must launch dozens (or even hundreds) of episodes, each of which has a beginning, middle, and end—which work separately from (but congruent with) any serialized plotlines continuing from previous episodes.

This is the biggest concept that newbie writers often miss when they initially develop their dream TV series. . . . They go for the big idea and miss that their series idea must have an engine behind it capable of "factory output." This offers potential audiences a complete (and satisfying) story experience, while also offering them potential for an unresolved conflict that will keep them tuned in for the next episode.

So the first question a television writer should ask themselves is not what their series about, but rather whom it follows. . . . Characters are the elements that drive great television. It goes without saying that a one-off feature-length film should have great characters too, but overall a feature's plot is centered around a clear and achievable goal that drives the movie. . . . A television series will certainly have objectives (e.g., Walter White earning money for his family by cooking meth in *Breaking Bad*), but it's really more about the smaller chapters in the lives of our main characters striving to reach that goal that fuels the series season after season.

On the one-hour dramatic front, the overall objectives of both *Homeland* and *24* involve stamping out international terrorists intent on doing harm to the United States. . . . Although we know this objective will never be resolved, the lives of the characters we're following keep us hooked. Both programs are giant ideas, but they are not giant singular stories.

On the half-hour sitcom front, the storylines are often more "situational"—meaning goofy yet very well fleshed-out characters are forced into inhabiting the same claustrophobic space. . . . The consequential interactions are what make each episode function. Living situations often funnel these together (neighbors in apartment complexes as in *Friends* or *The Big Bang Theory* work great, but it could also be job-related, like *The Office*). It's usually odd pairings that drive comedic television, again not giant far-reaching storylines.

Television's Gold-Mine Demographics

On the movie side we discussed the gold-mine genre types, describing each as nice, clean filter you should use to focus your spec script to gain better traction on the other side. . . . TV, on the other hand, doesn't have these preferred genres; instead it has gold-mine *demographics*.

The business of television is completely dependent on the data-mined details of those watching it (and the nightly ratings of "who watched what for how long"). The primary metrics—gathered by the Nielsen Company, therefore known as the Nielsen ratings—relate to surface-level things like gender, age, and zip code. But behind the scenes, they are taking into account attributes like annual household income estimates, level of education, religious affiliation (if any), and even details like which demographics are more likely to check their emails via smartphone during a commercial break.

Great television writing is simply great television writing; there isn't one type of program series for you to focus on and create (e.g., *The Walking Dead* and *True Blood* are horror(ish) themed—a genre to avoid as a novice spec script feature writer—but they're too layered and complex to simply be categorized as horror titles, and both are great series concepts that attract a wide viewing audience).

However, you should first get a real-world sense of what it is Americans are actually watching; hop on Nielsen's website and look up their top ten listing by TV platform (web address: www.nielsen.com/us/en/top10s.html). The list is a bit of an eye-opener and offers the top ten programs by prime-time broadcast (big free-to-air channels like ABC, NBC, CBS, and FOX), by cable network (basic channels including USA, TNT, A&E, Disney, etc.), and continues to breakdown which programs are strong in syndication and even what the top ten programs are for Hispanic households as well as African American homes.

Great television programs will speak to these giant audiences; even niche programs, like *Battlestar Galactica*, will take these demos into account. Aside from the fact that several non-scripted series will fill each of these top-ten lists (even worse during football season, which is also the start of the year's television season), you'll notice that the programs that exist in more than one category aren't exactly the big time programs you'd expect to be there. . . . As of this writing, long-running *NCIS* far beat out its competitors (yet is hardly the water-cooler talking program that *Breaking Bad* or *Under the Dome* were, for instance). Although the trendy water-cooler series get the hype and buzz from a more social media-engaged audience, the numbers generally show a much weaker performance than the noise would otherwise suggest.

Sturdy and stable programs tend to lead (and since Nielsen is crunching the numbers that Hollywood relies upon, studio executives and their writing staffs will focus on what the Nielsen ratings say over word-of-mouth any day). So the demos you should focus on are the ones that speak to Nielsen's largest audiences—meaning series that skew slightly older or much younger than you'd probably be inclined to first approach.

For instance, middle-aged Americans (classified by Nielsen as eighteen to forty-nine, but really represent an audience in their mid-thirties and upwards) are a fantastic demographic. . . . They have more money in their pockets (and advertisers are able to spend more cash during their commercial breaks). This demo has a small nudge toward female viewership and is the crowd that loves the slightly melodramatic programs ranging from *ER* in the 1990s, *Lost* in the 2000s, and the ongoing variety of *CSI* spin-offs today. They'll also take in a wide range of comedic sitcoms, like *How I Met Your Mother* and *Two and a Half Men*, or fantasy-based shows like *Charmed*. Writers able to speak to this demo are highly sought after by the big studios' writing teams; proving you've got what it takes to nail this target—or even just the talent to stay afloat until you master it—will get you noticed. This is a huge demographic, so generalizing what it is they want as we did with our gold-mine genre types just doesn't apply. . . . However, I can give you a great piece of insight an anonymous writer offered me for this space: Audiences in their mid-thirties, forties, and fifties have lives in motion, so your characters must reflect that. What he continued to explain was that it's important to ensure that each of your characters has a beginning, middle, and end already in full force when we meet them; it's the inciting incident in your pilot episode that now make their lives worth discussing—and offers the series a platform to continually generate new episodes. *Breaking Bad*'s Walter White found out he had cancer in episode one, but he was already established as a school-teacher and husband/father. *House of Cards*'s Frank Underwood is a well-established congressman who is "stepped over" for a position as Secretary of State, an inciting incident that launches his takeover of Washington. These characters have already lived full lives, but now a new element has entered to disrupt that trajectory. Even on the sitcom side, *Two and a Half Men*'s Charlie Harper has a successful life in full gear, until his recently divorced brother arrives with his son.

Another strong demographic would be kids programming, especially shows aimed at tween girls. The numbers aren't as encompassing or detailed on these demographics, since there are many rules and regulations against the data-mining of youths (as well as targeted marketing toward them). However, tween-themed programming (again, slightly skewed female) can work very well—for example, programs like Disney's *Jesse* and *Hanna Montana* or Nickelodeon's *iCarly*. And even though the laws are a bit complex around advertisements, programs in this space have the ability to take their young starlets and go on cross-country tours and offer book or merchandising opportunities, even concerts. Proving you can write for this targeted demographic showcases you're a writer that can offer several major TV entities what they need to stay in business.

Generally, you will need to skew your content slightly female. Women, by and large, are television's viewing majority. That doesn't mean everything needs to be pink-colored and soft—women are equally responsible for the success of crime series like *Law & Order: SVU* as well as lighter content like *Grey's Anatomy* and *Friends*. But as a writer, you should keep their opinions and thoughts close to heart.

Demographics to avoid would be ones targeted at older teens and those in their mid-twenties (ages fifteen to twenty-four). It's nothing against these targeted audiences personally—and yes, they are very likely to be out spending what little cash comes into their pockets on material items—but they are generally the least engaged television audience out there, meaning writing specifically for these audiences offers the fewest "showcase" selections for your work.

The Risk of Too Many Ideas

The most important aspect to keep in check when writing your sample TV spec script is that it must accurately reflect the better interests of your newly created series (and *not* just provide a showcase of your "best of" writing moments). In other words, keep your pilot script genuine, as if it were a real series you'd been assigned to write; don't fill it with too many ideas from the season. The goal is to give us a taste of all the amazing things to come based upon the interesting pull from your characters (without giving too much away). Hook us!

The true art of television writing is a much higher-level skill than that of a one-off feature film. Your objective is not to force your talents down the throats of those readers who pick up your sample TV spec script, it's instead to prove that *if* your talents were commissioned, you would be fully capable of not only producing a well-written episode of a TV series, but that your talents would truly aid the overall progression of that series forward—which would make you seem capable of fitting in with an actual writing team.

While on this note, there is absolutely *no* need to write out a full-on series bible. All readers want to see is that you're capable of writing a really solid pilot episode that showcases your ability to tell a complete story within a framework that offers potential for more episodes. The most you would ever be asked to present in addition to a sample pilot script would be a generic list of "next episodes," where you'd simply craft the next few installments of your invented series. I've personally never heard of any executives asking for an extra episodes list, but a few professional writer friends of mine have in the past.

Format and Structure

Regardless of whether you're pursuing comedy or drama, get your hands on actual TV scripts so that you can see *how* television programs are written. For instance, sitcoms are generally written for a three-camera "in-studio" approach, which uses a very unique formatting style, whereas one-hour dramas follow the more mainstream structure yet often place "act breaks" directly into the script, indicating where commercial breaks will take place.

Fortunately, in today's world, accessing legit TV scripts is now easier than ever—you can probably get yourself some PDF versions after only a few simple Google searches. But don't settle on just one or two episodes from a series, try to get several—preferably from more recent seasons—so that you can ensure your writing is up-to-date as possible. If there is a major discrepancy between one half-hour sitcom and another, choose the one that is most similar to the unique series idea you're crafting.

Even though your sample TV spec scripts will not be getting read with any real possibility of being put into production (because series are always developed within studio walls), your ability to write for real-world teams is still vitally important. Proof that you understand their way of writing is a telling sign you're a writer worthy of consideration.

Animated Series

When it comes to animation writing, it is better to write for a pre-existing series rather than inventing your own concept.

Since animated series exist in worlds unique to themselves (where the laws of the physical universe are different), they are simply much harder for readers to visualize than an animated series that's had years of life already fleshed out and is easily recognizable. For example, a sample TV spec script of *Family Guy* is very digestible for a reader. . . . We can "hear" Stewie's voice with that mischievous British accent and Peter's obnoxious laugh—a spec script for a newly created show, on the other hand, would not accurately reflect these nuances (no matter how blatantly they were detailed in the script).

A Final Note on Your Writing

The blessing (and curse) of writing a sample TV spec script based off your own invented series is that your work will primarily be judged by other writers. . . . Of course, in order to get there, your work will have to go through the hands of readers and/or other representatives (or filters), but ultimately those that will move you forward professionally will be actual working television writers.

The curse of this is that a fellow writer will always be more critical of your work. They will see the clichés coming much earlier than a normal reader, they can sniff out weak structure long in advance, and can spot every newbie mistake (and trick) in the book. . . . However, the blessing of having a writer judging your work is that they will give your work that extra bit of attention if they feel you have a natural talent at writing. They want to find new talents and bring them into their circles of staff writing teams, and they will be more receptive to a unique or fresh voice rebelling against the status quo.

Therefore, a fellow writer will respond to your writing similar to a film director working with an actor; both would rather see your work as "too big" or "too grand," which allows them the simpler task of reeling in and focusing your talents, rather than pushing (and hoping) they can build your skillsets to the level they need to be.

This means that, for you, unlike the feature-length spec script work, which follows a very rigid formulaic structure, the television world is slightly more open to expansive ideas and risk taking. (I say "slightly" because you must still produce a pilot episode that fits within the norms of television's limitations, but your pilot is also your true showpiece to express what talents you can bring to the table if given the chance.)

When starting out on the film side, your writing is much more about showcasing that you know how to play by the rules and can deliver what the industry needs; on the TV side, it's about showcasing you as a talented writing machine, capable of churning out one great concept after the other. . . . Keep the targeted demographics in mind—and work only with the same genre to show consistency—but don't be afraid to fully pursue a really grand idea to the fullest. Allow yourself to completely run with it!

REWRITES AND FEEDBACK

For your sample TV spec script, going out for a peer review is not the kind of thing you can just request of anyone because you need someone not just with general (or industry) writing experience, but actual *TV-based* script experience (with a legit emphasis on comedy or drama).

My personal advice, to give you the most well rounded approach, is to get two very solid opinions from these sources:

First, reach out to a close friend who's a complete TV geek. We all know one person who can recite every cast member of each season of nearly every

TV series currently on the air. . . . That's the type we're going for here. Just ask them for *basic* advice, not technical advice (on craft, theme, etc.); the question should really be, "Could you see something like this working on TV and would you watch it?" You're going for the entertainment viewpoint here, not the critical one. Let them speak openly and guide you on your overall story and series concept, and let them voice annoyances or concerns about your characters, or about the logic of the overall series concept—this friend knows TV and, moreover, knows how audiences respond to new programs. Take their criticisms to heart and rework your pilot as necessary. This is more to guarantee that your series concept (and its pilot episode) does indeed stick as an idea and does sync with a dedicated television audience.

For your second opinion, you will need to dig a bit deeper and get someone with real TV industry insight. I would definitely go into the professional realm here and ask people who are truly in Hollywood's inner circle. Of the two consulting names I mentioned in Chapter Three, Erik Bork would be a great pick here given his TV experience on *Band of Brothers*—but you can also check out UCLA Extension classes and Writer's Store classes focused on television. This is the arena to look in when you're taking an idea for a series you know sticks well with fans, but are better catering it for the eyes of the working staff writers who will be reading it—and judging it. Never get too bogged down with the exact credits of a professional TV reader; it's more important that they (1) have legit working experience in television and (2) that you get along with them. . . . Try to get them on the phone for a few minutes to chat with them—ask yourself if you would work well with them; for example, do they give criticism in a way that you are comfortable hearing? They will be reserved with what they can say, obviously, withholding the real meat of the conversation until you're hired, but see if you can set up a casual phone call as a sort of introduction to get a feel.

Both of these perspectives will really get the ball rolling by ensuring you have a strong conceptual idea for a series (that truly allows for factory output), as well as a great showpiece pilot vetted by a general TV fan and a veteran writer with which to display it.

WHAT TO DO *AFTER* YOU FINISH

One of the biggest differences between the film side and TV side happens after you've finished your spec script. . . . On the film side, as already mentioned, there's a clear-cut plan of action, however on the TV side, there's not.

You could send your sample TV spec script to the offices of an actual studio producing a series very similar to the style of your spec script. . . . But they will likely tell you they don't accept unsolicited submissions (meaning that they only work with represented writers—not the case with indie feature scripts). You could instead go after the big agencies and try to seek out legit representation, and use their clout to secure you a gig. . . . But they will most likely be more interested in seeing what else you have (like a movie script), or in looking for something a bit more "immediate," since most agents are much more focused on quick sale opportunities rather than building a long-term career.[1]

The real answer is rarely spoken: Hold onto your sample TV spec script.

As already stated, a feature-length spec script is a direct and simple one-off item, something that works completely in and of itself; however, a sample TV spec script is a longer term investment—it's a part of the overall package that *you*, as a writer, represent. A feature-length spec script is a calling card; it's the item you toss around openly to showcase you're the real deal. . . . Those sample TV spec scripts you've written, on the other hand, are very valuable tools you don't use often (but you're always very glad you have when the occasion requires it).

In some cases, your professional consultant might ask if they could show your pilot script to a close contact of their own, like a manager, agent, or fellow writer friend of theirs. . . . *Let them!* As long as you've taken the proactive steps to register your script with the Writers Guild of America (WGA), having your script passed along the ladder is the way this process really works—because to break the seemingly impenetrable walls of staff writing circles, you need someone on the inside to be willing to pass along your script. Obviously, you cannot expect your hired consultant to do this for you, but if they see enough promise in your work—and just happen to know someone looking for your exact qualifications—they could make that recommendation. And if not them, someone along the way will catch wind that you're a hopeful TV writer, trying to break in. . . . If they reach out to you specifically and ask if you have something available to show your talents, you are in the enviable position to confidently hand them a piece of your writing.

There's no one you can necessarily—and blindly—send your work to where it will not be seen simply as noise (especially since spec-written pilots stand no chance of getting produced as one-offs). . . . And "noise" doesn't get you or your work noticed by Hollywood decision-makers. So your real challenge is to get yourself into positions where you have the ability to strengthen valuable relationships that might, if you play the game, take an interest in your work and read one of your scripts.

The TV Credit Catch-22

In TV writing, there is no green light for new series ideas, unless they're coming from top studio executives or are being created by very well established veteran writers; therefore, the only real objective for a newbie writer is to get a job on staff for an existing series. Going back to our classic screenwriting catch-22, where no one will take you seriously until you have a legit onscreen credit, this logic is propelled to the extreme in the world of television writing. Until you have pre-vetted TV writing experience (with a legit TV credit), the notion of having your sample TV spec script reviewed by those in a hiring position, or joining a team of staff writers already in motion, is an extraordinarily challenging objective.

But there is a way to tackle this puzzle, it just involves a little outside-the-box thinking. After all, those writers currently on staff writing the big Hollywood series had to have gotten there somehow or another.

ENTRY POINTS

The real secret to breaking in is via tiny wormholes I like to call entry points. An entry point is a rarely taught-about shortcut toward fast tracking your way through the Hollywood system. They are the foot-in-the-door jobs you can take that allow you real-world opportunities to get your work read by professionals who, if they like your style, might just bring you in and see if you have what it takes to be full time. (If this sounds curiously like an internship, the logic behind it is not far off.)

As mentioned earlier, the majority of television is non-scripted. . . . However, it's the non-scripted side that offers newbie writers the most wide-open entry points; let's review a few examples specifically catered to television:

Gag Writing

Writing for the hosted late-night television shows can be a great way in—the creators of *How I Met Your Mother* broke through the studio walls this way.

Regardless of the host (Jimmy Fallon, Conan O'Brian, etc.), the majority of them open their program with a monologue. On screen this lasts several minutes and is the glue that captures an audience flipping through channels and keeps them locked-in for the entire program (or at least the first half).

Ever watched them and counted the jokes? There's dozens of them. . . . Some take as few as five to ten seconds to set up and deliver. Multiply that times five episodes per week and you're well into the hundreds of pre-scripted jokes—and they cannot be "evergreen" jokes, they have to be timely and current. Even the most talented and "on it" comedian/late-night host would never be able to sit and write twenty-five to forty jokes each day and have the bulk of them "sell" to an audience and garner a laugh.

That's why they have a whole team of staff writers to draft out that daily monologue, right? Not quite. . . . Instead, they have dozens of gag writers (or joke writers) under non-exclusive contract—many of whom have never set foot in the staff writers' offices. Every day, the gag writers submit a minimum number of jokes. . . . Sometimes it's three per day and for others it's seven; it really just depends on the program and the agreement. They email their joke submissions to their contact at the network, who then compiles all the day's joke emails into a list. The joke list gets printed out, and is handed to all of the full-time staff writers who work for the late-night show directly as salaried or exclusively contracted employees. Together, they review the jokes and start to arrange them into a logical flowing order (they're technically constructing the monologue, but in essence they're writing it). Ninety percent or more of the submitted jokes are discarded right off the bat.

What happens if you get your jokes thrown out for the day? Nothing. . . . You just submit your next batch of jokes the following day. However, if you do get a joke all the way to broadcast, with the host using your zinger on camera, you'll get a check anywhere from $20 to $80 for each joke used (prices vary, and sometimes you have to hit a certain minimum, such as an accumulated $500 over the course of several weeks before a check will actually get issued). The pay is certainly not incentivizing up front. . . . But if you are talented joke writer and are submitting a steady flow of quality jokes each day, even if they're not used during each broadcast, those staff writers will take notice that you've "got the chops" to write comedy.

In time, they might lose a member or two of their staff to other writing assignments. How do they hire replacements? Generally, they pull from the talented and steady gag writers already submitting material. If they've been at it for a while, and have had several jokes on air, then they clearly understand not just the value of writing a good one-liner, but also have an understanding of the type of content (and style) that's needed for the program. The head staff writer might just bring you in for an interview, or request to see that comedic sample TV spec script of yours.

If brought on for a staff position, they might have you temporarily write out a few "freebies" such as those silly sketches and bits late-night comedians do midway through each program (the segment used to keep a TV audience watching). From here, they can tell if you'd fit in with their style of comedy and their way of working on content.

Where can you go from here? Once you're in with a crew of staff writers, you will be settled within a pretty tight-knit bunch . . . *and* you'll be working at a TV studio directly. What do TV studios produce? Sitcoms.

If NBC has a new sitcom it wants to produce, it's much more likely to hire from within (by plucking a few of the "go-to" staff writers churning out quality comedic writing for the late-night shows and "promote" them into prime time). What would make you even more valuable is having a ready-to-go sample TV spec script to offer, already showing you're ready for the opportunity—are you seeing a trend in how having a few of these laying around are useful?

How do you get in with this crowd and become a gag writer? Start by going to a live taping. . . . Once you're at the taping, you'll be escorted into the big auditorium and seated. There will be a warm-up comic in front, keeping everyone alert and energetic before the program and during breaks. . . . That is your target. Get their name and contact details. Talk to them during a break or after the show. Tell them you'd be interested in being a gag writer or joke writer for the monologues, even if you don't get paid. They will tell you they're not the one to speak to, but that they can put you into touch with someone who can be of help. . . . Bingo!

Don't want to head to a live taping? Call the studio, there is a full-on department for each series in production. All you need is an office production assistant. Tell them you want to be on the "go-to" list of joke writers for the late-night show. . . . The "joke" team is always looking for new material to keep the show fresh.

Staff Writing Assistant

Essentially, a writing assistant is the grunt of the staff writing division. But nevertheless, these jobs are coveted positions that many fresh Hollywood newbies would be thrilled to accept. And although the dream scenario would be to join in on a team writing for a scripted series, there are numerous "reality-based" or non-script programs that need assistants too (that also happen to be working within the same buildings as, and sometimes reporting to, the same executives as the more "elite" scripted programs).

The bulk of your duties will be running errands, scheduling meetings, making copies, and juggling drafts from one department to the next. You'll also be in charge of handling all those unwanted submissions coming in from wannabe writers (the scripts and sketches that the studio is not legally allowed to review).

On the positive side, as with the readers on Hollywood's film side, this position does offer rare access to Hollywood's unspoken rules. . . . You'll learn how not to submit work into the professional world, you'll learn where the orders come from in a studio setting (realizing that more often than not, the staff writers are following orders from the program's showrunner on the overall direction and tone the show must follow). You'll also overhear countless staff writer meetings, where assignments are dished out, and later, where written works are reviewed and revised.

Whether for a big time studio dramatic series, a half-hour broadcast TV sitcom, or even a lower level project like a soap opera or talk show, getting in at the base level with the writer team will be a truly rewarding long-term investment. . . . The hours are awful and you will undoubtedly deal with at least one person you cannot stand, but stick with it. Regardless which TV show you're lucky enough to land a gig with, you will walk away having learned far more about the world of TV writing—and the entertainment business as a whole—than you even could have imagined.

Getting one of these jobs, on the other hand, is a very tricky endeavor. On the major studio-level shows, the writing assistants have their own hierarchy! You will have a head staff writing assistant who has his or her own group of assistants to the assistant to boss around. I would advise going smaller, getting leaner, and not directly approaching a studio-level job (besides, you'd have to cash in a great deal of connections and favors just to be interviewed for an assistant to the assistant position). Save yourself the trouble.

The route I'd offer you is the seemingly unglamorous—yet rewarding—path toward daytime talk show TV programs, soap operas, or late-night comedy shows. The line is not nearly as long to get in and they need just as much work completed. You generally also have more in-check egos to deal with (which is worth its weight in gold on some days). You can approach these in much the same way as you would a gag-writing position, by calling the studio and asking for the [fill-in-the-blank] show. Whoever answers, tell them you'd like to see if the staff writing team needs assistants. Chances are, they'll want to see a résumé—possibly a sample of your writing. If asked only to send in a résumé, do not include your sample TV spec script. Be professional about it. . . . Don't mention your interest in writing and instead emphasize your skills at all the things they'll need you to manage (computer programs you're familiar with, clerical skills, and other functional assets). If brought in for an interview and asked what you hope to do long term, it's perfectly fine to say "I do want to write for television, but I think it's much more important to truly learn the business of how it works first."

Often times, if you play by the rules, writer's assistants can end up getting to write a freelance script for the show. . . . Which will garner them their first onscreen credit.

(This same process can work on any form of reality TV as well—even though many reality programs don't have writers, they do have creatives on staff creating those magical scenarios that lead to grand reality TV moments).

Office Assistant or Personal Assistant

Too many people overlook these jobs, assuming they're just too beneath them to be of value. The hours are awful and the pay is terrible. . . . But if you are an office assistant or (even better) the direct personal assistant to a Hollywood decision-maker in the TV space (either scripted or non), then you will be in a fantastic position to fast track your way into TV writing.

The development, green lighting, and execution process of a TV series all takes place within high-level talks between a very limited number of strategically placed persons. There are many well-connected and talented comics or actors with fantastic ideas for long-running series that a studio or broadcast network would love to engage with (seeing them as long-term cash-generating enterprises). Studios acquire the rights to major book properties that have "hooks"—relevant concepts that could be expanded into a series. But producing, and scheduling, a full TV series is a very costly decision, one that must have back-end support before it's ever moved forward.

So, execs and decision-makers break it down into steps. First, they get the proper high-level parties involved to decide what the concept is going to be. Second, they commission key writers to draft up a "blueprint" for the series so that everyone can give their input into whether or not the series is taking on the right shape. This process continues until the blueprint is worthy of entering a scripting phase.

From here, we all know the next steps (production of a pilot commences and everyone waits to see if the series will move forward). Most series go nowhere and get dropped. A few make it and get cancelled after a few episodes. And a small minority go all the way and become major TV hits.

More often than not, the truly successful TV series come from proven TV writers (and occasionally feature-length film writers). Some are generated out of the offices of the big-wig execs, but it's generally the hired writer who does most of the heavy lifting in shaping the overall program. I stress again that these major companies are not looking for series ideas from unproven writers, only in very rare instances have top notch programs come from unknown writers (best example would be *Glee* (2009), where writer Ryan Murphy was able to get an A-list showrunner to read and push his work. . . . Meaning it only got to air via a powerful recommendation).

Why is this a great entry point for a personal assistant or office assistant? Because your job will be the one coordinating schedules with all of the key decision-makers in the room. You will be getting copies of episodes from one party to another. You will be on the phone and constantly emailing with the staff writing assistants about coordinating hand-offs or fixing their grammatical errors before the boss sees them.

By being in this world, you are exposing your name (and work ethic) to the very people who have the ability to pull you into their world, eventually ask you for your thoughts, and possibly allow you polish jobs or do other rare clean ups on actual written material. This is not the time to say something like "Will I get paid extra for this?" or "Can I write an episode?," it's instead about being there for the team to ensure that every project is moving forward in the most efficient way possible.

How can this position be effective if you secure a job at a non-scripted production company? You will gain true insights into how the non-scripted world is actually written, and you will find major opportunities to dip your toe in for experience. You will meet the producers who are whittling away narration on their lunch breaks or the editors sifting through pages of transcription notes looking for good interview inputs. Once you've developed an open line of communication with these teams (and your supervisor is supportive of you helping out), offer assistance to these individuals. . . . Make their jobs *easier*. They will be happy to hand off the assignment to you, since they already have mountains of other work to do. And in time, if you navigate the company in the right way, you can become a semi-"go-to" writer in the organization (whereby a supervisor with well-connected friends might just inquire if you have any sample spec scripts for TV). This scenario is not as speculative as it sounds. This is a very true path that many successful writers have followed. Going back to Erik Bork once again, this is essentially how he was first hired by Tom Hanks to draft out *From the Earth to the Moon* for HBO. . . . He went from an administrative assistant to a top-tier writer overnight, but in reality he spent years laying down groundwork as a smart and trustworthy employee (while writing spec scripts on his own time).

After a minimum of one year (ideally two) as a dedicated and loyal personal assistant to a Hollywood decision-maker, you will see huge progress in terms of how large your personal network has grown (and realize that several key contacts in your phone's contact list are direct links into the very staff writing teams you would hope to connect with professionally.

Again, in Hollywood, these assistant positions are very coveted and you will most likely need to cash in several favors to even garner a studio-level interview, so I would highly advise starting small, by going to mid-level production companies and breaking in there. Not only will you find the challenge of getting the initial job easier, your ability to navigate the job (and bring your own ideas to the table) will be much higher.

You can find assistant jobs on any of the job boards, but you can also check in with www.entertainmentcareers.net or even www.linkedin.com.

To really max this option out, you should never try to use an administrative-type production company job solely for the purpose of your own writing career advancement. . . . You should always keep your writing for a spare time goal. Over time, as you develop a strong reputation wherever you're working, your talents at writing can be mentioned and eventually you (with your supervisor's assistance) can merge these talents together to be more involved in TV projects when they get developed internally.

Keep Writing Gold-Mine Genre Type Features

One real (and consistent) entry point into television writing all stems back to your initial feature-length spec scripts. Those six gold-mine genre types we boasted about truly are the gateway into getting your foot wedged firmly into Hollywood's door (whether for indie features or for television)—because those are the exact films that are required to keep the industry functioning.

Spending a great deal of time to truly polish out and write several live action, feature-length spec scripts that match the gold-mine genre types outlined in Chapter Two *will* get you taken seriously by readers and development executives. However, they won't guarantee you any legit success, at least not right off the bat. Your scripts might receive a ranking of "pass" by Hollywood readers, but your *writing* could be a "consider." And if you play your cards right, that production company might just give you a chance by offering you a limited gig (such as taking one of their script ideas and drafting out a treatment, or polishing out a script that's being rushed into production). You could get your gold-mine genre type script optioned, or even purchased. . . . Or you might even be commissioned to write a new original script for that company.

When writing a gold-mine genre type spec feature, there are several variables in your favor propelling you into situations where you and your work are being taken seriously. The other great attribute of writing the gold-mine genre type scripts is that many of them don't make it into theatres. . . . They become straight-to-TV movies instead. And when you're writing TV movies, you're gaining legit TV credits.

When you're "in" with development executives or acquisitions executives, you can schedule annual pitch meetings with them; you'll become a go-to person rather than an email or phone call professionals are trying to dodge. And the more wide your network grows, the more information you'll become privy to. You'll learn who's doing what and which production companies are transitioning from one genre type or content format to another. You'll also hear updates regarding Company A moving away from movies and focusing on TV series. . . . And it is for precisely these types of networking moments when you can then follow up on such a lead and contact Company A about their "new growth in TV" with the confidence of knowing that you can provide them a sample TV spec script if requested.

RISKY BUSINESS: THE "BACKDOOR PILOT"

Let's go back to our favorite finance word, "hedge," for just a moment. Businesses are very good at doing one thing: Making money. If dozens of major TV channels—which were once a prime target for movie slots—are now shifting gears and taking an active role into acquiring TV series, it only makes sense for Hollywood's middle tier of distribution and production companies (the ones you'll be able to readily access when starting out) to have a vested interest in seeing how they can move into television space in order to satisfy the needs of their clients, the channels, in way that makes financial sense.

Producing a full-on television series is a huge investment. . . . It's equivalent to shooting three or four feature-length films back-to-back (but at least with three or four movies, you have better odds that at least one of them will be successful, whereas a series is all or nothing). The TV business therefore produces pilot episodes, or one-off episodes, to be used as a sample of what the fully produced series will be like. At the studio level, these are produced with the full knowledge that they can bankroll the series if they choose to move forward. On the indie side of the business, producing one episode isn't an option (since it would be too short to be a feature and, without at least a minimum number of five or six episodes, could never realistically be placed anywhere).

The answer has come in the form of a hybrid product called a backdoor pilot. It's literally a feature-length pilot that also works as a stand-alone feature-length TV movie. That way, if the backdoor pilot is fully produced but is never picked up as a series, there is still potential to sell the title into the marketplace as a one-off movie. This is not just a growing trend in the indie world of TV, it's also a trend for studios. This is why you're starting to now see many new programs either launch with a two-hour premiere or, if broadcast as only a one-hour, feel suspiciously like they had a rather abrupt ending.

The only writers I personally know who have been involved with backdoor pilots were heavily focused gold-mine genre type writers with writing careers built on feature-length scripts. However, each of them had a strong desire to segue into television. They did have sample TV spec scripts (usually of dramas) that they were asked to showcase—so they could prove they had at least some TV understanding. None of their backdoor pilots were turned into TV series, but all of them transitioned into TV movies.

Where this reality benefits you is that you can take one of those great TV series ideas and flesh out a first episode as a two-hour backdoor pilot—while making sure to utilize the basics of the gold-mine genre types in your approach. This is the best win-win you can get, in which you are able to express your interest in TV while also having an immediately sellable movie on standby.

FINAL NOTE

There is no need to play the game of "showrunner hand-off," where newbie writers track down (and seemingly stalk) high-ranking Hollywood show-runners in an attempt to give them their sample TV spec scripts—or in one embarrassing story, an entire series bible. Tactics like these are doomed from the start.

Take the pressure off your shoulders and realize that there are wide-open (and untapped) points of entry for you to break into Hollywood's inner TV circle, many of them in easy-to-get positions on the vast non-scripted end of the spectrum. Focus on your sample TV spec scripts and series ideas. Keep working and developing new concepts (keeping your arsenal fresh and up-to-date) and you will be fully prepared for the moment when television opportunity knocks.

NOTE

1   Please note that there are agents open to working with newbie writers who *will* aid them in shaping and building their work—and guiding them on career—however, there are many successful writers who have built their own careers independent of agents. . . . We'll discuss the pros and cons of agents, managers, and other writing representatives in more depth in Chapter 6.

FIVE

CLOSE ENCOUNTERS OF THE L.A. KIND

In this chapter, we'll outline the most crucial aspect of selling your screen-play: selling *yourself* as a great writer. Not only will we discuss who you need to contact, but more importantly, how best to approach them. And if the idea of cold calls, small talk, or social gatherings makes your skin crawl, don't worry; we'll discuss ways you can fake confidence so you can best pitch your script—and yourself—in a way that builds your reputation and gets the right people in Hollywood paying attention.

THE HOLLYWOOD SCHMOOZE GAME

In an idealized world, your script alone should be indicative of your screen-writing talent and potential. But in the real life day-to-day hustle of Holly-wood, your script is only part of the screenwriter equation. Just as there's an expected format and structure your script must follow to appear professional to those who'll read it, there's also a specific manner for how you, as the writer, are expected to present it.

Officially, it's called "pitching" or "networking"; unofficially, it's the "Hollywood schmooze game," full of classic one-liners such as "don't call us, we'll call you." If you want to gain traction with the decision-makers on the inside of Hollywood, you have to learn how to act, speak, and behave in the way they expect (otherwise they'll rarely take notice). As far removed from screenwriting talent as brown-nosing, social niceties, or mindless chit-chat might seem, these subtle personal interactions serve as a very effective filter in Hollywood, allowing agents, producers, and devel-opment executives to quickly assess who they choose to work with (and who they don't).

Thank goodness for technological intervention! In today's world, you no longer have to call all those intimidating Hollywood executives and play small-talk games. Instead, you can blindly email your script to hundreds of people in one swift click. . . . Too bad those same technological advances we thought were here to help us have only created additional screening filters to keep you (and your work) out. In fact, I would argue that there's never been a more difficult time to contact or communicate with real human beings in Hollywood, let alone with those capable of making actual decisions. And as filtering software and cybersecurity continue getting smarter, it's only going to get tougher for you to get your foot in the door (or inbox).

So what's an unknown, first-time writer supposed to do? The old standard of "find an agent who likes your script" certainly doesn't offer much guidance—especially when your blind submission seems doomed for the spam folder.

So, if you want to play the Hollywood schmooze game as a writer, you just have to learn the rules, right? Therein lies the problem—and this is the key point that continues to hold countless writers back from enjoying true success as Hollywood professionals. The Hollywood schmooze game has no rules; it has *principles*. What's the difference? Rules change constantly, because rules are always struggling to keep up with rapidly changing situations. Principles, on the other hand, stay the same regardless of whatever curveball you throw at them. . . . Example? Nearly a century ago when a frightening new invention called "sound" threatened the movie business in the 1920s, the situational rules of Hollywood (like what new filmmaking equipment would now be required) all flip-flopped and everyone panicked. . . . But the principles of the entertainment business (such as making a quality film that could be produced on time, under budget, and earn a profit) didn't change at all. And those same principles, which carried Hollywood through its sound crisis, also carried Hollywood through many other turbulent transitions including the rise of television and the advent of the VCR—and they will continue carrying us forward as Hollywood adapts to the evolving digital realm.

Rather than see another talented writer waste precious time through potentially years of trial and error trying to figure out Hollywood's ever changing rules, I'd much rather cut to the chase and not only spell out the principles behind the Hollywood schmooze game, but also give you plenty of great examples of where and when (and—most importantly—*how*) to apply them in the real working world of Hollywood.

AND THE PRINCIPLES ARE . . .

Principle #3: You Must Always Be *Fresh*

Being "fresh" means always having something new to offer—and for a writer it means you must *always be writing*! Isn't this a given? At the outset, of course. . . . But the way in which this principle applies to Hollywood schmoozing is that when you are asked that inevitable question, "What are you working on?," you'll always have a selection of intelligent—and situation-appropriate—answers to pull from.

Principle #2: You Must *Grow* and Maintain Your Network

Principle #2 is not about pitching yourself or your talents to complete strangers, or the big-wigs running the studios, it's instead about making a conscious step towards consistently building (and maintaining) your own personalized social network of individuals that directly link you to professional decision-makers. This means picking up the phone and actively communicating with people you know (and reaching out to those you don't)— not because you're a nice person, but because you (and your talents) deserve to be on the forefront of other people's minds when they suddenly find themselves in need of a person with writing skills.

Principle #1: You Must *Expand* Your Understanding of Hollywood

Sound clichéd? I get that. . . . But where most books will tell you to "read the trades" and "study the studios"—and other advice that will yield minimal results—my advice is to simply focus on learning everything you can about Hollywood that has *nothing* to do with screenwriting (even if only at a grassroots level). The reason, the more you know about how other people's jobs fit into the overall system, the easier it will be to find a way for you to pitch your work and/or talents to them in order to gain a foothold.

COME PREPARED, OR DON'T COME AT ALL

It'd be nice to believe that real Hollywood "foot-in-the-door" opportunities come in the form of prescheduled meetings or other situations that we have a fair amount of control over . . . but they don't. Hollywood opportunities come from random interactions, leads, and connections that sync up spontaneously—not just for writers, but for everyone including distributors, editors, actors, and so on. For me, if I hear of an interesting new spec movie in the works or nearing completion, it's usually by word of mouth—from friends who know what content I'm looking for, or who just casually mention it off the cuff. I'll then go out of my way to chase down that film and find out whoever is responsible for producing it (so I can secure it). The same goes with my development team and their interest in writers. . . . If they hear of a writer creating content that meets what they're in need of, they'll go out of their way to contact them. How these interactions develop can happen at parties, networking events, film and TV markets, or just casually as two friends catch up and mix business and personal talk over the same lunch.

The problem for most newbie writers is that they are taught the overly formalized forms of pitching without learning how to subtly pitch their work (and themselves) in these everyday casual events. I call these "soft pitches," and the vast majority of the potential work a writer might secure for themselves—especially in the early parts of their career—result from how well they've established a base of professional contacts with whom they can communicate with and share these soft pitch announcements of their writings.

Whether semi-planned (at a professional networking-type event) or completely random (at a party or casual outing), there will inevitably be a time when you meet a professional who asks you point blank "So, what do you do?". While some may see this vague question as yet another example of the shallowness of Los Angeles, a professional sees this as their moment to shine. When you respond proudly with "I'm a screenwriter," that professional will immediately want to know whether (a) you're just another Hollywood hopeful with minimal understanding of the business and little to offer—AKA someone who *cannot* help them—or (b) whether you're a newbie with a solid understanding of the business capable of becoming a professional—AKA someone who *can* help them. . . . Let's make sure you know how to secure option B.

How This Works

A Hollywood screenwriting career blossoms when one can prove they have the ability to deliver the industry a consistent and reliable output of steady work—all while making the jobs of others around them easier. Your most recent project is what showcases your value to the Hollywood system—and when you're starting out and don't yet have any credits to do this work on your behalf, you must be prepared to answer professionals with your industry-appropriate work ready to show (with more already in motion behind closed doors).

That way, when you do find yourself in one of these sudden face-to-face interactions and the casual "What do you do?," and "What are you working on?" questions pop up you will always have a collection of work in motion that allows you to best cater to them with your answer. Meaning, you'll be selecting the work that best represents what *that* individual would be interested in hearing about—what's most pertinent to *their* career needs, rather than just pitching the story you're most proud of.

By piquing their professional interest, the conversation can close more on a point of you asking, "So, how can we work together?" or "Seems we have similar content interests, maybe I can flesh out one of your [or your company's] story ideas?" There's also the real possibility that the producer or development executive before you might have a focus in a genre you aren't currently strong in. . . . That's okay; this allows you to move the relationship forward by inquiring if they know of any leads in the gold-mine genre type you're pursuing (they inevitably will and are generally be happy to make an introduction).

But remember, it's not all about you. . . . It's about your ability as a writer to support the needs of the overall Hollywood industry, which is why when you reciprocate the "What do you do?" question, you need to have an appreciation of what the other side's contributions (and needs) are within the system.

When you're starting out, it's very common to be interacting with people who serve—or are hoping to serve—very straightforward roles in the business. People want to be editors, directors, and actors (amongst many other clear-cut roles). . . . But as you begin to associate with people who are a bit more established, you'll find that they tend to have roles that are a bit harder to place: Line producers, producer's reps, acquisitions agents, and so on. So the more you know about their role within the Hollywood landscape, the more capable you will be at speaking at their level and collecting leads in an professional way. If they're a line producer or producer's rep (purely as an example), they'd know which production companies tend to create specific gold-mine genre type movies like the ones you're writing, so you might be able to get a direct contact or at least get a company name you can search for later on; an acquisitions agent might work directly for one of these companies!

Hollywood, like any industry, is purely a numbers game. Putting yourself out there, interacting with people in all facets of the industry (not just other writers) gets both you *and* your skillsets in front of new people. . . . The more people you're in front of, the more opportunities there are for you to take the lead on. And the more opportunities like these you get yourself involved with, the more your name is slowly (and firmly) planted into the minds of people who can reach out to you when they're in a jam.

I'm not suggesting this is an overnight achievement; it's instead a process of always keeping your work (and yourself) in shape so that you can (1) discuss and deliver "fresh" content immediately upon request when you have these encounters, and (2) so that you're ready to move when that *9.6 Mega-Tsunami* opportunity suddenly falls into your lap.

You get to this point by writing every day and constantly rejuvenating your writing arsenal all while honing your pitching skills whenever possible. But generic "write everyday" advice is not the same old "Stephen King writes 2,000 words per day" approach, nor does it mean you literally need to sit at a computer and punch the keyboard for a blocked amount of time each morning. . . . Writing everyday simply means not being idle with your work; you must always be consistently moving your current film and TV ideas forward toward a state of completion. And "pitching" doesn't mean only discussing your stories in formalized boardroom meetings, it means being able to intelligently speak about your work in a way that engages the other party (and not blindly spouting out a forced or memorized logline).

Let's tackle these one by one. . . .

Your Writing Arsenal

Before you approach Hollywood, you will need at least two (ideally *three*) fully completed feature-length spec scripts ready to show. In addition, you will need a list of at least *ten* structured (meaning fully log-lined and "beat-sheeted"-out) ideas ready to pitch. If you really want to approach Hollywood as a writer, then you need to show them you've got what it takes; and that you are a *writing machine*. Having two to three scripts to showcase proves consistency, and the list of ideas shows stamina and preparedness. . . . Plus, it gives you a great collection of stories to pull from to best engage your immediate professional audience when those inevitable "So whad'ya got?" questions arise.

Although this is a *very* large volume of work to achieve, it is an excellent target portfolio for you to work toward and to keep as a minimum. However, this doesn't mean that once you reach this target that you can simply press pause and wait until your career begins. Once you have two to three scripts you're confident in, you can then pluck one of your solid ideas from your "ten ideas list" and start fleshing it out as a new screenplay. Once fully finished with a completed script, it can then replace the weaker of the previous two to three spec scripts in your arsenal (and you can add a new concept/idea to your "ready-to-go ideas" list)—and this cycle repeats itself.

Here's another interesting point, as pointed out by Hollywood veteran Donie Nelson: The spec scripts (and the list of ideas) should all be *the same gold-mine genre type* (or at minimum, very similar ones). Most people make the false assumption they should present a diversified slate. . . . The opposite is actually what garners results.

Let's hypothetically say you are in discussion with the development team at a mid-level production company. You get along, your ideas are in alignment with their way of doing business. . . . You have a gold-mine genre script in front of them and they're impressed. Before they offer you a writing position for their new film, they'll want to make sure your current script isn't just some fluke anomaly (or, random win). They'll want to make sure you can churn out a workflow that is consistent (and fresh). If they ask to see other writing samples, and all you have is work from a different genre, they might not be convinced. However, if you had a second example, completely unique to the first script yet from the same genre type, you would be able to prove dependability.

But wouldn't a writer get branded for only writing one type of script? Yes! And that's a good problem to have. . . . I hope you do get branded! (As Donie Nelson continued, "If you should only be so lucky as to get branded. . . ."). Many people falsely see getting known for writing a certain type or style of script as a bad thing; however, being branded is a great thing for your professional career. Go ask a veteran actor, they'll tell you being typecast is a luxury. When you get a reputation for being able to consistently output a much needed gold-mine genre type, in a factory-style manner, the work will start coming to you, rather than you always chasing leads.

Coming prepared means coming ready to show Hollywood what it needs to see in your work (and from you). Hollywood doesn't want to see your ability to write any old genre, it wants to see your ability to continue offering fresh and unique approaches to a reliable gold-mine genre type day in and day out.

Still stuck on how you're going to go back and write two to three brand new scripts? All from the same genre? *And* come up with another ten ideas that are fully vetted out? It will take time. . . . But that's okay, because as stated in the opening of this chapter, writing scripts is only part of the battle; you still have all the other aspects of Hollywood networking to learn.

Don't panic about the size of this target portfolio. . . . Remember that it's more the *process* of constantly working to build and grow your arsenal that's most important. If you're midway through your first script, keep writing until it's complete. . . . Once you're finished, start on the next one. If you don't have anything yet, that too is okay! Just start with one story idea and build upon it, followed by another and another, until you're ready to take a crack at your first spec script. Picture any great writer and there was indeed a day when they'd never written a word.

PITCH PERFECT: HONING YOUR PITCHING SKILLS

Some people are naturally gifted at verbal communication. . . . They seem to be able to gracefully enter a room, open their mouth, and simply captivate an audience. But in truth, most people never started this way. Instead, they *learned* how to command an audience through practice and application. Many of us cringe at the idea of making small talk, cold calling, or public speaking. And there is no worse feeling than standing before someone, being asked to tell them about your script (or yourself) and being at a total loss for words, followed by experiencing an immediate loss of self-confidence.

I've been there—we all have in one form or another—and for those of us (including myself) that get overly self-conscious when pitching our ideas, there are many ways to learn how to *fake* confidence and teach yourself how to handle any social encounter Hollywood might throw your way.

What follows are a few basic steps you can take action on today (while writing your scripts and working towards your target portfolio) that will not only aid you in how you view your own writing work, but will also improve your self-confidence, so you can pitch your scripts more effectively, and expose you to other facets of the film business, all while helping grow your social network—that's win-win-*win* thinking. Before you dismiss these, really read through how each of these can help you (not just to be a more effective writer, but also to more effectively manage your own career):

Improv Groups—Improvisational acting is probably one of the best skills you could ever hope to acquire. Whether you live in Los Angeles or not, your town will have a band of actors with an improv group open to new members. What should you say if asked why you've joined the group? The truth! Tell them you are a writer who is trying to gain better confidence and public speaking skills. You will instantly be seen as a non-threat by all the other actors, and believe me, they will want to help you improve your skills and get better. After that, fall into line and have some fun! Let loose. They'll have you perform all kinds of weird and crazy exercises (breathing exercises, training exercises, etc.). Then you will be placed into groups and given scenarios. You will invent scenarios of your own, which should come naturally to you, given your writing strengths. You will learn the rules of improv, such as accepting whatever piece of information, however ridiculous, your scene partner has introduced to the scenario. Why are these skills so vastly important? Because every business meeting I've ever been in literally feels like an improv session! I'm not kidding you. It's a back-and-forth volley of ideas, opinions, and corporate culture. How you speak, and what you say, will literally be part of the act. You will also learn how people communicate, and you will learn the "beats" people use when telling jokes or presenting ideas (which will also allow you to find those clutch points to jump into the conversation and get your ideas on the table effectively). You will learn how to more quickly consolidate your ideas and get your concept in front of the group as fast as possible, if you want your scenario to be used. (Know what this sounds like to me? Pitching!) Improv classes are not only a lot of fun, you will also make friends who share an interest in the same business, but with a completely different focus (which allows you the opportunity to learn the ins and outs of other professional avenues).

Acting Classes—Joining an acting class accomplishes several objectives that improve your professional writing abilities. First, you will be forced to read scripts from the point of view of a person using it as a tool, not as the bible to a film; and second, you will realize that many actors do not actually read their scripts, they simply scan the pages looking for how many speaking lines their character has (which they do to judge "how important" their role is). . . . Seems outlandish? That's Hollywood. But don't get discouraged, see the silver lining. This will force you, as a writer, to ensure your smaller characters offer just as complex and interesting acting decisions as do your bigger roles. Third, you will learn the importance of good dialogue versus poor dialogue. You will hear idiot dialogue or forced resolutions in speaking parts, but you will also hear well-crafted subliminal dialogue that allows an actor (and director) the opportunity to draw interesting conclusions in an exchange. Acting classes are also a great deal of fun and will also introduce you to completely new people (hoping to accomplish different goals but in the same industry).

Hollywood Pitch Fests—These are very interesting events; as with most markets and conventions, there's a steep entry fee along with your standard bag of swag (which typically contains mostly coupons and advertisements—AKA, more stuff for you to spend your money on). But during the actual pitch event, for a small fee (between $15 and $30) you can schedule a ten to fifteen minute pitch meeting with a staff member from a major studio. What will you find once you enter your meeting? A giant room full of small tables, each with a very young (twenty-two to twenty-five year old) intern. This is who you're going to pitch. Their job is to attend this event on the very off chance some brilliant material comes in. . . . In short, their job is to take detailed notes of the submission, the writer, and any materials that might be handed off, just so it can be back-logged and catalogued at the studio in the very unlikely chance that their work takes off at some point in the future. Are these events worth it? If you expect to pitch your idea and see it optioned, then no, these events are a total waste of money. But if you are looking to (1) hone your pitch craft and build confidence by pitching to a real person, or (2) make youthful connections who are also excited about making their own Hollywood dreams come to life, then a pitch fest might be a decent **one-time** investment.

VOLUNTARY NETWORKING

You're going to have to keep your social network growing if you ever want to get your scripts into the Hollywood hustle. . . . And that means you're going to have to get out there and network. The problem is that most of Hollywood's networking scenarios force us into awkward situations and yield zilch in terms of results when all is said and done. No thanks! (That time would be much better spent writing!)

Fortunately, there are very interesting ways you can approach Hollywood networking that are absolutely one-way tickets to seeing huge returns for your efforts. The irony? You'll be heading to the exact same markets, industry events, and festivals that everyone else will suggest you should approach, only you'll be experiencing them in a way where you'll glean more insight, contacts, and results than everyone else around you.

Film Markets

Now that I annually attend the world's largest and most prestigious film festivals and film markets, I can give you the piece of advice I wished I had learned back when I first moved to L.A.: **Don't attend a film market,** *volunteer* **for one.**

Believe me, whether it's the American Film Market (AFM) or Cannes, markets need people to handle all the grunt work. They might bring you in several weeks, possibly several months, early. . . . maybe even for a paying job—minimum wage, of course. But you will be helping orchestrate the market itself and will be dealing directly with decision-makers. You will have access to buyers and exhibitors lists, catalogues, and the client/contact lists of production companies. You will witness all the screening schedules. You will get firsthand access to see which companies handle what genres of content. You will see firsthand the sheer volume of movies (and how many are in the gold-mine genres). You can also volunteer as an intern for the companies exhibiting at the market. Sure, you'll essentially be the "doorman" or "receptionist" for the company, where you filter out people walking in and so on. But you will be on the inside. As a volunteer, you will witness wannabe writers entering the room and listening to them as they fumble through their pitches. Smile, nod, and *learn* from their mistakes. But the best part is that there will be downtime. . . . You will talk with this company about everything and nothing. **Don't make the newbie mistake of actually pitching your work to them during the market**; keep your ideas to yourself at the moment. Simply listen to them, and be accommodating whether they ask you to make coffee or fetch supplies. Listen to them talk about movies with others in the room, especially with their clients; listen to them discuss ideas. You will overhear meetings about collaborations and development, about money, even about content that works and content that doesn't. They will learn to trust you. And, when the market comes to a close, you will have several close contacts that have seen you perform under pressure and will know you are able to deliver what's needed. Attending a market costs a lot of money, volunteering costs nothing but your time. . . . And you'll probably get a few meals covered, as well as more direct access to real working professionals than you could ever imagine.

Annual Markets and How to Participate

American Film Market (eight days in November); Santa Monica, CA—Unlike the splashy film festivals located overseas, AFM is a U.S.-based business-focused event. The market is organized by the Independent Film & Television Alliance (IFTA), which utilizes both paid and volunteer staff members for support. To get involved, here's who you need to contact:

- *American Film Market* (AFM, www.americanfilmmarket.com) regularly updates its site with market related employment opportunities as well as volunteer information.
- *Independent Film & Television Alliance* (IFTA, www.ifta-onling.org) has a dedicated team year round planning and organizing the event. You can reach out by phone at (310) 446-1000 or by email at AFM@ifta. online.org Just let them know you're interested in volunteering or getting hired and they'll guide you the rest of the way.

Cannes Film Festival's Marche Du Film (twelve days in mid-May); Cannes, France—The Cannes Film Festival receives all the attention, but the real business behind the event is at the *Marche du Film* ("Film Market"). Unlike AFM, a great deal of financial support from the French government is provided to the Cannes Film Festival and its *Marche du Film*, so they are one of the rare events that can afford to pay its entire workforce—as long as they're French citizens. . . . However, there are two external (third-party) services which *non*-French citizens can utilize (for a fee) to gain access to both the *Marche du Film* as well as the world famous Cannes Film Festival:

- *The American Pavilion* (www.ampav.com) offers student programs, which allow you to work directly with larger-scale U.S. distribution companies. Accommodations are included in their prices. For specific questions, their phone number is (310) 202-3375.
- *The Creative Mind Group* (www.thecreativemindgroup.com) is an internship program open to everyone. I have personally worked with

many interns supplied via the Creative Mind Group and was very impressed with their services. Students come from all over the globe and seem to have very engaged group leaders showing them the ropes. Accommodations are included in their prices. You can reach out directly at (310) 674-7466.

European Film Market (February) Berlin, Germany—Running alongside the world famous Berlin Film Festival, this market rounds out the top three film markets. . . . The problem is, speaking German is a must for anyone working directly with the event (for those with Deutsch language skills, they have jobs posted here: www.kbb.eu/de/jobs_ und_ausbildung/stellenangebote/jobs.php); anyone else must receive sponsorship directly through a company and probably pay their own accommodations.

The reason for not putting more of the famous film festivals (such as Sundance, Toronto, and even smaller—but growing—goodies like the Heartland Film Festival) is because few of these have a business market taking place during the event. In this example, both Cannes and Berlin are film festivals, but each has a convention style market where distribution companies attend for the express purpose of buying, selling, and packaging (putting together the financials of) new movies. Film festivals are celebrations of cinema (and are great to attend for fun), but your professional networking time will be best spent at one of the markets instead of the festivals.

Film Commissions

Volunteer for your local film commission. Even if you're not in a major metropolitan area, you will be directly associated with professional individuals in and around your community that have a strong interest in films (and who are in the business of bringing film productions to your region). Film commissions offer interesting opportunities on new productions that cannot generally be found if only using Google or IMDb searches. Film Commissions have entire databases on Hollywood production companies (and development entities). Ask permission to copy email addresses, and also ask if you can be a point of contact for regional productions. Everyone you work with will have years of experience for you to glean insight from, and most of them will have legit contacts in the business who are working professionally.

Be An Extra

Contact a company that hires extras and tell them you want to become a film extra. You will get paid a minimum wage; however, you will gain access to the production office as well as to the film crews and the sets. Very politely, during a break, approach a member of the department you have interest in working for. Simply state, "I'm working as an extra in order to meet professionals in the [fill-in-the-blank] department. If you need any help on this film or on future projects, I'd be interested in helping out." You're not there to enter into a dialogue, just to announce you're available. . . . It's not a crazy idea to print up some business cards (it's cheap as heck online these days) with just your name, cell phone, and email address. Keep it short and to the point, hand them your card, and walk away (after saying "thank you," of course). They are busy and cannot get into deep conversations about your love of cinema. Do not use this approach with the director, nor should you use this to become an actor/actress. This is more of an approach to use with production office personnel, production assistants, and other (lower-ranking but well-connected) team members. One other note, *you must actually do the original job you were hired to do*, which is to be an extra in the film. . . . Have fun watching the crews set up the shots, you're getting paid to network!

THE MYTH OF GOING TO THE TOP

Bypassing the hierarchy of a production company and attempting to speak directly with the head-honcho decision-maker (such as the president or CEO) certainly sounds like it'd be the most effective way of moving the ball, but in reality it's the most counterproductive . . . and often times detrimental to gaining any real traction with that company.

I see it happen all the time, pushy producers or pesky screenwriters calling into our offices (sometimes several times per day) trying to reach the CEO or head of development. We've even had a few incidents of persons just showing up at the door unannounced claiming they had a meeting with so-and-so (or insisting they're longtime friends and just happened to be in the neighborhood and wanted to say hello—which is fishy considering they don't know how to pronounce our CEO's name properly).

The logic here makes perfect sense: If you can get in with the decision-maker, then you must be able to get a decision made in your favor; however, the above actions are seen as very unprofessional and reek of desperation.

Don't forcibly reach out to whomever you perceive to be a decision-maker; go instead to the more approachable employees who are already on the inside and have direct access to the people you need (and who will actually hear you out). They're the interns and assistants! If you want your spec script to have a higher chance of being read (and have more favorable coverage written on it), then don't waste your time going to the top of the food chain in a given company.

It's not only hopeful writers who've broken this unwritten principle; filmmakers and hopeful producers make this mistake all the time. Most people have this false impression that they must fight through the barriers of interns and assistants to get to the top executives at a company in order for action to take place. Instead, you should befriend interns and assistants. Empower them, don't think of them as useless—they are extremely useful and strategically placed individuals. After all, interns and assistants are already on the inside of the very organization you're trying to get your material into. They know the company politics and how their particular supervisors like not only their coffee, but how they like material to be presented to them (including at what time of day and in what temperament).

WHO YOU NEED TO KNOW

What follows are the three most likely candidates for direct access to whom you can reach out to when making first contact with a production or distribution company. . . . Not just who they are, but what they do, and how they like information presented to them:

Acquisitions Assistants—Executives serving in the acquisitions department are generally so pressured to find new quality content in advance of their competitors, they're willing to go the extra mile and take phone calls (or accept unsolicited submissions) more freely than others. Again, this doesn't work in the studio world, this is more of a mini-major to indie-zone practice—but that's the zone you'll see the most results. Most of acquisitions execs have assistants who do the grunt work (logging data, putting little research overviews of submissions together, endless IMDb trolling, etc.). They're your target. Although acquisitions executives (and their assistants) are really on the hunt for completed films, they're always working hand-in-hand with their internal development teams (or have an interest in cultivating projects from scratch to serve as future producers on). The interesting thing about most acquisitions agents that I know is that they so often deal with producers—and have dealt with more troubling/annoying ones than easy ones—many of them have a mindset that they could easily stamp out their producer competition and take on a film project themselves; makes sense, they already know what works and have a powerful contact list. As a result, the acquisitions department in general is a great place to be connected both for the short term (for your immediate spec scripts) as well as the long term (for more—like co-production opportunities if you really hit it off), but reaching out directly to an acquisitions agent's personal assistant is one of the most direct pathways you can take to getting your work into the right team member's hands.

Directors (or Coordinators) of Development—Not development executives; go for the director or the coordinator of development (still a prominent connection, though not the top of the food chain). The development team is sort of a collection of in-house producers; they're on the hunt for new projects, but also are assigned productions based on upper management decisions and corporate relations. Development executives are a major part of those decisions (and are directly involved in those major high-level relationships); the directors of development (who are one step below the executive level) and their respective coordinators and assistants, are part of that key executive's immediate team of go-to people. That means directors of development are crucial (and well-connected) inside an organization, but still have quite a bit to prove before they can move up that next rung in the corporate ladder. As a result, they are eager to find new writers, new projects, and new opportunities—not just for the company they're working for, but also for themselves. Directors of development are at that beautifully hungry point in their professional careers, where they're willing to put in eighteen-hour days while still accepting the grunt work. They are not only open to taking your call, they're also looking for their own big ticket opportunity to make it on their own. If you're scrolling the development team's titles and aren't seeing a director of development, then the coordinator is your next best match. After that, just call the reception desk and inquire which assistant on the development team would be best to speak with.

Sales Teams—This one's a bit more out of the box, because the first instinct for a writer is to approach those in a company that can actually make a film from their script. . . . But think big picture for a moment. If you, instead, go directly to the sales team (the employees whose job it is to make money for the company by selling its films), they will be much better suited to either (a) give you practical advice on your script or (b) push your script/contact info through to the right person within the organization—if a sales executive gets excited about your script and they tell the production team to take a look, the production team will take note—because if the films aren't selling, no one continues working. . . . And sales executives must know what's most likely to sell at the end of the day.

Notice that agents aren't on this list? By and large, and despite common misperception, agents aren't all that interested in hearing from new (un-produced) writers. We'll discuss agents in detail in Chapter Six, but to quickly touch on the main point here, if you stick to writing the gold-mine genre types, agents will actually be the ones coming to you. Agents are interested not in finding new writers, but in earning 10 percent off the success of scripts that are easily selling. Therefore, you will actually first need to develop a reputation as a writer and garner some deals before you go dealing with agents.

Know who else didn't make the list? Producers. That's because being a producer really isn't a job description or title all by itself. Instead, producers actually come from all areas of the industry (usually from development, acquisitions, or simply any zone within distribution) or serve other roles within a company or organization. A producer can really be anyone on the business side who has already built a strong network and simply gets either passionate about a script you've written, or sees you as a strong writer who could potentially pen something they have interest in producing. Occasionally, when scanning titles at a production/distribution company, you might come across a few producers listed on the site, but these are generally not full-time employees of that company, but rather freelancers brought in for a single project.

Stick to the principles of the Hollywood schmooze game (always be writing, always be networking, always be learning about the rest of the business), and you'll find your circle of contacts growing, your library of scripts improving, and your understanding of where you can fit in becoming more refined. Focus on contacting the people that can move your career forward as opposed to those who will do nothing.

These three first-contact points are a great start to entering into Hollywood's mysterious business world.

NAVIGATING THE RECEPTIONIST'S DESK

All companies (big and small) have a person designated to answer calls (or one who manages all those blindly submitted "info@company" emails). Ideally, this person is designed for guiding all those messages and delivering them to the right persons within the organization. But in reality, the reception desk is every company's first line of defense against allowing the crazy and annoying writers and producers to gain entry. As a result, no matter who else you wish to speak to in any organization, you will first have to navigate the reception desk in order to be properly passed along (either to get directly connected by phone, or to obtain key contact names and email addresses).

1. Respect the reception desk—They work very hard and take shit from everyone. . . . Don't continue that cycle! Treat them like people, not like a switchboard. They have all the leverage when they pick up the call as to whether your call actually goes through to the right person, or whether it goes straight to voicemail.
2. Get to the point—It's okay to admit you're a newbie! It's okay to say the truth, that you have some scripts that are in line with what the company produces and that you'd like to see if there's someone you can speak with to see if there's "synergy" or opportunities. The more forthright with them you are, the better able they will be to get you to the right person who can actually handle your requests.
3. Don't put them on the spot—It's okay to say, "If it's not appropriate to put me through, that's fine, I can always reach out to [the person you are calling, or his/her assistant] by email if that's easier." You'd be surprised how reluctant some people are to push you through a direct line, but how readily they'll hand you a name and email address.

THE QUERY LETTER IS DEAD

The most effective way to communicate with people is face-to-face (and that's not going away anytime soon). The second most effective way is by email.

A lot of individuals will jump in here and try to persuade you that the phone is number two in terms of reaching out, but I argue it's email.

Some will push you to just call blindly. . . . But more often than not, you'll end up with one voicemail recording after another (and most professionals these days let those VMs pile up). So is Hollywood now devoid of phone calls? Of course not, the phone is a great way to really get a lot of quality work done in a short period of time, but now you need to make a written request for a call by email.

But this is very good news for you! Many new writers are freaked out by the phone and get nervous discussing their ideas verbally. An email you completely control (and can read and reread before sending it off to people). And, after all, you're a writer, so typing (and retyping) an email should be second nature.

TIMING THE MARKETPLACE

Don't reach out unless you have something to offer. It's okay to reach out and inquire if a company has interest in what you're working on, but certainly don't get them excited about it **until it's complete and ready to deliver**. There is no worse way to tarnish your image than building up your capabilities and not being able to follow through after you've cast the line (essentially, over-promising and underdelivering). There is no worse missed opportunity than the one where you pitch what you're working on and having the other side say, "Sounds great, send it over," only you're far from completion.

This happens in my world all the time. Filmmakers reach out with movies, only they're not completed. I can't do anything with it, so the conversation goes to waste. With your script, sure you could send over a draft just so they can get a feel for what the script is, but you can never prove to someone you're a talented writer at the rough draft phase (for all the other party knows, your exploratory draft is actually your finest writing—and they think it stinks).

ASK FOR A PITCH MEETING

First, they're rarely called "pitch meetings." They're simply "meetings." And second, there is no formula for how to obtain one other than by simply asking someone from the acquisitions department, development department, or the creative team.

After you've made first contact by email or phone, and after you've presented the goods (emailed a *requested* copy of your script and/or discussed a few ideas that are in alignment with what that particular company is looking for), you simply need to ask for the meeting. Nothing overwhelming here, just a simple: "Would it be possible to meet in person to discuss some of these ideas?" Or the old, "Maybe we could meet up to see if there's any upcoming projects of yours that I could help out with?"

I find it's best to always be in the position of moving the ball forward—meaning being the one who's asking. And as a writer, that means utilizing the skills you've developed from places like your improv classes to introduce the idea of a face-to-face meeting into the conversation. Assure them your schedule is flexible and that you understand they're busy.

You always need to be the one traveling to them. Meet at their offices (or at a coffee shop or other location that they suggest). Their time is limited and your objective is to show them you're a person who understands (and respects) the time they've carved out to hear your ideas.

THE PITCH MEETING

You've finally secured the coveted pitch meeting, a half hour of legit face-to-face time with a Hollywood professional for the sole purpose of sitting down and discussing *your* scripts, *your* ideas, and how *you* can write to meet their needs. Has the panic set in?

Problem is that far too many writers look at the pitch meeting as a job interview, which adds unnecessary stress to the scenario and causes them to second-guess their talents and abilities. The truth is, you *are* talented and *do* possess the ability to write. . . . Otherwise you wouldn't be there. So it's much more important to view the pitch meeting for what it really is: A first date.

Although it's quite true that the quality of your pitches (and ideas) are absolutely important during your meeting, this is only a small percentage of the overall purpose of the meeting. The pitch meeting is really more about seeing how well you can interact with the team—and how well can you take criticism and hear others' ideas. And if the development executives start tossing around curveball ideas on how the script could be improved, do you go with the flow or do you get defensive or not participate. And if you do play ball and contribute ideas, are they ideas that mesh well with the common core values of the company with whom you're speaking, or are they too far out of line?

Again, these are generally informal meetings. Just as a job interview begins with "So, tell me about yourself" (which translates to, "What have you done that proves you're worth hiring?") and a first date generally begins with a "So, what do you do for a living?" (which translates to "Tell me what you do so I can get a relatively accurate sense of your net worth, income level, stability, and level of maturity"), the first question during a pitch meeting is usually "So, what do you have?" (which means, "tell us some of your ideas so we can see where our ideas overlap").

Out of all three, I think the pitch meeting is probably the most informal and the most fun. Remember, you're in the room because you have command of the craft and have secured the confidence of the team, and you have already been vetted as a quality writer. All you need to do now is enter the room and have fun!

Keep the room relaxed and the conversation flowing. It's inevitable that as you begin presenting your ideas, the team might interrupt you in the middle of your pitch and say, "That doesn't work for us, we do more family content." Don't get distracted and focus only on the first part, "That doesn't work for us," listen to what they're telling you (we think your ideas are very good, but we need your ideas focused on the gold-mine genres that work best for us). Don't think twice, just shift gears and keep your concepts focused on the genre style the team is looking for.

FOLLOWING UP (WITHOUT LOOKING DESPERATE)

Following up is a delicate art; it's really part of the same game as pitching and accurately presenting all your points during a meeting. When you follow up appropriately, you are announcing that you understand business etiquette and Hollywood's social norms and procedures. However, if you follow up in an unprofessional way, you can unintentionally give off a very negative image.

The best way to really master this is to simply follow standard dating etiquette to time your follow-up moves. If you had a successful pitch meeting (similar to a first date), send a quick email note, such as, "Thanks for your time, looking forward to the next steps." If during that meeting you discussed action items (such as sending material elements back and forth, like additional story ideas), go ahead and send them along. Otherwise, mention an approximate ETA so that the other party knows when to expect them. Also, as with dating, it's important to know when you might be coming off a little too strong. . . . A simple pitch meeting (as with a first date) does not guarantee automatic movement forward, and following up with emails and/or phone calls several times in the days thereafter can quickly put a sour taste into the other party's mouth.

There's no rulebook here (such as a "wait three days before following up"). If the other party is interested, they will respond and be receptive to your emails and phone calls. If they are not interested, it's okay to continue a soft push for a bit, but it's also important to understand that after a few attempts without any response it's most likely just not going to happen. Move on. . . . There's plenty of other fish in Hollywood.

IMAGE MATTERS

Just as your screenplay starts getting judged before the reader even opens it to page one, you too are getting this kind of attention from those around you.

When we think of "writers," we often see awkwardly (sometimes sloppily) dressed individuals, who spend much of their time inside their own heads and very little interacting with the real world—making them anti-social and strange. This is quite far from true—most writers I know are very sociable; they have to be. They're out hustling their work each and every day.

Dressing the part for a writer doesn't mean wearing baggy jeans and a stained shirt, it means dressing professionally. You must know how to enter a room, appearing as a person who takes care of him/herself, including good personal hygiene. Some wannabes have a vision that they should project an image of "I don't care" to the system, that their work is too personal and important for Hollywood to rip apart.

Okay, I get it, but if your work is too important for Hollywood to see, then who will? And if you have a standoffish attitude and dress horrendously, not too many professionals will want to invite you to corporate meetings.

What I'm saying is that image is very important. It is the first thing people see of you. The image of your email, the image of your clothing, and the image you present as you speak in public situations. All of these elements create *your* overall image. . . . And the best part about your image is that you have 100 percent control over it. You only have to be true to your own styles and tastes—while being respectful of how those styles and tastes are received by those around you—in order to be seen as unique and interesting to work with.

". . . IT'S ABOUT *WHO* YOU KNOW"

It's not just Scorsese and Tarantino working with the same people project after project, it's everyone. And the reason is very simple: It's just easier that way.

When you work with someone you've already collaborated with on a past project, there's no risk. . . . You already know you can rely on them. (Just like our development executive calling up his friend to write *9.6 Mega-Tsunami*—all the guesswork and stress were simply taken out of the equation.) What Hollywood professionals need at the end of the day is a writer they can depend on, who understands what *their* side of the table needs in order to make a film work, and who won't make them look bad by missing deadlines or turning in shoddy work.

Therefore, the writers who get hired for legit writing jobs are the writers whose names are already firmly planted in the minds of those agents, producers, and development executives *before* they need to hire one. So, the real challenge is not getting someone to take your script seriously, it's getting yourself in front of the right people and getting them to take *you* seriously—well ahead of when they need you.

So keep writing and working towards your target goal, but also keep communicating with as many people *outside* of writing as you possibly can all while learning about the overall business. Constantly improving your writing arsenal is a given, but you need to people to showcase and discuss your work with. Gain your professional foothold by consistently maintaining (and expanding) your network of connections and by understanding the business behind Hollywood—so that you can always find a unique way to wedge yourself into Hollywood's ever-changing landscape.

Is it worth submitting spec scripts to screenwriting festivals and contests?

Yes! If your spec script is shortlisted by a festival or contest—and especially if it wins—you can absolutely use this triumph as a way to get this same script to the head of the line during submission to production companies for review. And you can also use this win to pitch *yourself* when reaching out to production companies to submit future scripts or when requesting pitch meetings. It's also not unlikely for directors of development to be the judges in some of these events, who might also reach out to you directly to commission your talents regardless of whether you win or not. And in a worst case scenario, if your script does not "climb the ranks" and come out on top of a festival or contest, understand that you will generally receive detailed feedback from whomever made the decision to pass on your script—this feedback is extremely valuable to your overall growth as a screenwriter, so take this criticism as a constructive way to build your talents and strengthen your writing muscles. Festivals and contests are a wise investment.

SIX

TO LIVE AND WRITE IN L.A.

In this chapter, we'll prepare you for the day-to-day hustle of Hollywood. From building a reliable reputation to negotiating your own contracts. . . . We'll transform you from a novice writer into a screenwriting entrepreneur, capable of inventing your own paid screenwriting opportunities, all while protecting yourself (and your ideas) along the way.

"NOT MY DEPARTMENT. . . "

The fantasy for many of those on the creative side of the movie business is that one day their talents will simply be recognized and they'll suddenly find themselves being represented by Hollywood's ultimate trio of defense: (1) A major Hollywood agency, fighting tooth-and-nail on their behalf for every project; (2) a big-wig talent manager, running the show behind closed doors while inflating their image in the trades; and (3) a Harvard-educated legal team so ruthless and crass they could star in their own reality show. For a writer, this wall of protection would allow them complete space to simply focus on their scripts while leaving all that intimidating "business stuff" for the professionals to deal with.

But there's more than meets the eye with this idealized scenario. Think about it: If you want to be represented by Hollywood agents, managers, and lawyers (and actually believe that they'll do all this daunting and tedious work-stuff for you), you will still eventually have to put pen to paper yourself and sign your own name over as a client to these entities. And believe me, they're not in business for you, they're in business for *themselves* (and your name will be just one more line item on their clientele list); and if you don't know how to read agreements, negotiate like a pro, and construct deals on your own with *your* best interests established (in a way that's fair to both sides), you'll never see true protection for your work nor advancement in your career.

It's easy for us to imagine Aaron Sorkin or James Cameron simply sitting back, feet kicked up, thinking about their next great project while an army of minions handle all other aspects of their lives, but this fantasy just isn't the way the real world works. Most of the breakout hits that writers or filmmakers experience, which are often labeled by the media as "overnight successes," are really more in the realm of ten to fifteen years in the making. That's ten to fifteen years of constant hustle, ups and downs, and (above all else) persistence. Most big-wig writers and filmmakers that I know are very professional and astute with all aspects of their careers and take an active role during contract negotiations and project management; they generally have agents, but at the end of the day they use *their own* judgment, insight, and wherewithal to make the decisions that affect their careers. And many distinguished Hollywood professionals I've known have pretty in-check egos, even after much success; their current and continuous levels of success are not from a brash attitude of know-it-all-ism and "take no prisoners" contract negotiation, but rather from one of compromise. It's about what works, what doesn't, and where the middle ground lies to *get the project done*.

If you want to truly succeed in Hollywood, then you must fully understand the business behind the movies and how it operates, from beginning to end. You must be able to read agreements, understand term structures, and negotiate what's important (while leaving behind what is not). As we've stated before, it's not the writing aspect that holds most novice writers behind, it's the inability to manage their own careers. That means you need to be the one taking an active role managing your own screenwriting career.

Don't panic! Before you get antsy or nervous about the prospect of taking on all those intimidating contracts or business negotiations, remember two things: First, you can Google any legal phrase and get a very clear definition of what it means, and second, if the person on the other side of the table knows something (anything) about contracts, negotiations, or the movie business in general, there was a time when they *did not* (meaning *everything in this world is learnable*). Even if they're using acronyms you don't understand or terms you've never heard. . . . There was a time when they'd never heard them as well. And if you think a power trio of agent, manager, and legal counsel makes you untouchable, just imagine how well-off you are when you're the one calling your own shots (and not having to pay all their commissions)!

As the old saying goes, if you want something done right, you're better off doing it on your own. Same applies here. . . . So let's get started.

HOLLYWOOD MYTH BUSTING

Myth #1: You Need an Agent to Get Work

A common set of assumptions held by most writers is that producers and production companies contact agents when they either (a) need to hire a writer to draft a work-for-hire screenplay or (b) if they've come across a spec script they wish to acquire. There's some truth to these assumptions, with a 'Hollywood twist' of course . . .

If a producer or development executive at a production company stumbles upon a spec script they really like, they're only reaching out to that agent because the writer signed with them; if there's no agency agreement (and no agency info listed on the cover pages of the script), then those same producers and production companies would, instead, reach out to the writer directly. And if that same producer or development executive reaches out to an agent to find a writer to complete a work-for-hire script, they're not reaching out blindly.... There's often a long running ad hoc "friendly understanding" where they each cash in favors with one another.

But wouldn't an agent who likes (and signs) a brand new writer go out of their way to find them available opportunities in the marketplace? Isn't it the agent's *job* to ensure all of their clients (writers) are getting promoted and receiving work? Not really.... Agents are busy enough dealing with the workload already on their plates. And since agents work purely for commission (taking 10 percent of every dollar a writer earns), they're much more focused on whichever writer is already getting attention (meaning, whoever is already selling properties). If you're the newbie, signing up with nothing but a few spec scripts and the hope of Hollywood success, you fall way down into the "out of sight, out of mind" category. That agent won't be out in the marketplace trying to hustle work for you (cashing in favors on a writer they're not 100 percent certain will deliver); they'll be focused on whomever on their clientele list is already selling (and is the most direct line for them to earn their commission).

You'll have to *prove yourself* first. That means you will have to be the one out hustling to secure yourself with writing jobs and getting your talents noticed (no agent will do this for you, not when you're a beginner). During your early years as a newbie writer starting out in the business, you can either sign with an agent and then hustle all alone to get yourself some legit writing credits (then pay your agent, who did nothing, 10 percent of *your* money), or you can enter the marketplace—doing the same amount of work with the same results—and pocket 100 percent of what's paid out (while building all those valuable Hollywood connections directly).

Once you're out securing your own jobs, building a stellar reputation as a writer who can deliver, agents will be coming to you.... But until then, you'll have to be the one creating your own opportunities for work; no one will be doing that for you. Signing with an agent will *not* put you ahead or increase your odds of getting screenwriting work. Signing with an agent does *not* make you appear more valuable or incentivize production companies or producers to hire you.... *Only your talents and your ability to present yourself in a professional manner will secure you with legit writing gigs*—which is something you can do entirely on your own.

I would only agree with the myth "you need an agent to secure you with work" if you were trying to be an actor.... Talent agents have privileged access to casting lists called "breakdowns," which are detailed reports "breaking down" all the available acting roles that production companies need working actors to fill (down to things like weight, race, hair and eye color, gender, etc.). But as a newbie screenwriter, whether you have an agent or not makes very little difference since no breakdown lists like these exist for writers.

Many television writers I know have a much more positive view of agents than feature writers. . . . TV writers will insist that you need an agent in order to get your work before studio-level staff writing teams—which is totally true. However, the likelihood of a staff writing team plucking an unknown writer to join them based upon a spec script is extremely unlikely—and if that writer were so talented, they'd be able to land that position without the help of that agent.

When you're starting out, go solo, pocket 100 percent of your money, and build a valuable network of connections—with real Hollywood decision-makers—directly.

Myth #2: You Need an Agent to Negotiate Your Contracts

Contracts of any kind are intimidating; they're always long and overly complex (and screenwriting contracts are no exception). However, if a producer or production company is going to hire your writing talents for their needs in exchange for money, then a contract of some kind will be involved, and you will have to be the one signing it in order to secure the job (whether you have an agent or not). And precisely because contracts are so intimidating and complex, you should have an agent negotiate all contracts on your behalf (so you don't get screwed). . . right?

Of course not! If you're reading the words on this page then you're perfectly capable of reading (and understanding) an agreement. And if you've ever given a specialty order at a restaurant ("Could I get a salad instead of fries?" or "No mayo, please") then you're perfectly capable of negotiating terms within a written contract as well.

Negotiating a deal is about finding common ground. Break it down to basics: If a producer or production company needs a screenplay written, and you have the ability to write the screenplay they want, it seems to me there's plenty of common ground for both parties to engage in a pretty straightforward agreement. Adding an agent into the mix (a third party) makes finding that common ground much more difficult because *their* common ground would require both you and the production company giving something up. You as the writer must give up 10 percent of your payout, but the production company loses out on something vitally precious to them: Their time.

True story: I once overheard a loud speakerphone conversation in our office between our head of production and an agent. The head of production really liked a script one of this agent's clients had written and wanted to commission this writer for an upcoming TV movie. She and the agent had been going back-and-forth for three weeks trying to work out a deal to hire the writer. Our head of production was furious with the situation, but she remained calm and kept trying to meet the agent's needs while remaining true to the budget she had to work with. This particular conversation was to be the final negotiation call. The agent saw it as yet another opportunity to play hardball instead of actually working a deal out. What resulted was the agent holding out over the difference of $500 from the overall deal. Our head of production finally just said: "Look, I've really tried to make this work, but it's obviously not going to. . . . Thanks, but we're in a time crunch and my gut is telling me this just isn't worth it. . . . Sucks for the writer cause he's really good." The agent then tried to rebut saying "No, no, no, we can make it work, we can go at your price"; my head of production paused, then said: "Sorry, I'm sticking to my guns on this one, I've given you plenty of opportunities and it's been a battle every time. We'll pass, thanks." She then hung up on the agent as he again tried to argue his point.

In the end, because this agent muddied up the situation, he blew it for everyone. The head of production really wanted that writer. . . . And that writer really wanted the job. It was the agent (as a third party) trying to make the situation more favorable for himself that caused the deal to fall apart—and blew it for the two legit parties that already had common ground. Our head of production had to go find another writer—which wasn't difficult, but the irony was that the writer who secured the job represented himself (meaning he had no agent). He had basic and simple terms, ones that were very in line with how our production company could operate; they signed a deal in two days.

Conclusion: You Do *Not* Need an Agent!

So, if you don't need an agent in order to secure yourself with writing jobs and you don't need one to negotiate your contracts, then what real reason is there to sign with an agent at all? Truth is, there is no reason—at least not at this early stage in your career. When you're first starting out, an agent cannot do anything that you cannot do on your own. And, let's be blunt, no one is going to value your talents or put as much focus and attention on your career than you will.

Most agents are not really looking for talented writers as much as they are looking to keep talented writers from slipping through their fingers and getting gobbled up by their competitors. . . . At the end of the day, the majority of agents really only care about one thing: Getting their cut of *your* money. There are certainly great and stellar agents out there, ones who will work with you—for a period of time—to get your portfolio into strong shape. . . . But if your work isn't selling soon after, just watch how quickly all that attention and accommodation fades away.

As already explained, the majority of screenwriting books on the market spend most of their pages first discussing how to write a spec script, followed by a very thrown-together chapter explaining that the next phase of your journey is to simply "get an agent," leaving you with the false belief this "magical" agent will take the reins from there. This has resulted in many talented writers entering Hollywood with the objective that after they write their spec scripts, they *must* secure an agent, which is simply not true—that time and energy would be much better applied to writing and pushing their own scripts!

As a newbie writer, you cannot view an agent as some sort of "career messiah" who will make all your dreams come to life after entering a deal with them. At the end of the day you must only think of an agent as a tool, one that assists you in managing your workload, and not as the gatekeepers of screenwriting success.

You are more than capable of representing yourself at the beginning of your career, and later you'll be able to secure the right kind of representation (after a few legit paying gigs). Agents will always be there, waiting for their 10 percent of your income. . . . So build your own career to begin with and obtain a qualified agent—one who you like and want to work with—later on when you start getting the kind of volume and reputation that *requires* proper representation.

WHEN *IS* THE RIGHT TIME?

So if so many successful screenwriters have agents, when is the right time in your career to sign with one? *When you actually need to outsource the work!* Once you're able to secure yourself with a steady flow of work, you might eventually find yourself negotiating back-and-forth with a new production company while simultaneously trying to meet writing deadlines for a different production company. Rather than overworking yourself or risk missing deadlines, this would be the right time to hire an agent.

Yes, they will be taking their 10 percent fee from your income. . . . But now that 10 percent commission is worth it, since they are *aiding* you in maintaining a steady flow of consistent work—paying 10 percent without the volume is when it's a big-time waste. And for real-world context, the time to start looking for an agent is when you find that negotiating your latest writer-for-hire agreement is starting to interfere with your ability to meet an already existing professional screenwriting deadline; for example, the writer of *9.6 Mega-Tsunami*, who's well-known enough to receive writing work out of the blue would be considered to be in a good position to begin *initially thinking* about agency representation.

Can you see how the tables have now turned? Rather than going out and sucking up to agents in the hopes of securing one, you are now the one hiring an agent to serve *your* needs, which is how it's supposed to work. You can audition them, meet with them, see which ones you like. You now have clout and understanding of basic contracts and will be able to discuss with them the ways you like to work and the ways you do not.

Again, the timing is right when you have a need for an agent. If this seems like a far-fetched dream for you, it's completely within reach. Once you start writing what Hollywood needs (gold-mine genre type scripts), rather than what you want to write, doors will open. And once you network and get a good sense of who's who and how you can serve *their* projects rather than your own, they will take notice and give you a shot.

Whereas an agent's true purpose is to broker individual deals on a project-by-project basis, another form of representation that writers can work with are managers. A manager serves as a career coach for a screen-writer and helps guide him or her during professional transitions—including aiding in deciding which projects to take versus which projects to pass on. They also work for 10 percent of your pay, but will some-times work on a retainer basis (a pre-negotiated monthly fee). There is no storefront you can head to in order to find a manager, but they will be available through recommendations via connections once you're gaining a steady flow of work. . . . However, as with an agent, in the short term when starting out you really don't need one; you can get great career development advice, if you desire it, from writing consultants or instruc-tors (as outlined in Chapter Three).

A BUSINESS OF COMMISSIONS AND FEES

If there's a dollar trading hands in Hollywood, then there's someone not far behind trying to wedge their way in to take a cut.

After you work your fingers to the bone writing your spec scripts, promot-ing your talents, and securing yourself a legit writing deal, it might suddenly feel as if the floodgates have opened up. Out of nowhere, agents, manag-ers, and producer's reps will all be calling, telling you how much potential you have (and how far—and fast—they can get you there). As explained above, their job is not to find new talent and promote it, their job is to find a Hollywood-related financial transaction and figure out a way to wedge themselves in, for their cut.

But commissions and fees are perfectly reasonable since screenwriters make millions, right? Some do, but most don't.

I consistently come across articles in the trades boasting some new hot screenwriter who inked this-or-that script and who's now under contract with [insert huge agency and studio combo here] for a $4 million deal.

Wow. . . . That's impressive. I mean, forget the fact that *if* that writer actu-ally received that lump sum up front that they'd owe $1 million in taxes (possibly more); it's still a huge sum of money. Now let's also consider that if that writer were paid the full amount as a lump sum up front, they'd also now owe (and let's be conservative here) 10 percent of the gross to their new big-wig agent and another 10 percent gross to their manager. That's another $800,000 gone. But hey, they're still pocketing over $2 million right? I mean, how could that possibly be bad? Minus of course the fees they'd owe to the Writers Guild of America (WGA) or any other affiliations they might be involved with, they're still making crazy money up front. . . .

The problem with the above scenario is that rarely do these big million-dollar script deals get paid out in a lump sum; they get paid out in stages or "steps," which has led to these agreements being structured (and referred to) as "step deals." And each of these contractual steps are "hedged" to protect everyone involved in the process with money on the line (not the writer). The contract might be worth $4 million on paper, but it only *pays* $4 million if each step of the agreement is met.

This writer must first enter into the agreement (meaning they must sign the deal). One of the first components might be that he/she sign with the WGA (the writer's union), and that his/her new agent and manager get set fees off the gross for every dollar earned. Okay, a small price to pay to be associated with such great entities that exist to help you and secure you with more work. On the positive side, there's usually a signing bonus on such an agreement, which is really just a tiny portion of that total figure paid out as an advance. Once you sign and accept that money, you're committed (contractually locked).

The first actual step of the contract might be to draft a treatment for the studio's development team so that they can begin work on your next idea. You write and write and come up with something brilliant. . . . Only they reject it. Technically you've completed the step, but since they didn't accept it and don't intend on going forward with the treatment (meaning from *their* side the step was *not* completed), they'll decline payment and you must start over.

See where this can get tricky? On one hand, you have a talented writer who has just been touted as Hollywood's next "it" screenwriter. He or she is now secured with the top players and is under contract. Even though the deal is for $4 million on paper, this writer might not ever get past the treatment/pitch stage for their next idea. And they're now forbidden from writing any ideas for anyone else. Even if another studio thinks their initial idea is great, they're locked with their current studio and cannot sell that property. Meanwhile, they still haven't received any payouts since that initial signing bonus. Sure, the writer could attempt to hire a third party legal team to yank them out of this deal. . . . But that would cost a great deal of money—remember, the contract might be worth $4 million, but that writer's signing bonus is probably long gone by now, given the taxes, commissions, and union fees spent. And unlike Hollywood's agents, managers, and producer's reps, L.A.'s everyday lawyers wouldn't be working on a commission basis, they would most likely require an up-front fee on a case like this, one that's probably now unaffordable (unless there was a clear breach of contract).

So who in the above scenario has the writer's best interest at heart? Other than the writer, no one. All other parties have laid out all the groundwork for their own financial success in the event that the writer takes off. . . . However, if that writer's work does not take off, they lose nothing while the writer loses big time.

SCREENWRITERS MUST BE ENTREPRENEURS

You're going to have to be the one promoting your talents, building your connections, and securing your initial professional writing opportunities. Waiting around for others to swoop in and kick-start your career on your behalf just isn't going to happen. Essentially, you're going to have to represent yourself.

No successful entrepreneurial CEO blindly opens a division to offer a product that the market doesn't need. They instead look for what the market *wants*, then make themselves available as the best company to provide that product. As a screenwriter, you already know what the marketplace wants: Gold-mine genre-type scripts. You also possess the skill to produce them.

Most wannabes write a script, then go shop it around Hollywood hoping someone will buy it. However, if a novice writer (you) utilizes the lessons from Chapter Five (meeting people and building a professional network) and then add in the reality stated here in Chapter Six (that most producers and development executives are only in business for themselves), you are suddenly in a prime position to learn what it is these Hollywood insiders want. And with that knowledge, you can position yourself as the screenwriting answer to their prayers.

With this scenario, you are no longer shooting blindly in the dark; you are identifying a relatively common occurrence in Hollywood—well-connected producers and development executives with great ideas who are looking to get ahead in their careers but don't have the time to write the scripts they know will sell—and you're strategically aiding their career objectives while also building your own.

Think a busy development executive with a great idea for a movie (and all the connections to make it a reality) has time to go home each night and pound away at a script? No. . . . But *you do*. Think a busy producer constantly hustling and schmoozing clients has time to personally write the perfect script to satisfy both the money people and the talent they're current wrestling with? No. . . . But *you do*. And, just to rub the point in one last time, do you think an agent will put two and two together and link up any of these real world Hollywood needs with your ability to write? No. . . . But, *you can*.

Just as you wrote a spec script that made the readers' and line producers' jobs easier, you can make the career objectives of the producer and development executives easier as well. Utilizing the skills learned in Chapter Four about schmoozing and pitch meetings, you can wedge your way into their professional lives just as an agent or manager would attempt to wedge their way into yours; you're coming to them offering the answers to their problems ("I could write that script for you, if you have the means to produce it"), rather than trying to add one more task, which is what most wannabes do ("You wanna read my script?"). One scenario *helps* a producer or development executive, while the other one hinders them. Which do you think they'd be more receptive to?

DON'T SAY "YES" TO OPPORTUNITIES. . . . *INVENT THEM*

When opportunity knocks, my best advice is to simply open the door and say, "Yes!" The problem is, opportunity doesn't knock very often, and when it does it rarely arrives in the way you imagined.

That's because *real* opportunities begin as broken leftovers or disjointed ideas—in other words, opportunities usually show themselves first as problems. What transforms these problems into opportunities is when *you* see a way to solve them by applying your skills or talents in order to fix them. That "knocking" that everyone talks about has nothing to do with an opportunity being presented to you; it's your own realization that you're able to see a way to apply your skills to fix it.

Sending a blind email pitch to a production company, trying to sell your screenplay to them, does not solve any of *their* problems—it only adds to their workload. But learning directly from the heads of development at that company what scripts they need written in order to lighten their workload will help them tremendously. That's opportunistic thinking. . . . It's more about approaching the situation in the way others are not that usually gets the job done.

You don't have to be a genius to be an opportunistic thinker, you just have to be observant—and as a writer, you're already hardwired to observe the world. Thinking "outside the box" has very little to do with inventing the next great "it" thing, and is much more about simply stepping up to the plate when you see a reasonable chance where you can assist.

Success in Hollywood, as with any industry, is about *making* situations work in your favor.

HOMEWORK ASSIGNMENT: THE MESSAGE BOARD SCREENWRITER

I know a guy who produces down-and-dirty schlock pictures. Action films, martial arts pictures, and some *really cheesy* sci-fi stuff. He has no shame (almost a modern day Roger Corman). He even produces "mock-busters," extremely cheap knock-off versions of the legit multi-million dollar studio films (my personal favorites are *Metal Man* (2008), released just after *Transformers* (2007) and a film called *Star Quest: The Odyssey* (2009), released at the same time as *Star Trek* (2009)—terrible movies, but commercially profitable). Go ahead and knock the movies, they make money. He produces what he *knows* will sell. . . . His productions are extremely cheap, but his poster art is fantastic.

During the development phase he comes up with an idea, types it up a bit (as a general treatment or outline), then hops on Craigslist or some other public message board and puts an ad out for "Screenwriter Wanted—Low Budget." His rules are simple: The writer must be non-union (a given) and they must be willing to write a feature-length film for $500. That's right, $500 bucks! $100 for the outline/treatment (which is his way of vetting if the writer can actually write); then $200 for the first draft and $200 for the final draft.

But, if you are a fast writer, and you're writing something that you're not emotionally attached to, the above formula isn't all that bad. If a script averages 100 pages, you're getting paid $2 per page. It's shit money, yes. . . . But it's money *you're getting paid* to build a portfolio and get script after script out of your system (while learning to write for what others need and being mindful of budget), all while getting legit writing credits.

Perhaps you're rolling your eyes at the above premise, thinking *$500 is chump change!* However, writing at $2 per page is far better than *zero dollars per script*—which is what most wannabes write for. And once you get your $500 in pocket, this producer will go off and turn that project into a movie (and you'll get your screenwriting credit). Ashamed of what you're writing? Don't worry about it, just use a pseudonym. Many of the best writers have done so. But remember, professionals don't judge you for having started out working on less-than-savory projects. No one arrives in Hollywood and gets picked up for an A-list project overnight.

If you hop on Craigslist right now (or a multitude of other message boards for that matter), you will find dozens of people actively looking to hire a screenwriter. Take a risk: Contact them, interact with them. . . . See what they're looking for.

The people on message boards seeking screenwriters are no different than producers actively working in the business. They have ideas and concepts, but they don't have time to actually write themselves. . . they're willing to hire a third party to do the grunt work. It's not Academy Award-winning stuff, but they're real movies—with real money behind it. (And the last time I checked, Coppola, Scorsese, Bogdanovich, and even Cameron ALL started out working for Roger Corman before gaining their own notoriety.)

HOW SCREENWRITERS GET PAID

$500?. . . I must be kidding, right? Those above examples are the bottom-of-the-barrel, of course. I brought those types of writing opportunities up for two reasons: (1) proof that you can actually go out and get a paying screen-writing job today, and (2) proof that screenwriting opportunities are liter-ally everywhere—it's just that most people overlook the real ones. I'm not suggesting that you'd ever use those scripts toward your target portfolio (to garner professional writing work with larger independent companies), but reaching out to a message board screenwriting opportunity when you're first starting out is a great way to build stamina, build confidence in negotiating on your own behalf, and learn the workflow that is used at the grassroots level all the way up to the studios.

Rather than writing spec script after spec script for free, you can actually go get paid (a small amount of cash) while learning all the valuable lessons regarding writing for budgets and time constraints. But if we started this chapter with examples in the $4 million zone and have now dropped to $500, then what can you actually expect as a real-world paycheck for your efforts?

So let's say you follow the steps listed out in Chapter Five and are able to successfully pitch yourself (and your talents) to a development exec-utive. . . . What kind of money are we really talking about for a real production? And we're not assuming anything crazy, like a $30 million theatrical film, we're being fully realistic about Hollywood's 'indie zone' and are focused on a straight-to-home entertainment product that might get a bit of TV play—hypothetically, a movie with a $500,000 budget. As a writer, you've schmoozed up the development executive(s) and they are willing to offer you a deal. What can you expect?

The answer: You will be paid about 5 percent of the film's total (actual) out-of-pocket budget. Your paycheck will always be dependent upon the budget of the movie. Bigger budgets have bigger paychecks; smaller budgets have much smaller paychecks. The problem is no one will ever tell you what the exact budget of the film is. . . . And, as explained in Chapter One, there are numerous reasons why production companies might want to hide the true budget of a film from different audiences (for different reasons).

Using our above (hypothetical) $500,000 budget, 5 percent would be $25,000. (That would mean that $500 writing opportunity would equate to a budget of $10,000—and that is actually the ballpark budget that guy works within!)

That's for a commissioned script, so what kind of money are we talking for a spec script you've written that a production company has interest in acquiring? Rarely do screenplays get purchased, they sometimes, however, get "optioned." An option is when a company likes your script and acquires permission to shop it around town. How much can you expect for that privilege? On the higher end, you're looking at a couple thousand dollars. On the low end, as little as $1. Usually option agreements are for a period of one to two years (after which the term is renewed or you get your rights back). But by the time you get your rights back, the script is now virtually worthless; it's been broadcast all over town and no one has bought in. It's yesterday's news (and just to be clear, the likelihood of garnering a sale from an option is already very low). My advice, if you ever find yourself with a company wanting to option your script, simply say "I'll just sell you the thing to you in perpetuity," meaning forever. How much should you ask for? Let them make you an offer—assuming they're interested. Even if the figure is slightly lower than you hoped, it's probably much better than $1 with zero guarantee of anything further. (Some writers have scoffed at this advice, telling me that I'm too business-minded to appreciate their efforts; but the successful—and steadily working—screenwriters I spoke with have all agreed with my point of view. For you to make your own determination, let me ask you which of the following options you find more valuable: An unsold yet already exploited script on your desk collecting dust, or money in your pocket coupled with a professional screenwriting credit?) And, just for clarity, if you propose them simply buying the rights and they're not interested, then absolutely say yes to the option.

However, the real money (for a real-world newbie writer) is in the process of getting commissioned to write scripts for hire—not writing blindly and hoping your script gets picked up. And whether you're the golden child "it" writer a studio is touting (as in the $4 million example), or seeking out writing gigs on the message boards (in the $500-zone), all of these deals work as step deals.

Here's a classic example—and for simplicity sake, we'll use the example of a $500,000 budget, meaning a writing agreement for $25,000:

Three Step deal (one treatment, two drafts)

- Price—$25,000 (flat—no royalties)
  - $2,500 upon signature of Agreement (AKA a "Signing Bonus")
  - $2,500 upon approval of Treatment
  - $10,000 upon approval of First Draft
  - $10,000 upon approval of Second Draft
- Credit, First Option for Re-Drafts upon Need.
- Time frame: 90 days.
  - Treatment due 2 weeks
  - Draft 1 due 45 days
  - Draft 2 due 90 days

The above deal structure takes a writer who knows how the system works and wants to be a team player. It takes a writer who is interested in writing, but also in delivering what a team needs in a very short period of time. He or she would need to understand there is no time for games and that a company is really putting a great deal of trust into them. It's his or her job to deliver according to the contract and not deviate from the expected results.

Let's go back to our Chapter One example of *9.6 Mega-Tsunami*: the film had a budget of $450,000, but the screenplay cost $25,000 (big win for the writer). That film followed the above step deal exactly as listed. The writer made no royalties. It was a non-exclusive deal, meaning the writer was free to enter into deals with other companies at any point.

LEGALESE

After you've played the Hollywood game successfully (and have secured yourself a verbal understanding for a writing opportunity), the next step is to enter into an "agreement". . . . But agreements are not one size fits all, and the type you receive is fully dependent on the specific situation you've negotiated for yourself—or on what the company is willing (and able) to offer. In addition, each company has their own preferred style and format. So let's go over a few basics of common Hollywood legal docs just to get the ball rolling.

As an aside: Please understand that I am not a lawyer and do not take this section as any form of legal advice. For further reading on entertainment law, including full breakdowns of real Hollywood contracts, check out any of the books written by Mark Litwak; you can also check out Agreement breakdowns in Appendices II and III of this book.

Submission Release—This document is probably the most familiar to a newbie writer; it's a straightforward (one to three page) document essentially announcing that you, as a writer/author, are formally submitting your finished work (treatment, screenplay, or outline) to a production company for consideration. Who does it protect? A submission release protects the production company because the writer is promising they're responsible for the literary material (and no other person can rightfully claim story theft later on).

Letter of Intent (LOI) or Term Sheet—These documents are generally formal, but usually non-binding (meaning neither party is promising anything). The purpose, instead, is to simply document that both parties engaged in a professional conversation about a writing opportunity and discussed financial terms or deadline time frames; however, at this moment there is no formal agreement binding either party to a task. (On some occasions these documents can be binding; it all just depends on the language used.) The real incentive for the writer is proof you discussed a clear writing opportunity (story concept) with a production company (1) in case they produce a strikingly similar film in the future without your awareness (to prevent story theft) and (2) to be used as a written record that a certain dollar amount had been associated with the opportunity, in case the agreement is put on hold then returned to at a later date. LOIs and term sheets are used as a form of protection by the production company and can also be used by a producer or development executives as they attempt to raise funds to package the project together.

Option and/or Literary Purchase—These documents are getting more involved; they are for situations in which a producer or development executive wants to acquire (buy or "borrow") the rights to your material for their needs. The literary purchase would be a full-blown purchase of your script or treatment—generally with a flat, up-front fee. Once you sell the material, it's out of your hands forever (or at least for a staggeringly long amount of time). These are very rare for newbie writers. To option, on the other hand, is when a producer or development executive wants to borrow the rights to your material. As stated earlier in this chapter, gaining a purchase (or green light) out of an option is also quite rare. . . . You will get your rights back later (sometimes after six months, sometimes after a few years), but by then all the players in town who might have had interest have already been approached (and they've passed), meaning your project has already been seen. My advice would be, as already stated, turn any offering of an option into a purchase (even if for a seemingly small figure). You'd be surprised how many hopeful producers might hand over a few thousand dollars to own your script. And since you're already writing every day, churning and burning your way through a few scripts each year, you'll have better content within a few months' time.

Writer's Employment Agreements—These agreements are your real target; you've used your spec scripts as proof you can get the job done, and your Chapter Four-honed schmoozing skills to be seen as trustworthy (and dependable) by those producers and development executives who need a specific script written. When producers or development executives wish to commission your writing talents, they will be employing your talents to produce a screenplay. There will be a financial payout (which is generally equivalent to 5 percent of the actual budget) and there will be hedged steps to follow along the way (deadline for treatments, drafts, and a final delivery date). And since you're starting out, you will be working in the non-union world as a non-exclusive "work-for-hire" employee.

When you are presented with any of the above legal documents (or any others which Hollywood might throw your way), never feel like you must handle the negotiations completely on your own. If you're uncertain how to handle a specific legal document, hire a lawyer—with experience in entertainment law, of course. Yes, you will have to pay them a flat fee, but it's much cheaper to pay a lawyer one time for their opinion than to be locked with an unhelpful agent for the long haul. Ask your growing network of contacts for references.

IF THERE'S MONEY ON THE TABLE . . . TAKE IT!

To get a better understanding or feel of the different types of deal structures, hop onto the WGA's website (www.wga.org) for a full overview.

You'll also find a pay scale associated with the WGA outlining standard industry minimums. Even if many indie-zone production companies are specifically seeking out non-union writers, they will usually play ball at (or reasonably near) union pay scales.

Getting paid for your talents is very important. After all, you are being commissioned to draft out the blueprint and floor plan the entire cast, crew, financial team, and sales force will use to produce a marketable product. However, being realistic about what those talents are worth in an actual marketplace is something different.

There will be countless times in your career where you know you're getting an offer slightly lower than you were expecting—sometimes dramatically lower. But, if a lower-end production company is offering you a writer-for-hire agreement with a total payout of $8,000 instead of $25,000 (and you've never been paid to write a script for a movie that's guaranteed to actually get produced and distributed in the professional world), should you say "no" out of principle? Personally, I wouldn't. I would say "yes" to the opportunity, and secure a first real-world writing credit and use the opportunity to get a good professional reputation. Perhaps only a handful of people would say yes to the $8,000; if so, you might get two or three script-writing jobs from that team by year's end (and you'll learn how they work, meaning you don't have to scrounge as much on the back-end). Suddenly your $8,000 payday became $24,000 and you have three writing credits to boot. It's not always about principle; sometimes it's much more about common sense.

TO UNION? OR NOT TO UNION?

Almost all indie-zone films you'll be working on during the initial stages of your career will be non-union productions. That means, any writer with membership in the WGA will not even be considered for a writing job (of any level). There are numerous reasons as to why, but they all pretty much boil down to costs. However, after writing a non-union indie-zone film or two, you might be tempted to "up the ante" by approaching a WGA-signatory production company to get commissioned onto a WGA-covered project, but I certainly wouldn't recommend that—at least, not yet.

Once you sign with the WGA, you can no longer write non-union films (similar to restrictions against actors joining SAG). You are locked—and there are stiff penalties if you try writing under a pseudonym. I'm not suggesting the WGA is a bad deal at all—it is a great organization and has paved the way for many beneficial rights now considered industry norms for writers. But joining the WGA *does* prevent your ability to write smaller low-key projects (which are the most vital writing jobs when starting out for building your reputation).

The admission requirements to the WGA work on a "point" system. If you have received a paid writing job via a WGA signatory company (on a WGA-covered project, whether an all-out commissioned script, or even just hired on for the appropriate amount of rewrite or "dialogue polish" work), you're given a different set of points for your efforts. Once your points all add up to the minimum required number, you can apply and become an accepted member of the WGA. You pay an admission fee (a few thousand dollars) plus your quarterly union dues and you're in.

However, going in too early can really stunt your career progression. You'll only be able to work on 'union' jobs (or with WGA-signatory production companies). And if you don't yet have the career reputation already established, you might have a really difficult time getting projects into motion at this much more advanced level. Does the WGA assist you in securing potential work? No, it does not. . . . That responsibility still falls onto your shoulders. Just like the illusion of having an agent, many young writers mistakenly see WGA membership as yet another milestone or status symbol in their careers without realizing how far back they can get pulled by joining too early.

You don't even have to think about the WGA until a project is presented to you that would *require* you to join the WGA. Even then, you don't have to accept the offer. The only time to join the WGA is when you are first obligated to (and then only doing so if you truly believe there's ample WGA-level work waiting for you after signing up). Don't worry about the WGA when you're starting out; focus on building your career and marketing your talents to the right people first. The WGA will be waiting for you when the timing is right (and you'll know in your gut when it makes sense for your career).

A COMMENT ON STORY THEFT AND
PROTECTING YOURSELF

One of the many overwhelming fears ingrained into new writers' heads is that they'll present their ideas or writings to the marketplace only to have them stolen or in some way ripped off. The reality? Writers do get exploited and story ideas have certainly been stolen, but there is a rational line you must walk as an individual embarking into the brave new world of Hollywood screenwriting.

First, if you want your work to be seen then you will have to show it to people. That means mailing (and emailing) your work, discussing your ideas with strangers, and pitching your stories to professionals. Although you cannot copyright an idea, you also cannot secure a pitch meeting with a "you just have to trust me, my ideas are really good" approach. Register your works with the WGA (script registration is open to both members and non-members); other than that, you just have to follow each company's protocol and send in your submissions. If they require a submission release (where you give up your right to sue them), I wouldn't stress about it too much. They receive hundreds of script submissions (and I think only someone in the reader's seat could truly appreciate how many scripts mirror one another).

Second, not only is story theft incredibly difficult to prove, it's also an incredibly rare occurrence. Why would a producer or production company risk their entire reputation (and financial status) to steal a blindly submitted spec script when they could simply request you and they enter into an option agreement? An option agreement, as already stated, can be entered into for as little as $1, or at most a few thousand. . . . A real company would not steal your work, they would reach out to you and enter into a formal agreement (so that a paper trail shows your grant of rights to the material to them). They might try to stiff you a bit in the contract, but that's just normal show business—and as mentioned previously, if money's on the table (even if slightly lower than you expected), say yes and move on!

And third, the only real threat you might encounter (and this can be optimistically seen as a true milestone in your career) is to have to deal with legitimate exploitation of your talents. Examples can range from being required to write too many revisions (far outside your contractual obligations) before receiving payment, or being brought on as a "story consultant" where your concepts coincidentally become the backbone of a film project (yet you receive zero credit). Other examples could be "collaborating" on a project with a producer, where you're writing their script completely on spec or allowing a producer to shop your work around town without any formal agreement. These are scenarios that really require you to trust your gut above all else. If a situation seems fishy, cut your losses and get out. You might walk away with a few cuts and bruises, but it's better than staying on board for the full collision. When in doubt, get it in writing. Professionals are very comfortable putting informal agreements into writing and will be perfectly happy entering into an agreement (even one that is non-binding and simply lays out the general terms of the current discussion, such as an LOI or term sheet).

Above all else, relax. In order to get your talents into the marketplace, you *will* have to show the goods. If you're expecting a producer or development executive to hand over some cash in exchange for an agreed promise that you'll deliver the screenplay they're expecting, then you'll most definitely be required to show them writing samples and openly discuss your ideas well in advance. Protecting yourself in a general sense is a very wise thing to do, but getting carried away can completely isolate you—and your work—from the very professionals with whom you're attempting to do business.

Any artist's portfolio is ultimately a display of what they have to offer the marketplace. This concept is no different for a screenwriter, so show off what you've got! Let Hollywood know who you are and what you can bring to the table.

To be a successful screenwriter, do you have to live in Los Angeles?

No, you don't ... But it's very important to have *L.A. experience*. Some of you are fresh out of film school and can simply cram your cars full of your belongings and head west, while others are a bit more rooted in your current location—with work, kids, family obligations, or perhaps you don't even live in the U.S. At the end of the day, it's more about *what makes sense for your specific situation*. But I can assure you that Hollywood will listen to anyone that is able to deliver what it needs to keep the system in motion (wherever they're from). Gaining L.A. experience simply means taking initiative to visit the City of Angels (perhaps for a market, screenwriting expo, or simply on a personal vacation where you also include a few initial meetings to develop some contacts). You need to be able to understand the feel of the city and get an idea for how things flow in the real world of working Hollywood. Before traveling to L.A., schedule out your trip by securing a writer's workshop in advance, or perhaps reach out to volunteer for the AFM ahead of time. Both give you time in Los Angeles and experience in the business (without breaking the bank if you aren't in a situation to make the move permanently). The beauty of the gold-mine genre types is that they grab the attention of readers and distributors alike, regardless of your zip code.

SEVEN

"GOLD-MINE" GENRES ... NOW AND *FOREVER*

As the Hollywood machine moves ever faster into the digital realm, how will the role of screenwriter evolve (let alone keep up)? In this chapter, we'll examine where the film business is going and how you, as a novice screenwriter, can stay ahead of the curve—not by blindly guessing what the future might hold but instead looking at how the *principles* of the film and TV business have (and will continue to) remained constant through all of Hollywood's transformations.

INTO THE DIGITAL REALM

Hollywood will always follow its audience (never the other way around). Now that audiences are "cutting the cord" with their cable providers and buying internet-ready smart televisions, Hollywood's next chapter—which has already commenced—will exist purely within the digital realm. But relax. . . . Despite what people may say, the only things changing are the technology and a few key phrases of industry terminology. What audiences choose to watch and *how* Hollywood functions as an industry will be continuing down the same old path it always has—meaning Hollywood will always have a need for *someone* to write all that film and TV content required to keep the supply lines in motion and the industry afloat. And there's no reason that "someone" cannot be you!

So, What Is This "Digital Realm"?

When we describe Hollywood as "going digital," we're not talking about the explosion of "cute cat videos," gimmicky web series, or multi-channel networks on platforms like YouTube; we're instead talking about the business behind the film and TV industry's content delivery systems—things that happen long after a movie is wrapped but that consequently affect how films are developed early on.

Audiences are still hungry for entertainment; they're just purchasing that entertainment in new ways. For decades, Blockbuster was the king of home entertainment . . . until Netflix nearly put it out of business. After going bankrupt, Blockbuster was bought out by Dish and now sells movies as transactional video on demand (TVOD) rentals on cable channels instead of in physical stores. And where people used to buy physical DVDs in retail stores like Wal-Mart and Best Buy, these companies have launched online home entertainments of their own (Wal-Mart sells online movies at Vudu.com and Best Buy sells at CinemaNow.com); each platform offers the big-time studio hits without all the expenses (e.g., replication costs, shipping/stocking fees, or limits on shelf space)—costs that were previously passed on to the consumer. That means that today, *more* content can be acquired by these majors, which can also be held on the "digital shelf" for longer periods of time, all for a discounted rate—a savings that is then passed on to the consumer in the form of a cheaper per item price.

And as consumers continually grow more accustomed to purchasing things online, the overall landscape for how movies get from point A to point B has started to shift a bit. What does this mean for Hollywood's independent zone? Three things:

1. *Better placement for indie titles*. With lower costs and the seemingly infinite volume of titles potentially offered by digital shelf space, the door is now wide open for indie titles to receive placement alongside mega-Hollywood blockbusters on top-tier go-to sites (like iTunes and Amazon—a dream scenario for hopeful screenwriters and filmmakers everywhere). But this doesn't mean these outlets will take just anything. . . . They do have to account for things like limited bandwidth and consumer drive—which has resulted in nearly all platforms focusing their efforts on acquiring the safest types of indie content: Gold-mine genre types.

2. *Indie titles must be produced on smaller budgets*. Given all the new costs savings by cutting out the physical manufacturing and in-store placement, digital platforms can now offer highly competitive (cheaper) pricing for their offerings—which means these companies are spending less money to acquire these films from distributors, which results in the immediate shrinking of indie production budgets. And when production and distribution companies need to tighten their belts, they invest conservatively in more reliable content (AKA gold-mine genre types).

3. *Innovative marketing trends*. Studios and indie companies alike are quickly learning that the digital space offers completely new ways to promote their films to audiences, and to do so in much more targeted ways. A simple Tweet or behind-the-scenes Instagram post from their leading star can drive more business to their films than all the billboards or banner ads money can buy—to such an extent that now

casting agreements are introducing "call-out" clauses specifically requesting their socially engaged talent to send out such postings. Indie distribution and production companies are into this trend as well. And when indie distribution and production companies take a gamble on producing movies with innovative marketing campaigns, they tend to choose projects that stand to be successful even if the innovative marketing element fails—the most reliable candidates are gold-mine genre-type movies.

See a trend here? While digital enthusiasts will express their views that Hollywood is on the verge of some kind of "digital revolution" and that user-generated content will somehow soften the grip of the studio system, I beg to differ. . . . Hollywood going digital is yet another case of "the more things change, the more they stay the same." This is why all you need to do as a newbie screenwriter is to simply keep your eyes focused on the gold-mine genre types. Not only will you be able to ride this current "trend wave" Hollywood is experiencing, you'll be prepared for every single transitional curveball Hollywood will experience in the decades to come.

Keep following the gold-mine genre types and making sure your work is reader-friendly. And keep hustling! The concept of *Writing for the Green Light* is to never follow fads and instead only follow the principles of Hollywood. Attempting to predict what trends will be popular in Hollywood in the years to come is a fool's game—and even if you were spot on correct in anticipating a trend years in advance, your ideas would be ahead of everyone else's, meaning they wouldn't even be able to see your work's potential yet and you still wouldn't sell anything.

As the years and decades continue to roll past us, we as consumers will still seek out and watch entertaining content—even if we presently have no concept as to what crazy contraptions we'll be using later on down the line to view it. Young girls will still enjoy their tween-aged romance films about cute boys, ice-skating, and ponies. Young boys will still enjoy their rampaging creature features (no matter how ridiculous they might be). Women in their thirties and forties will still be drawn to an overly melodramatic woman-in-peril thriller and the whole family will still gather each holiday season with a soft spot for a family-safe Christmas film with an adorable and funny dog.

Writing for this space does not make you a sellout, it simply gives you a huge advantage in terms of breaking in to Hollywood. After you gain some traction, pull out your dream ideas and get cracking. . . . But to kick-start your career, the gold-mine genre-type scripts have been—and will continue to be—Hollywood's safest go-to genres to produce, which is why they should be your initial focus when you're starting out. As in the past, in the present and forever into the future, all one has to do is look to the principles that guide Hollywood and your odds of being ready regardless of what trend is all the rage will certainly help you beat out the odds.

NOW IS THE BEST TIME TO BEGIN

The doors of Hollywood will always be open to writers who are there to serve its needs. Hollywood does not give a whit about your age, gender, race, or background. Great screenwriters have ranged from Harvard grads to former drug addicts who've gathered their lives together from the streets. Hollywood does not care about anyone's past or circumstances, it only cares about finding those rare individuals who can deliver what it needs to continue functioning.

Therefore, the doors for talented writers will always be open to those who can deliver what's needed on time (both today and well into the future). Any writer coming with the mindset to *serve* the system can find a relatively steady flow of work because those Hollywood decision-makers will always hold sacred the writer who can put all the zany pieces together and simply make a concept work that appeals to the needs of industry producers, investors, and audiences.

Want to know what else never changes? The lack of success found by those Hollywood hopefuls chasing trends and following blind leads. There will always be new trends to follow and new fads to chase; for the writers that follow these pathways, the opportunities will always be long gone by the time they finish a script that meets the fad.

Now it falls back to your shoulders. If you took just twenty minutes today to write out a few ideas related to one of our gold-mine genre-type scripts (no matter how awful or broken they felt when you started), you would be taking a major step toward seeing real change and progress in your writing career. It really is that simple.

ALL YOU HAVE TO DO IS *START*

What's stopping you from truly taking control of your dreams and making them a reality? By truly taking to heart the lessons and concepts described in this book (that is, by truly understanding how the logic of Hollywood operates) you *can* get your writing career into motion in the professional world of Hollywood. No tricks, no gimmicks, just the straight-faced practicality of serving the needs of an industry.

What's stopping you from writing a script? You don't have to complete it in one sitting. . . . You don't even have to complete it within one month. But each day you *don't* write is one day added towards delaying your goals in life. And what's stopping you from meeting people in the business? From reaching out and growing your social network?

Write every single day, even when you don't want to—only the writers who can consistently output words get ahead. If you're unable to write, at least be working to move your projects towards a state of completion (revising, editing, or even just brainstorming). Be open to learning about things completely different than screenwriting (the more well-rounded you are, the more sociable you'll become and the better writer you will be), and constantly reach out and grow your social network (one simple phone call or email each day will move your career monumental distances over time).

Regardless of whether your ambitions are for Hollywood's TV side or its film side, both require their writers to constantly keep their minds actively engaged. In the end, the process of gaining traction and building a career in television or film are pretty similar. What's most important for new writers to understand is that their goal should be a continuing effort of growing their craft of storytelling until they can consistently output ready-to-go ideas that the people "behind closed doors" will see potential money-making value in. Once writers can consistently output great ideas that also offer studios and production companies the chance to profit, the rest will solve itself.

As you begin your journey into professional screenwriting, start slow. Do not expect overnight success, because true success takes years of effort. You must prove to the marketplace you can do all you promise before anyone will truly pay you for the effort.

THE ROAD TO SUCCESS IS PAVED WITH PERSISTENCE

Success is not awarded to those who are simply the smartest or the most talented. It's awarded to those who put in the effort. Writing a screenplay, even just a rough draft, is a major accomplishment in your life, *but keep going*. Keep pushing yourself forward, toward building your portfolio, and toward building your network. I have met plenty of talented people who never put their talents to work and I have met plenty of highly educated people who kick back and wait for success to magically arrive at their doorstep—neither group accomplished much. But I have never in my life met a successful individual who was not persistent as all hell.

Persistence is about big-picture thinking and not sweating the small stuff. It's about accepting that some days you will attempt to write and feel like every idea is a cliché—it's okay, that's part of the process. It's about being realistic that there has been and never will be a perfect script—all of them have flaws, even the ones from the best screenwriters in the business, so take the pressure off your shoulders. And the beautiful part about persistence is that *it's okay to make mistakes*, just as long as the needle is moving in the right direction.

Taking the initiative to pluck something from your imagination, committing yourself to putting that concept into motion, and seeing the results of those efforts in the form of a completed work is one of the most rewarding experiences you can ever hope to feel. It is that sense of accomplishment (and empowerment) that drives successful individuals forward, toward the next project and the next one after that. And from this persistence derives success.

Be passionate about what you write and love what you do—because if you're not, no one else will be.

A LITTLE SELF-MOTIVATION

No one on this planet will make you write today (or tomorrow, or even the next day). And it's not anyone's job to do so. . . . It's *your job* to move that needle on your own. One of the things that's universally true about writers is how damn independent they are. They crave that absolute freedom of space and time to explore projects on their own. But what separates the successful writers from the unsuccessful ones is getting the job done.

The hardest part of accomplishing anything in life is simply starting. Not the physical aspect of starting, but the mental component. Without absolute commitment you will struggle with any objective you set yourself out to achieve. But picture it all just like a movie in your head. . . . Start with your goal (the resolution) and simply map your way backwards to where you're sitting right now. Think about all the ups and downs you might pass through along the way. Think about all the crazy Hollywood characters you might meet (and all the amazing ones too). Think about the times you'll feel ecstatic and on top of the world. . . . And think about the times you'll feel beyond beaten and broken down. You will feel all of these emotions when setting out to accomplish any goal in life—at least any that are worth going after. (If the goals were easy, where's the challenge?) Think about the story of your future and how you (the protagonist of that story) might deal with each of these moments . . . the good times, the bad, and the completely unexpected. Keep working your way backwards, past the ten page point decision, past the theme on page three, all the way back to exactly where you're sitting right now.

Look around you. Consider where you are at this moment, what's happening in your life, what situations you're in the middle of (work-wise, relationship-wise, and even financially). The smells, the sounds, everything. This is page one. Get up and go look in the mirror. That face you're staring at is your protagonist. How are you going to get them from page one to success at "The End" and "Fade to Black"? Doing the same things you've been doing? Or taking a chance and approaching Hollywood in all the ways no one else ever taught you about by building a portfolio of gold-mine genre-type scripts?

There is only one thing left for you to accomplish your goal . . . to start it. Get started writing today and don't stop. And when you're finished, you might just meet someone like me on the other side (a business guy, looking out for writers to fill only one selfish need, to write the very scripts we need written to keep the Hollywood machine in motion. . . . Because I can tell you point blank that we sales reps and distributors in Hollywood are absolutely *desperate* for writers who can deliver gold-mine genre-type scripts—and so few writers actually write them!!

I've said all I can for this lesson, so I hope you'll go back to that project sitting on your desk (or the one simply bouncing around your head) and now actually apply it. Now, go get to work, cause I have a big slate of movies that need to get made next year and only half of them have finished scripts.

I wish in film school they actually taught about the kinds of writers we need in the professional working world of Hollywood, because we're desperate for them! And I hope that you'll now get to work, with a slightly more authentic breakdown of how you can get that first phase of your career into full swing.

APPENDICES

For me, nothing works better than real-world examples. And, just as important as it is for your writing education to get your hands on actual film and TV scripts in addition to just reading how-to books, the same holds true later in your career when you enter the phase of selling your work and commissioning your talents—seeing samples of what to expect will help immensely.

What follows are three of the most likely types of forms/documents that will be associated with your work during your professional journey: (1) Script coverage, used by readers to analyze and judge your work, (2) the Non-Union Writer-for-Hire Agreement, used when your writing services are being commissioned by a third party, and (3) the Option/Purchase Agreement, used when your actual script (or other submitted materials) are being licensed or acquired by a third party as is.

Please note that *I am neither a lawyer nor a legal professional; this section is simply meant for educational and informative purposes only.*

For each of the following samples, I have kept only the look and style similar to the real-world examples on which they're based. . . . All of the text I personally wrote—in layman's terms—to explain what each paragraph actually means and how such overly wordy language applies to you. Although the terms, formats and structures of these three documents might differ from one company to the next, the general headers and parameters outlined within each of the following are pretty "cookie-cutter" across the business.

There is no need to let legal documents or agreements intimidate you; contracts are an integral part of the Hollywood landscape and you will encounter many throughout your career. Even though they might seem intimidating at first, in time you will be able to negotiate many of these agreements on your own (with confidence). But when starting out, always feel free to seek out a lawyer to assist. He or she can help you simply review and understand the basics of the agreement, or you can always hire one to negotiate the deal on your behalf. And never feel embarrassed about asking a knowledgeable friend for advice before signing anything.

SCRIPT COVERAGE

It's not that decision-makers in Hollywood don't want to read spec scripts; they just don't have the time! Their schedules are booked solid, their inboxes receive hundreds of urgent emails each day, and—to be frank—there's just too many poorly written (*non*-gold-mine genre-type) scripts clogging up the system.

Be that as it may, these busy Hollywood professionals absolutely value talented writers (and want to find them), but with all of their attention pre-allocated at the start of each workweek, there's little time to start hunting. To make their jobs more efficient, they hire readers to handle this chore for them. Readers take all those piles of blindly submitted spec scripts and review them one-by-one. They break down each script, summarizing the overall story while highlighting its pros and cons. They'll then type up their notes into a generalized summary, which is commonly referred to as "script coverage."

Although script coverage is discussed in many screenwriting books, it's rarely broken down in a way that gives a novice writer true insight into how "the other side" (readers and their executive bosses) receive and evaluate the coverage of a submitted script. And unlike many other documents and forms dealing with the writing side of Hollywood (e.g., letters of intent, option agreements), any coverage drafted in reference to a spec script you've written will most likely be off limits to your eyes. However, that's not to say that you don't have a strong amount of influence in how the coverage of your script is ultimately drafted.

We discuss earlier in this book the concept of making the job of the reader easier, specifically because their analysis of your script is crucial in how your work—*and you* as a writer—are seen by Hollywood's decision-makers. Even though you will most likely never meet the individual who will cover your script (nor will you have any control over their level of experience or capability to perform the task at hand), if you're able to make their job easier they will be better able to relay the positives of your spec script when they draft its coverage—which will give you that much needed boost to get your work noticed.

What follows is a sample of script coverage, broken down in a way that gives you true insight into how the indie development team on the other side might see your future work—after it's gone through the filtering hands of a reader first.

SCRIPT COVERAGE FORM

TITLE: [Spec Script Title]　　　　　　**PAGES:** [Number of Pages]
AUTHOR: [Your Name Here]　　　　　　**DRAFT DATE:** [Date on Script]
SUBMITTED TO: [Development Exec.]　　**ANALYST:** [Name of Reader]
SUBMITTED BY: [Your Name Here]　　　**GENRE:** [Gold Mine Genre Type]
SUBMISSION DATE: [Date Received]　　**SETTING:** [Recurring Location]

IN BRIEF: Here the reader generally invents their own logline for your script. Occasionally they will reference the logline you've crafted (from your cover letter or cover email), but only if you've phrased it in a way the truly nails the *commercial* style and feel of the film. More often than not, the reader's opinion of what your script is about will be completely different than how you've been pitching it, but nevertheless it's their opinion that will be summarized here. This "In Brief" section is generally the first block of text a development executive or producer will read; if they don't see a fun concept with commercial value expressed clearly within this summary block (high concept with a hook), they won't continue reading. Although the reader's interpretation might be far from how you envision your work, it's preferable to let them pitch it in their own way. . . . After all, they know what their boss is looking for!

(Rated on a 1–10 scale)
　SCRIPT: CONSIDER　　　　　**WRITER(S):** RECOMMEND
　PREMISE: 7
　PLOT STRUCTURE: 6　　　　**CHARACTER DEVELOPMENT:** 4
　PLOT DEVELOPMENT: 3　　　**CHARACTER MOTIVATION:** 3
　CHARACTER DESIGN: 7　　　**DIALOGUE:** 5

SYNOPSIS: The synopsis in spec script coverage is boringly detailed. It reads exactly as a treatment would (i.e., in the present tense, limited quotes or dialogue blocks); it's simply a line-by-line breakdown of what the script is about in a very matter-of-fact tone. Every time a CHARACTER (Age, Description) is introduced in your screenplay, the reader will list them in detail here.

The synopsis generally contains 250 to 500 words, which means it averages about 2–3 pages in length. But in that we're not covering an actual script here, we'll use this area to breakdown the basics of the overall script coverage form.

First, check out the block of text at the very top of this sample form. . . . Can you see how meticulously your script is broken down from the get go? Note that it's not just the title and author details being listed, it's everything. This is why it's crucial for your script to have all the right parameters in place before it enters the marketplace. For example, one of the sections asks for the number of pages. If your page count is coming in way too high or low (even with high rankings for plot, character, and genre), a development exec might just place this document in the trash and never give it a second thought. Sound harsh? Think about it from their perspective for a moment; development execs have dozens of coverages to skim through (in addition to yours) that *will* have the right number of pages, meaning they won't require additional work to expand or reduce the scripts. Even with high rankings, a script with too many (or too few) pages screams out "too much work" for it to make sense.

Also take note of the "Draft Date," where the date stated on the submitted script is listed. Many newbies like to place their dates of completion on the title pages of their spec scripts. I would advise against this. Placing a completion date on your title page can quickly age your script and make it appear old. Decisions in Hollywood are made at a notoriously slow rate of speed. . . . As your script gets more and more dated, development execs will (rightfully or wrongfully) wonder how good it could possibly be if no one else has picked it up. (I offer producers of finished films the same advice, to not list their titles too early on IMDb or to cover their poster art with too many festival notices; both of these can unintentionally devalue their work and make it appear older than it might actually be.) Leave the date off. In the coverage, if there's no "Draft Date" listed, the reader will simply leave the section blank or place an "N/A" in its place.

Moving on to "Genre," although the reader fated to analyze your script might not list the gold-mine genre type with the same wording used in Chapter Two, they will be indicating what your film is about in this space (which, if you've followed Chapter Two's advice, will clue in your potential development executive that there's something worth checking out in the synopsis). Add in a witty, "on-the-money" title that represents your script's hook, and you'll see results. Remember our example of a family Christmas dog adventure film titled *Santa Paws*? . . . Adorable.

Once you've coupled together a gold-mine genre-type script with an "on-the-money" witty title—that also has the right number of pages and lacks an aged draft date—any development executive will most certainly skim down to block #3, which outlines your reader's ratings of your work.

Block #3 is truly the selling point because this is where the reader sells you and *your abilities*. Notice how both the script *and* the writer are listed, and that each is worthy of its own unique score? It's completely possible to have a *pass* associated with the script, but a *consider* or *recommend* for the writer. In addition, there are the numbers ranking other aspects of the script following a one through ten format (with ten being the best). Check out the numbers used in the sample above (which are based on an actual, blindly submitted, yet acquired) spec script. Does anything jump out to you? (This wasn't an anomaly; I based these numbers on a recurring trend I noticed with spec scripts that received high rankings with regards to several readers' opinions of the writer). . . . The scripts that moved forward had high rankings for "Premise" and "Plot Structure." The other elements (i.e. dialogue, character motivations, and even plot development), could all have medium (or even low) rankings, yet the writer's talents were still *seen* as quality. Why is this? Because (again) it's *very* rare for readers and development executives to receive scripts that truly nail what it is they *need*! The premise and plot structure fill this void; great characters (although a must in your scripts) will not sell you or your work by themselves.

As a writer, it's of the utmost importance to constantly improve and develop your talents. But there are legitimate aspects of your efforts that can "move the needle" even if other aspects of your work are only seen as "good" (or even "average"). Again, focus on the gold-mine genre-type scripts and really put your emphasis into the *concept* of your film. Even if your dialogue is a bit too "on the nose" or your characters are a bit too one dimensional, you can still see results that propel *you* as a writer forward.

Incidentally, I found numerous examples of legit coverage that had high ranks for original characters and sharp dialogue but that lacked concept or had a genre that was too far off from the sellable zone. Not only did these scripts receive a "pass," so did their writers . . .

Make your reader's job easier and the rewards *will* pay off.

COMMENTS:
The "Comments" section (or sometimes, the "Notes" section) of the coverage is where the reader essentially makes an argument leaning one way or the other regarding both your spec script and your writing capabilities.

By this point, the development executive has (more often than not) already made a decision about whether or not they're going to read your script, but they'll generally skim this section to get a sense as to *why* the reader made the comments he or she did (and hone in on a few points such as why they defended your premise yet noted your plot development as seemingly weak).

If you've made the reader's job easier (and you've offered an entertaining read in the process), they will generally praise your work here and give you a subtle push into the "consider" or "recommend" direction. This section is not only about your work, it's also about how your work seems to fit within that particular production company's overall corporate culture. Are you writing material—or could you if your talents were commissioned—that could mesh with the types of films that particular company produces? That question will be answered here (even if not directly).

It's not uncommon for an inexperienced reader, out looking for the next "epic" indie hit, to oversee the value of a gold-mine genre-type script. They might spit out a large essay on how the intellectual concepts of your gold-mine genre-type story are clichéd and dull, or that you're way too invested in the commercial (rather than the conceptual) aspects of cinema. Let them; if these words were ever used against you, in the eyes of Hollywood's decision-makers and gate-keepers (the ones responsible for making the decisions based upon a projected return being made for any monies spent), being an overly commercial film is a good thing!

Although you may never lay eyes on any script coverage drafted regarding one of your scripts, it is a vital document for the life your spec script sees within a production company. You will most likely never meet the reader who drafted coverage of your script (and you will most likely never see the actual coverage with your own eyes), but what type of script you write (and how much effort you put into making the job of the reader and potential line producer easier) has a major influence in how that coverage will be written—and, thusly, how it will be seen by those receiving it further down the decision-making line.

THE NON-UNION WRITER-FOR-HIRE AGREEMENT

This agreement is specifically used for the commissioning of one's writing *services* for a particular film or project. In short, a company likes your writing style (and knows you have the skillsets to get the job done), so they are offering you a one-time writer-for-hire gig for a project they need written. Perhaps it's just for adapting an executive's script idea into a treatment for internal review, or maybe it's to clean up someone else's script and make it more filmable. Regardless of the reason, when a small-to-mid-sized non-WGA-signatory company (which will be the most common entities you'll be working with when first starting out) has a writing job to offer, they will hand over an agreement looking very similar to this one.

So, for the purposes of all practicality, we're going to assume the following scenario (which can just as easily be yours): A novice screenwriter, named Jessica Screenwriter, has successfully pitched herself as a young talent to a production company called Hiring Production Company, LLC. She has shown works that she's written (her gold-mine genre-type spec scripts), which are commercial in nature, reasonable in budget, and follow the norms of what "working Hollywood" (and Hiring Production Company, LLC) is on the lookout to produce.

Based on her willingness to contribute (and her sample spec scripts), Hiring Production Company's readers and development executives have vetted Jessica's talents. With a new production on the horizon, Hiring Production Company has now offered Jessica a $25,000 contract (*go Jessica!*) to write a screenplay for their new production, *NEW COMMERCIAL FEATURE FILM*.

What follows is an example and overview of how her contract and how her general terms might appear:

**NON-UNION FEATURE-LENGTH MOTION
PICTURE SCREENWRITER AGREEMENT**

DATE: As of _____, 20___
COMPANY: Hiring Production Company, LLC
            123 Sunset Blvd., Suite 456

Hollywood, CA 90028
Tel. (323) 555-5555
Fax (323) 555-5555
Email: legal@production.com

WRITER: Jessica Screenwriter
789 Novice Street, Apt. 3D
Los Angeles, CA 90028
Tel. (310) 555-5555
Email: Jessica@screenwriter.com

(If Jessica Screenwriter has an agent, Jessica's address will still remain as listed above; her agent's company and contact information would be written as a second billing, meaning exactly where you're reading this text block.)

TITLE: "NEW COMMERCIAL FEATURE FILM"

The Parties Hereby Agree as Follows:

1. **SERVICES**—Here is a block of text that is overly wordy and legal-sounding, which essentially outlines that the Company above is hiring the Writer to render a Service (which means "to write"), to the best of the Writer's abilities, a Screenplay—hereafter called "Literary Material"—for a feature-length Motion Picture tentatively titled *"NEW COMMERCIAL FEATURE FILM"*. The terms of the Agreement are considered non-exclusive (meaning Jessica Screenwriter can enter into other Writing Agreements as long as they don't interfere with her ability to perform the Services required here) and shall be considered on a "freelance" basis (meaning the objective of her efforts are only to produce the script and that the relationship can continue or end at any time).

2. **LITERARY MATERIAL**—Some more overly wordy language essentially stating the Writer needs to complete the following steps in order to be in good standing with the Company; these are stated as full breakdowns for each phase of the writing process and allow both the Writer and the Company to collaborate on the project, while ensuring the Company is getting (and paying for) a script it will actually be able to work with:

(i)   Outline for a Screenplay of the Title [the "Outline"] (meaning Jessica must write an Outline or Treatment);

(ii)   Provided Company notifies Writer to continue—(meaning Company can end deal at any time)—Writer will supply a first draft of the Screenplay ("Screenplay") based upon the Approved Outline of the Screenplay (meaning that if Jessica turned in the Outline and the Company has heavily revised it, they are expecting a first draft which *includes* their changes);

(iii) Provided Company notifies Writer to continue, Writer will supply a second draft of Screenplay (again including any changes made to first draft by the Company);

(iv) Provided Company notifies Writer to continue, Writer will supply a rewrite of the Screenplay (this can mean a variety of elements, but at this point the second draft is most likely the skeleton everyone's approved, but the Company might want certain characters more enhanced, etc., so Jessica should be prepared for a nearly full rewrite of the script at this point);

(v) Provided Company notifies Writer to continue (see a trend here?), Writer shall supply a polish of the Screenplay (again, this can mean a variety of things, but it's best to assume the worst by preparing for *much more* than a few small corrections).

3. **DELIVERY AND READING PERIODS**—An overly wordy block that basically outlines your expected due dates and how long the Company has to provide you with a response. Important note is that while the Company is allowed to be a week or two late getting back to you, Jessica Screenwriter needs to be ON TIME, ALL THE TIME. It's not a two-way street here. Generally, a Writer will deliver the materials on a set date and the Production Company will have anywhere between two weeks and thirty days to respond--but the Writer should always be accepting of delays on behalf of the Production Company.

4. **TERMINATION/SUSPENSION RIGHTS**—Here the Company clearly states it has the right to fire the writer, terminate the agreement, or put the agreement on hold for any reason. At whatever point the Company decides to terminate or suspend is where its obligation to pay the writer ends. Again, this is not a two-way street. . . . The Company holds the power here because it has the money. But don't sweat over this one, it's a very standard clause.

5. **COMPENSATION**—Provided Writer is not in Material Breach of this Agreement all compensation shall be payable as follows (meaning that if you've followed all the points listed and met all deadlines—which is why it's really important to meet all of your deadlines—then the Company will be paying you based upon the following criteria):

(For our purposes, we're assuming Jessica has been commissioned to deliver a script for a flat $25,000 price—not bad!)

(i)   Upon Delivery (meaning they've approved it) of the Outline: $2,500 (which actually means the check will be printed
thirty days after Jessica turns in the outline, BTW).

(Doesn't Jessica get a signing bonus? Not quite yet in her career. . . . Once
she's secured two or three scripts, *then* she can start requesting signing
bonuses, but until then she's still in the process of proving herself.)

(ii) If applicable (meaning if they keep you on board—and
this language is only for their protection, don't think of it
as mean), upon delivery of first draft of Screenplay: $5,000
(again, thirty days after Jessica turns in the screenplay).

(iii) If applicable (again, if they still continue with the agreement), upon delivery of second draft of Screenplay: $5,000
(thirty days later).

(iv) If applicable, upon delivery of the Rewrite (regardless of
how in-depth the "rewrite" might actually be): $5,000.

(v)   If applicable, upon delivery of the Polish (and the polish
could be a few tweaks, it could be starting from scratch):
$2,500.

(Have you been doing the math? If you've gotten this far, you'll
realize you're now short $5,000 from the total $25,000. That's
because another major component of most flat Screenwriter deals is
the "Production Bonus"—the amount of money the Screenwriter is
issued on the first day of principle photography. Not all deals have
this clause; some writers would prefer to just get paid for their work
regardless of whether the film goes into production. . . . Why would
that be? The Company isn't paying the writer a "Production Bonus"
to congratulate them on writing a script that's now in production,
they're paying them so that the writer is "on call" during the production in case the Company needs a last minute rewrite or polish
to the script during the filming process.)

(vi) Provided Writer is not in Material Breach (you know by now
to follow the rules), the Writer will get a Production Bonus
of $5,000 payable on the first day of principle photography.
During the production period, if Company requires polishes
or rewrites of the screenplay, for any reason, the Writer shall
be considered available and on call for these services, which
are to be considered already paid for. . . . Meaning they can
come anytime with absolutely ridiculous requests.

ROYALTIES: Overly wordy statement generally goes here all about a Writer's royalties. It will essentially say: "If a Motion Picture is Produced which was Based upon the Literary Material herein referred to as a Screenplay (see how overly complicated they make stuff?) and the Writer is not in uncured material Breach of this Agreement, then Writer shall receive 1% of 100% of the Net Profits in Accordance to Company's customary profits definition, attached herein as Exhibit 1, blah, blah, blah, in accordance to the laws of blah, blah, etc. So, you'd get $1.00 for every $100 the company earns right? Not quite. . . . You are entitled to $1.00 for every $100 the company *reports* that it earned. Essentially, most Companies (not all) will find a way to apply expenses against their earnings; and if there are no earnings, there's no royalties to pay out. At this level, it's not even worth the fight (most novice writers and producers spend all this time fighting these clauses without understanding how royalties in the real Indie Hollywood world work. . . . Do yourself a favor, think of the deal as a flat offering and move on—if you ever earn a royalty check, cash it ASAP! For the details on what 1% of 100% of Net Revenue looks like, feel free to review Exhibit 1 of this Agreement).

6. **SCREEN CREDIT**—Again they'll list here "as long as Writer is not in Material Breach" that they'll give you a Written By credit for your work in the main credits, and that the on-screen credit is equivalent to the font and text size on screen as everyone else. If the writer chooses to be credited under a pseudonym, that can also be addressed within this clause.

> *Note*: Generally there will be a note dictating that this Writer's Deal is NON-UNION and that it is not bound to the rules of the Writers Guild of America, *but* that it will follow the general principles of the WGA in determining writing credits, etc.

7. **RIGHTS**—Here they'll state that the Writer doesn't own the script. It's a work for hire, therefore the Company owns the script, they're just commissioning the service of the writer.

8. **SEQUELS, PREQUELS, AND REMAKES**—If, within a certain time period (let's say seven to ten years) after the film, which is based on Jessica's script, is released, a Sequel, Prequel, or Remake is desired, the Company must first go to Jessica before anyone else to make a deal with her. Since this was not a spec script out of Jessica's imagination (the Company hired her to write the script and therefore the Company owns the content) they don't owe her advanced money if they move forward with a Sequel, Prequel or Remake and she wouldn't be owed any royalties. . . . But generally they would go to her first for alternative versions. This is why it's really important to stay in good contact with all entities you've entered deals with, especially if you

move and so on. This even would be very rare, but it's generally outlined or brought up in an agreement. Also, according to WGA rules (and even though this agreement is a non-union agreement, it's stated above the rules of this Agreement follow the WGA principles) Jessica would have to be credited since a Sequel, Prequel, or Remake would be based on a script, characters, or story/stories Jessica first wrote.

9. **INSURANCE COVERAGE**—All companies have blanket/umbrella insurance policies to protect themselves in the event Jessica is plagiarizing material. Jessica wouldn't be required to have insurance (called Errors and Omissions insurance on her work), but since this is a work for hire, all material she turns in would be insured by the Company.

10. **STANDARD TERMS AND CONDITIONS**—Attached to this Agreement will be long list of definitions outlining each term, condition, or phase of this Agreement, so that anything disputed has a very clear and overly complex explanation.

AGREED AND ACCEPTED: HIRING PRODUCTION COMPANY, LLC

Name: JESSICA SCREENWRITER   **By:** _____
SSN: 123-45-6789   **Its:**

STANDARD TERMS & CONDITIONS
To the Agreement by and between Hiring Production Company, LLC ["Company"] and Jessica Screenwriter ["Writer"];

This Standard Terms & Conditions (sometimes abbreviated as "ST&C") portion of the Writer Agreement is also found in almost any agreement that you'll ever read, including those outside the movie business. It essentially is the opportunity for the hiring company to define—to their advantage, of course—how each and every possible definition should be viewed and/or seen by any third party should there ever be some kind of dispute. This is often the portion described as the "small print" and is actually the real nuts and bolts of any agreement.

For ease and sanity, we won't get as detailed as earlier in the "agreement" sample, but I will take a bit of page space to outline the common words that would receive a definition, and will provide some detailed breakdowns on the more complex terms, etc.

1. **Definitions**: The following terms mean the following herein:

(a) "Picture"—or "Motion Picture" or like words referring to a feature length movie;

(b) "Name or Likeness"—Name, Professional Name, Photographs, Voice Recordings, or any other actual or simulated "likeness" to an actual person, living or dead;

(c) "Person"—Important to note that in the legal world, a "Person" means any Corporation, Partnership, Joint Venture, Trust, or any other Business Entity as well as any Natural Person, meaning by default, both Jessica Screenwriter *and* Hiring Production Company, LLC are both "Persons" in the eyes of the law and within this Agreement.

(d) "Writer"—In this case Jessica Screenwriter is the Writer, but it is the Person within this Agreement to which all of these definitions apply.

(e) "Company"—In this Case, Hiring Production Company, LLC who has sought out and commissioned the Services of Jessica Screenwriter, and to whom all of these definitions protect.

2. **Screen Credit**. A big statement on how Screen Credit shall be assigned and how it shall appear within the completed film. On studio films, this section can be huge, but on smaller indie films such as this one, this section is pretty much a cut-and-paste from the Writers Guild of America.

3. **Principle Services**. A breakdown of the roles each "Person" (meaning the Writer *and* the Company) will play. Statements usually begin with "Writer shall blah blah blah" meaning Jessica Screenwriter needs to listen to and

work for the *Company's* needs and expectations. The Company shall honor its payment structure and deadlines listed herein, etc.

4. **Suspension**. This is generally a full page of text about all the different reasons the Company might put this agreement on "Suspension" (meaning on hold until they get back to it later). There is usually a grace period of two to three weeks that an Agreement like this could be "suspended," otherwise it'll be considered Terminated.

> Common reasons will be:

> "Incapacity" (meaning the Writer's inability to write (if Jessica has an accident) or if the Company becomes incapacitated (Legal issue, head of production has a baby, actress they based their presales on no longer wants to be involved, etc.)).

> "Force Majeure"—A French phrase found in all contracts stating things that are out of our control, like a flood, war, political protest, or any other unforeseen and unstoppable event.

> "Default"—When one of the Parties (Jessica or Hiring Production Company) is in breach of the agreement and the Parties need to settle the issue.

> Then several more paragraphs go into how a Suspension will be decided upon and resolved after the fact. Also, this will be the place where questions get answered such as how the "due dates" get adjusted, etc.

5. **Termination**. Different from Suspension, to Terminate would be an all-out abandonment of the Agreement, cancelling out *both* parties' responsibilities and obligations.

> We won't go too heavy here, but there will be extremely well-phrased paragraphs that protect the Company but also guarantee that at whichever point the Agreement was Terminated will be the point where the obligations cease—which means if Jessica turns in her Second Draft of the Agreement and the Company decides to Terminate, she will get paid for the Second Draft. Also, if by WGA rules and principles, a certain portion of Jessica's Second Draft is used in the final version of the Produced film, then she will receive appropriate credit. However, she would not get her Production Bonus, since the full reason for receiving a Production Bonus would be to have an on call writer during Production, which wouldn't be Jessica.
> There will also be language about how each party can propose to end the agreement. The Company has more ability than the writer, but let's say hypothetically the Company wants Jessica to write something she's morally opposed to, she would be able to cancel the deal.

6. **Rights.** In short, Jessica is being hired to write. She will not have any ownership of the script at all. For all practical purposes, she is producing

a "work made for hire." Any unique ideas, brilliant speeches, or amazing characters she creates are done so for the Company, not for herself. Granted, she will always be credited accordingly, but she doesn't own anything . . . not even the Copyright. That's why she's getting paid (to render a service on behalf of the Production Company).

7. **Warranties**. Sometimes called "Warranties & Representations" this section is another standard in any Agreement. But unlike a Warranty offered to you as an up-sell at an electronics store, this one has a little more clout for both sides.

   (a) First, the Company wants to make the Writer promise that she has the right to enter into this Agreement (that she's not under an exclusive contract with another company, that she is who she says she is and that she's not misrepresenting herself to the Company).

   (b) Second, the Company wants Jessica to promise that all the work she'll be creating and submitting is original work (and not plagiarized or stolen from another source). That way, if the Company were to ever be sued by another writer or entity for plagiarism, the Company could pass along the damages to Jessica for submitting non-original work. Don't panic on this point, it sounds scary, but theft of literary material is actually quite rare in Hollywood and it's very difficult to steal and/or even prove work has legitimately been stolen.

   (c) Third, the Company Warrants and Represents similar things, that it has the right to offer this job to Jessica and that it's in good standing professionally and financially to fulfill its promises.

8. **Indemnity**. Another standard. In short, this Agreement is only between the Company and the Writer. In a legal dispute, all of the Companies' employees, investors, partners, etc. would not be personally affected. Same for Jessica, this Agreement only extends to her and cannot be used against partners, spouses, parents, etc. Also, this will go into other protections—let's say the finished film gets sued by an organization, or a piece of music in the film wasn't cleared and a record label is suing the production company. . . . None of this affects Jessica; it's not her problem. This stuff seems scary, but it's to your benefit too. Just follow the rules listed herein and you're good to go.

9. **Remedies.** How both sides make a note of issues/conflicts and a procedure of how both parties can work through them. Again, follow the terms and you're fine.

10. **Assignment**. If Jessica Screenwriter decides to quit, is terminated, or for any other reason, the Company may "assign" this exact agreement (and

Jessica's project) to another Writer. On the other hand, Jessica CANNOT assign this agreement to another company or another writer.

11. **Conflicts.** This section defines what a conflict is in a legal sense. It also outlines how a conflict would be resolved. Generally, it would go into "arbitration" (a third party to hear both sides and make a judgment). Realistically, if Jessica weren't performing up to speed, the company would simply terminate. If Jessica is making a big enough fuss about something to go into Arbitration, she will probably never get another screenwriting job. In a deal like this, there's very little to complain about from either side. Company wants a script and Jessica says she can provide it. If Jessica decides she doesn't like writing the script, the Parties go separate directions. Jessica doesn't own the work anyway, she simply owns the talent that can give the Company what it wants in a short period of time.

12. **Confidentiality, Publicity**. The terms of this Agreement would need to remain confidential. Jessica shouldn't talk about how the Company works or what the real budgets of the movie she's writing for are, for example. That might be in a separate "Confidentiality Clause" or it might be defined here.

Another point here is the Publicity. This states that if Jessica receives Screenwriting credit in the main titles of the film, then her name will also appear on the billing block (that block of names on a movie poster for Actors and Crew), and if Jessica were to ever become one of those rare household name Screenwriters (like Kauffman or Towne), then the Company could use Jessica's name to promote their movie in the future.

13. **Use of Services or Products**. Your film school professors might hold great screenwriters (and their scripts) on pedestals, but the law looks at a script as a "Product" and the screenwriter as a "Service" provider. This clause states the Writer gets paid only when the Service Jessica is providing results in a finished Product (each of the steps listed previously like Outline, First Draft, etc.).

14. **Non-Union Production**. Here the Writer (as initialed below and signed for on the whole) acknowledges that she is Agreeing to write as a non-union writer on a non-union film. If Jessica is actually a member of the WGA, she is here acknowledging that she's breaking the rules of her organization. This protects the Company. Also, Jessica cannot come back later and try to use the film to springboard herself into a union with back pay on previous projects since this film is non-union.

15. **Attorney**. Jessica has the right to show this Agreement to an attorney. She has a period of X days (let's assume five days) to send this Agreement to a lawyer and get a legal point of view on elements she doesn't fully understand. She is allowed to make minor changes (that the Company

may or may not accept) based upon her own, or her lawyer's, wishes. If Jessica hires a lawyer, she can add her legal representative's address to the front below where her agent's name and contact information would be written.

16. **Governing Law and Jurisdiction**. Yes, they even get this detailed, so that in the event of a dispute, you know the exact State, County, and City with which the laws will be reviewed. Ninety-nine times out of hundred, in the movie business it will read: "in accordance with the internal laws of the State of California in the City of Los Angeles." But it can be anywhere.

17. **Miscellaneous.** Yep, everything else they can squeeze in. Let's highlight a few simple terms, but go ahead and assume they've thought of every contingency here:

(a) Entire Agreement—Just because one sentence on page three could mean one thing, but another sentence of page four means the opposite, an Arbitrator or Lawyer should only be reading both in context within the "entire Agreement" or how they related to the whole Agreement.

(b) Definitions of what "minor tweaks or polishes" mean in relation to the act of payable service "polish" or "rewrite."

(c) Definitions of what submitting a "draft" are. How these elements are to be submitted, and to whom, what format everything should be in, etc.

(d) Payment obligations (this is where it states the Company must pay within thirty days after a step is considered complete).

(e) More details on non-union projects.

(f) More details on the Writer's non-ownership of the script but full right to accurate credit.

(g) Time constraints, etc.

(h) Blah, blah, blah, ongoing details that have very little to do with writing a movie.

    And then both parties again sign. . . .

AGREED AND ACCEPTED: HIRING PRODUCTION COMPANY, LLC
_____
Name: JESSICA SCREENWRITER   **By:** _____
SSN: 123-45-6789   **Its:**

CERTIFICATE OF AUTHORSHIP

This is very similar to a release form that an Actor must sign before he or she appears on camera. The Certificate of Authorship is essentially a statement saying that all words, ideas, characters, scenes, sequences are unique and original, coming only from the imagination of the Writer, and that the Writer is providing the Company with a script that cannot be seen as anything other than original. Or, that in the event another Screenplay were to surface from a third party that was strikingly similar to the script our Writer is turning in, it would be a complete coincidence and that the Writer would be able to prove drafts, progression, and notes detailing the personal origin of the script.

If there would be any conflict, the Writer agrees to work with the Company to clear the originality of the work he or she has submitted.

Face it, there's only so many scripts/stories out there. Every writer has worked hard to produce a spec piece of work, only to find out something very similar is in the works or is in production. If you turn in a script, chances are there are dozens very similar to yours. It doesn't mean someone stole your work or that someone will think your work is stolen. Truth be told, the vast majority of Hollywood execs are legit and want to do the right thing. And the vast majority of original scripts—even if very similar to others—are in fact original and only coincidentally have resemblance to others already in the marketplace. All this ongoing legal speak is because of the one or two times where someone has actually sold a script that was knowingly ripped off. Don't ever worry about this stuff. Just do good work, turn in the work you create, and you will be fine!

Sometimes, in these statements, you might come across one of the most confusing terms in contracts: "Droit Moral." This phrase refers to the moral rights of you as an individual. With regards to a screenplay, since you are a person and you have "created" this script, you somehow own a piece of it because it wouldn't exist in quite the same manner if your fingers never graced the keyboard. The Certificate of Authorship further considers the Company the owner of the material and that you are being paid for your services. Don't put up a stink about this. Take the money and move onto the next script so you can build a career. If you want to hold onto your script rights, then sit in your apartment for the rest of your life writing on spec for readers who will never read your work.

The Undersigned hereby agrees and executes these Terms:

_____

Jessica Screenwriter

EXHIBIT 1

Net Profits Definitions

Look, I'll keep this simple. The chances a writer makes a penny on royalties for non-union low-budget indie productions is slim to nil.

First, this Agreement is based upon a production that doesn't yet exist.

Second, the Writer is in last place to receive any royalties that would trickle down anyway.

Third, your agreement will only ever say "net profits." If it says net, you probably will never see anything. Why? Because "*net*" means *after* other costs and payouts have taken place. Sure, money will come in. But then the Company must make other payments (like its full-time staff, costs associated with selling the movies, etc.). Real costs, not invented ones. They also have to pay the accounting staff to keep track of all these payments and payouts, plus there are the costs associated with paying taxes and printing/shipping checks out. Long story short, there's thousands of costs and deductions to be made on each dollar the Company earns from the film, so unless it turns into a billion-dollar franchise, you'll most likely never see a penny. . . . And even if it does become a billion-dollar franchise, you don't own it anyway, the Company does.

Instead, I'm going to list common phrases that are used against the gross profits of the movie before any net payouts take place. You should view this as a fun fantasy and accept that the crux of this agreement is a $25,000 flat payout (which is what it really is). Don't spend time arguing percentages like other novices. Production companies will go through the motions with you, but they know it's wasting time.

"Contingent Amounts"—Can mean any cost the Company decides relates to the movie.

"Material Costs"—Can mean any "physical material" cost (shipping, DVDs, postage stamps, etc.).

"Sub-distribution Costs"—Cost of having other companies sell certain rights.

"Collected Taxes"—Taxes collected against earnings of the film

"Distribution Expenses"—Means, without limitation, the cost of duplication, advertising, phone call expenses, foreign language dubbing costs, collection costs, litigation costs—the list is endless.

"Audit Rights"—Sure, you can audit. . . . But you pay for that, and your auditor won't find anything that the Company doesn't have the right to hold.

Be a professional, fight for the flat fee and don't make a big fuss over percentage points. Deliver what the Company wants and move on!

────────── *APPENDIX III* ──────────

THE NON-UNION OPTION / PURCHASE AGREEMENT

If a Production Company likes your script as is, they have two ways to acquire its rights: They can either "Option" your script (or "borrow" its rights for a limited window of time in exchange for a small fee) or they can outright "Purchase" your script (meaning you'll be handing away all rights into perpetuity in exchange for a larger bulk payout or payment offering).

Production companies and producers like to keep their hands inside as many cookie jars as possible (and by optioning instead of purchasing, they spend less money yet have access to more scripts).

If you are ever presented with an offer of Option on any of your scripts, push to see if they would just outright purchase it from you. . . . How much should you ask them for? *If* they're open to the idea, let them make the offer—your target should be to get them to approximately two to three times the "Option Fee" or "Initial Option" price they offered.

Although the total figure you'd receive would much smaller than if the script were to be purchased after a successful option cycle, the truth is that most options never progress to a green light. On rare occasions, producers might do the math and see the purchase of your script as a worthy investment (which means you can simply cash your check and move on to the next project). However, most companies would prefer keeping the deal on an Option/Purchase basis only—and that's still a *fantastic* spot to find yourself in. If you've tried pushing the idea of a purchase and they're still leaning toward an option, *don't force the issue*. . . . Just move forward with what's on the table and play ball.

To give you a better sense of how an Option/Purchase Agreement might work in the real world, we're going to assume the following scenario:

A young novice screenwriter, named Jessica Screenwriter, has successfully pitched her latest screenplay *SELLABLE FEATURE-LENGTH SCRIPT* to a new Production Company, called Purchasing Production Company, LLC. Her spec script was quickly vetted by the readers and came highly recommended to the production team, who've decided to move forward in acquiring the script's rights.

The head of development reached out to Jessica by email, asking if she would be interested in optioning the rights to *SELLABLE FEATURE-LENGTH SCRIPT* to Purchasing Production Company, LLC for a period of 1 year for $1,500 (a very reasonable offer). Jessica replies by asking if there would be any opportunity for a purchase of her script rather than an option. The head of development explains that Purchasing Production Company likes her script very much, but that they're not in a position to move forward with a purchase; however, they'd be open to sending over an Option/Purchase Agreement to secure the rights in the short term (with the opportunity for a purchase at a later time).

Being a smart young woman with a strong career ahead of her, Jessica decides to move forward with this fantastic opportunity knowing that an option for $1,500 (even if it never progresses toward a green light) is better than *no* option for zero dollars.

What follows is a sample of how Jessica's contract might appear:

SHORT FORM NON-UNION OPTION/PURCHASE AGREEMENT

DATE: As of _____, 20___
PURCHASER: Purchasing Production Company, LLC
                    123 Sunset Blvd., Suite 456
                    Hollywood, CA 90028
                    Tel. (323) 555-5555
                    Fax (323) 555-5555
                    Email: legal@production.com

OWNER: Jessica Screenwriter
                    789 Novice Street, Apt. 3D
                    Los Angeles, CA 90028
                    Tel. (310) 555-5555
                    Email: Jessica@screenwriter.com

(If Jessica Screenwriter has an agent, Jessica's address will still remain as listed above; her agent's company and contact information would be written as a second billing, meaning exactly where you're reading this text block.)

This confirms the agreement (hereafter, "Agreement") by and between PURCHASING PRODUCTION COMPANY, LLC (referred herein as the "Purchaser," which shall also include any possible entity, or assumed entity, that the Purchaser can in any way, shape, or form, mildly prove is "related" to itself—meaning once you sign this, Purchasing Production Company, LLC holds all the cards), and JESSICA SCREENWRITER (referred to hereinafter as the "Owner," but shall *only* refer to *her* and no successors, heirs, or representatives), with respect to that certain feature-length Screenplay, which the Owner solely has created, currently entitled "*SELLABLE FEATURE-LENGTH SCRIPT*" (referred to hereinafter as "the Property").

    1. "**Non-Union Agreement**": At the onset of your career, the non-union indie world will be your most likely entry point to early screenwriting success—meaning the production companies you will be dealing with will *not* be affiliated with the Writers Guild of America and, therefore, will *not* be bound by their rules or operating procedures. In addition to the clear "Non-Union" title heading of this contract, there will usually be a clause (just like this one) clearly explaining that this is a Non-Union Agreement. . . . But this is not here to freak Jessica out or cheat her out of anything; it's actually here to *protect the Purchaser*. Once a writer joins the WGA, they cannot work on any non-union production (even if they use a pseudonym). As a result, non-WGA-signatory companies will use very clear language announcing the project is non-union to avoid any confusion should a claim about misrepresenting themselves ever be made against them in the future.

    2. "**Option**": In consideration hereof (and a bunch of other legal text), *if* this Agreement moves forward as an Option Agreement rather

than a Purchase (or Buyout), then the Purchaser shall pay the Owner the sum of One Thousand Five Hundred United States dollars (US$1,500) upon executed signature of this Agreement. Upon receipt of said monies (meaning once Jessica cashes her check), the Purchaser shall have the right to Option said Property (attempt to sell Jessica's script) using its best business judgment during an Initial Term ("Initial Term") of twelve (12) months.

(The amount of money for the Initial Term of an Option will always be a relatively small amount; but even one (1) dollar is enough to legally obtain the rights and legally shop Jessica's script around—and yes, you might actually receive a request for a $1 Option/Purchase Agreement at some point in your career. The general rule of thumb is that the Option Price is about 2.5 to 3 percent of the anticipated budget of the title. . . . But the inherit problem here is that since so many things can change in the script before it's ever officially green-lit, an estimate on budget is nearly impossible. In real life, you'll actually be looking at a very small amount of cash. My advice: any money is good money in the world of indie non-union deal making.)

At Purchaser's sole discretion (meaning their decision, not Jessica's), Purchaser may elect to extend the Initial Term for an additional period of twelve (12) months ("First Extended Term"), upon payment of One Thousand Five Hundred United States dollars (US$1,500) ("First Extended Term Payment").

They will undoubtedly have more language explaining a pay-out structure for yet another term hereafter, but there are no guarantees the option will ever go past an Initial Term. Concluding this section will be a block of text essentially stating that during a "living Option Term" (when Purchasing Production Company holds the rights), the rights belong exclusively to them and Jessica will not engage in conversations with the intention of soliciting her own screenplay with any third party. However, at the end of the Option Term(s) if no progression towards a Purchase is made, the rights will be returned to her. There will probably be a claim that the purchaser will provide Jessica with a breakdown or summary of all entities with whom it openly discussed her Property, but this will also be followed by generic "within reason" or "to the best of its ability" text, which basically means she'll never exactly know who has been pitched her work and who hasn't.

3. **"Set-Up Bonus"**: In the event Purchaser assigns this Agreement (sells off the rights to Jessica's script) to a third party and/or enters into an Agreement for further development and/or production of a Picture based upon the Property, then Purchaser shall pay Owner a lump sum amount, called a "Set-Up Bonus," In other words, once Jessica signs over her script, the Purchasing company has the right to "flip" the rights to her script to

another entity—either as a one-time sale, or as a partnership, in order to get a production into motion (and Jessica will have no control nor approval over the terms of that deal). Sometimes there might be language offering "With Owner's Written Consent," but not always. The amount of the "Set-Up Bonus" will always vary (again, dependent on a variety of factors), but for practical purposes, we'll assume Jessica's "Set-Up Bonus" to be valued at Five Thousand United States Dollars (US$5,000) in the event Purchasing Production Company, LLC ever sells off her script to another entity during their Option Period.

4. **"Exercise of Option"**: This paragraph can be listed with a multitude of different titles, but the gist is to define the exact moment when this Agreement transfers from a simple Option (or "borrowing") of Jessica's script rights versus an outright Purchase of those rights. This clause is here to protect *both* the Purchaser as well as the Owner. Example: Purchasing Production Company, LLC could flip the rights to Jessica's script to another entity it already owns (and pay Jessica the Set-Up Bonus), then simply never inform her that the company they've flipped it to is changing the name of her script and going into production under a different title—which would require the Purchasing company to pay Jessica the remainder of her Purchase Price. . . . This also protects the Purchasing company against any wild claims Jessica might make (such as assuming a film of comparable style and tone is based off her script when it is, in fact, just coincidentally similar). The generally excepted "moment" of an Exercised Option (or an Option that has transitioned into a Purchase) is the moment a camera captures an image, while on a set, depicting a scene from the optioned script (whether that film is produced by Purchasing Production Company, or any future entity Purchaser engages in business on behalf of Jessica's script) that can reasonably be traced back to this Option/Purchase Agreement (whether that film is going by another title or not).

5. **"Purchase Price"**: Once the Purchaser finally places and secures a deal to officially green-light and produce a Feature Film based upon Jessica's script, her script has become "Purchased." And with this new transition comes (1) a lump sum payment owed to her, along with (2) a long list of protections and contingencies that all hover around Purchasing Production Company and any future claims brought against them.

First, about the "Purchase Price" payment: Sometimes there is a minimum amount herein (a flat dollar amount, or a minimum benchmark of some kind to be used as a reference), but not always. More often than not, it is a more vague and open-ended price based upon bits of data you're simply not privy to. For instance, the Purchase Price might be, "the amount equal to five percent (5%) of the total production's budget as defined herein as Production Budget ("Production Budget") less initial Option fee, all financing costs, completion bod fees, contingency services, bank or financial institutional charges and respective interest, insurances, general overhead, subject to a minimum 'floor' of not less than Fifteen-Thousand United States Dollars (US$15,000) ('Minimum Purchase Price') and a maximum 'ceiling' of not more than One Hundred Fifty Thousand United States Dollars (US$150,000) ('Maximum Purchase Price')." What does this really mean?

It means Purchasing Production Company's minimum check to Jessica would be $18,500 if they secure a deal through a third party, and $13,500 if they simply move into production themselves. . . . Sure, the minimum "floor" is $15,000, but that amount is less the initial $1,500 Option Fee. If a Third Party is involved, Purchasing Production Company must pay Jessica that additional $5,000 Set-Up Bonus on top of the $13,500 owed to her. But what if the Production Budget soars and Jessica's script turns into a major Hollywood Studio film? Very slim chance. . . . All of these figures are really based upon a hypothetical Production Budget (one that also has several other costs and factors which can be added or removed at will). And what have we learned about Production Budgets? The numbers change depending on who's asking and who's telling. The way the payment structure is spelled out here, the smaller the budget, the less money Purchasing Production Company would owe Jessica (which means it's to their advantage to find a way to make the budget as small as possible).

Key point to look for here: You want a flat Purchase Price, one that is very clear without a bunch of floating variables. A percentage of a high Production Budget is a definite floating variable to be avoided. Sure, it could be a jackpot, but the truth is Production Budgets are rarely reported accurately and indie films get shot for much less than you'd imagine. Only sign on a contract where you clearly understand the exact amount you'll get paid, while trying to avoid "if/then" scenarios—they'll always be used against you.

6. **"Contingent Proceed Compensation"**: This paragraph, which can go by a number of different titles, essentially exists to discuss hypothetical royalties. Well-intentioned indeed, but don't royalties always seem to be contingent on something? As long as Jessica isn't in Material Breach (meaning, as long as she hasn't broken any of the terms within this Agreement), then she could be entitled to a small amount of "back-end," should it exist—but this amount will always be "net" of something (meaning she'll only be gaining a small percentage of what are often referred to as "Defined Proceeds," or the amount the Production Company will actually "recognize" (or "acknowledge") as legit profit. Again, when working in the non-union indie zone, do not get held up by the notion of royalties. These are often used as barter tools by the contract negotiators to get you to sign for a lower Purchase Price or Initial Option Fee. Jessica should only be looking at the guaranteed minimums in this deal (as should you). That's not to suggest that Production Companies are all crooked, it's just that in reality there's rarely anything left after they've added up all their conceivable expenses and paid out everyone else in the royalties line.

7. **"Grant of Rights"**: When the "Option is Exercised" (meaning, once the Purchaser legitimately Purchases Jessica's script), the Purchaser shall own, in perpetuity (forever) and "throughout the Universe" (yes, real contracts say this) any and all interest to the Property excluding only those certain "Reserved Rights" ("Reserved Rights") as defined below (collectively, the "Grant of Rights"). Notwithstanding the foregoing (in addition yet separate from the above), Purchaser acknowledges that decisions made by any Third Party regarding individual appearances, etc., shall be negotiated separately between Third Party and Purchaser (meaning they can essentially do whatever they want to Jessica's script after they Purchase it from her). Without limiting the generality of the foregoing, the Grant of Rights shall be defined as:

(a) *Audiovisual Works*: Here, the Purchaser will breakdown that they have the sole right to produce any conceivable audiovisual work derived from Jessica's script. The key point is that the end result must be some type of Motion Picture (even if in short form); however, they would also own all the audio rights to that said product (including soundtrack rights). It's not out of the question that occasionally Soundtracks featuring the music from a film might also include quotes spoken on screen. Those quotes, even though derived from Jessica's script, would "belong" to the Purchasing Production Company. In short, if Purchasing Production Company is "buying" the script, they want to own (or at least have a piece of) any altered or derived version adapted from the Audiovisual Work (movie, TV pilot or Web-series) they create. If Jessica is allowed to hold onto any rights related to the Script (such as the ability to adapt the same script into a stage play or book), it would be spelled out here.

(b) *Copyright & Exploitation Rights*: Generally, when you sell a property to another entity, they take on the copyright. If Jessica's script were still in the Option phase, she could hold onto her copyright, but at the point of Sale, the Purchaser would inherit that copyright. They may or may not directly manage the actual paperwork with the Library of Congress, but there would be an official transfer of these rights at some point after the Purchase. Once the copyright officially belongs to the Purchaser, they forever have the right to "Exploit" that copyright and renew any "soon to expire" copyrights.

(c) *Alteration Rights*: This block essentially hands the Purchaser the right to change Jessica's script to meet its own needs. Blasphemy to some, but practical business sense to others. . . . The truth is, there are so many parties and entities that come and go during the process of making a film that her script will never end up word for word how she initially presented it. . . . Whether there are additions, deletions, translations, or any other modifications, Jessica is fully granting exclusive decision-making rights to the Purchaser.

(d) *Name, Likeness, and Biography Rights*: If Jessica closes on this deal today, then in five years turns into a mega writing phenomenon, you'd better believe the mid-tier Production Company who Purchased this script will fully exploit her name, likeness, and biography for its own needs. . . . Sometimes, if Jessica's script was adapted from a novel or other written source, this clause would rightfully assume you had the right to that author's Name, Likeness, and Biography—and by the nature of this agreement, those rights would be handed over to the Purchaser. In addition to the above interpretation, this clause could also imply that if Jessica's script were to be based on the "Life Rights" of a real person—and she acquired those Life Rights in order to write her spec script (which is now the property of the Purchaser)—then those Life Rights would also be considered the property of the Purchaser.

(e) *No Obligation to Proceed Rights*: Don't mistake this as an exit clause that Jessica can use to get herself out of the deal; No Obligation to Proceed means that after Jessica enters this Agreement and has her rights Purchased, she's no longer required or expected to perform any further actions. In some instances, the writer might be requested to remain "available" or "on call" for a period of time to perform any rewrites or necessary tweaks to the script, but more often than not, at point of Purchase, the rights are stripped from the Owner, which here simply allows Jessica to move on without hesitation. (If Purchasing Production Company would hereafter wish to bring Jessica on board to perform a rewrite or tweak of her already Purchased script, they would then issue her a Writer-For-Hire Agreement, as seen in Appendix II.)

8. **"Reserved Rights"**: These are all of the remaining rights that Jessica (as the Owner) would get to hold onto even after her script is Purchased. It's important to note that at no point would the Owner of the script ever have direct rights to any media that the Purchaser produces based upon her script. . . . She could license clips from the finished motion picture, for instance, but just because she wrote the script does not mean she's entitled to everything associated with it. However, even if her script is both Purchased and later Produced by the Purchaser, she will always hold onto at least a few rights to her script (though these will differ by company). Examples could include:

(a) *Publishing Rights*: Jessica could be permitted to certain publishing rights, usually limited to excerpts, from her script (not from the movie). There will usually be a certain maximum preventing her from using the entire work, such as a maximum number of words or a capped percentage from the overall work. But, let's hypothetically say she follows her career path and becomes a very well-known screenwriter, and she later decides to put together her own "how to write a screenplay" book based upon her industry experiences; under this reserved right, she could possibly use excerpts from the script she sold as an example within that book. Although she couldn't use the whole script, she could use a few sections to exemplify things. In this particular Agreement, Jessica is having these Publishing Rights reserved just for her, meaning she holds onto all rights related to "Publishing" (including Print, Audio Recorded Readings [e.g., a human voice], and even Electronically Read Editions [including any computer program capable of 'reading' from a page and modulating an audible verbalization]). Within this clause, there's usually language referring to how the Owner must notify the Purchaser of this type of decision, if ever exercised.

(b) *Radio Rights*: These rights would be equivalent to any fully performed version of the script (either in full or simply an excerpt). It could constitute a full-on production—with sound effects and multiple actors for each role—down to a simple verbal reading. The catch here is that any recorded version of such an event would be accessible (usually for free) by the Purchaser for potential exploitation or for advertisement purposes later on.

(c) *Stage Rights*: These are a bit interesting. Although here Jessica would get to hold onto her right to put together a live performance based upon her script, there would usually be a "holdback" (or a finite period of time that she must wait before doing so). This could be one year, all the way up to ten years. It essentially forces all potential revenue toward watching the motion picture version produced by the Purchaser versus any other version, so that there's no marketplace competition.

(d) *Author-Written Prequels and Sequels*: If Jessica Screenwriter were to be commissioned by a Company to write a script for them that later grew to be so popular it would merit a prequel or sequel, she would not be automatically granted any rights—because the Production Company would own those rights, since it was a "work-for-hire" work. . . . However, in the situation of an Option/Purchase, it was Jessica's own organic idea for the film (or its characters) that she took the initiative to craft a story from, that later grew into a popular film, she would certainly be entitled to keep or hold onto her creation for purposes of prequel, sequel, or even book franchise opportunities. But that's not to say that *if* her idea were so powerful that the opportunity for a sequel (or prequel) made financial sense, that the Purchasing company wouldn't want a piece. . . . Here there would most likely be language constituting another holdback period and/or a requirement that Jessica must present the Purchaser with any opportunities by a third party regarding a prequel, sequel, or other intellectual property opportunity and give them a first attempt to make an offer. However, there will be further language explaining her Holdback.

(e) *Holdback Period*: Jessica technically wouldn't be able to simply go out and exploit the Author-Written Prequels and Sequels rights on a whim or even at the first sign opportunity. . . . There will be certain parameters, which she must work within (and which usually include some minimum amount of time before she could actively exploit [or even work with] the concept of writing or pitching a sequel or prequel). And even after that Holdback period comes and goes, the Purchaser might just add another block of text explaining that they would have the "First Right to Negotiate" on (or "Match") any offer in the marketplace related to those sequel or prequel rights.

Don't panic about these nuances, they are very rare. . . . And if you ever happen to be lucky enough to be dealing with such problems, you will have so many other opportunities in the works that arguing over nickels and dimes won't even be on your radar.

9. **"Representations, Warranties, and Indemnities"**: Within any Agreement, both parties must always Warrant and Represent (promise and assure) that they're legit and legally able to enter the Agreement; if one party is later found not to be Warranting or Representing itself properly here, then they could be considered "in breach" of this Agreement. And if such an issue were to ever arise, they would be indemnifying (keeping out of the "legal complaint") any of the successors or partners associated (or attributed) to that other party. This is a very common block of text, which is generally very large and wordy. It essentially boils down to the fact that both parties (Jessica

as the writer and Purchasing Production Company as the Purchaser) have the right to legally enter into this deal and that both parties are being legit in their claims. . . . For Jessica, this means that *"SELLABLE FEATURE-LENGTH SCRIPT"* is legitimately her property and that no one will come out of the woodwork and be able to make a statement that she somehow "stole" this work from them; it would also mean that Jessica is not part of the WGA. For Purchasing Production Company, this clause would mean it is a legit organization that is up to date regarding paperwork with the State; it would also imply that it is not misrepresenting itself as a non-WGA signatory, etc. And if any issue were to arise and a lawsuit were to be filed, Jessica would have zero right to include any of Purchasing Production Company's employees or partners into the suit directly, just as Purchasing Producing Company couldn't legally go after Jessica's parents or her siblings if she'd somehow misrepresented herself.

10.   **"Additional Deliverables"**: If any clause in an Option/Purchase agreement could ever come back to require Jessica to perform more work, it would be this one. . . . "Additional Deliverables" are essentially all the add-on requirements that the Purchasing Production Company might require if the "Option is Exercised," transitioning this Agreement from an Option to a Purchase. There is generally no locked time on this (meaning, at any point, Purchasing Production Company could make a request for an Additional Deliverable). Generally, these deliverables are clearly identified, or at least "limited" in scope. They could range from requests to see Jessica's WGA registrations or Copyright notices to seeing Jessica's "work in progress" drafts to either (1) verify that she organically created the script, but more often than not it's to (2) see if they can harvest any material she might have deleted from earlier versions. The "limitation of scope" would be to prevent any "Additional Deliverable" being anything along the lines of a rewrite or polish of the script.

11.   **"Screen Credit"**: They'll list here "as long as Writer is not in Material Breach" that they'll give Jessica a Written By credit for her work in the main credits, and that the on-screen credit is equivalent to the font and text size on screen as everyone else. Generally there will be a note dictating that this Writer's deal is NON-UNION and that it is not bound to the rules of the Writers Guild of America, BUT that it will follow the general principles of the WGA in determining writing credits, etc.

12.   **"Creative Control Clause"**: The dream scenario here would be the Jessica (as a skilled and talented artist) could fight to see her vision of how *"SELLABLE FEATURE-LENGTH SCRIPT"* should be seen on screen once all is said and done. On a few occasions, writers might be given permission to approve the edits, trims, and revisions a Purchasing party is choosing to move forward with regarding their script, but certainly not always. And rarely would a writer, with the exception of a mega name, like a well-known

author, get to be a part of the process of choosing directing or acting talent for the project.

13. **"Irrevocability" or "Non-Equitable Relief"**: Lawyers have this funny way of drafting contracts to be overly clear without being redundant. . . . Except when it comes to hammering over one's head the fact that after this Agreement is signed, it's permanent and that all pertinent rights have forever been handed over from one party to the other. And the "Irrevocability" or "Non-Equitable Relief" Clause essentially reflects such an occurrence. . . . Here, they are simply reiterating that once the Owner signs this Agreement, the Purchaser has all the rights to the script into Perpetuity. There will certainly be other wonky nuances spread throughout this paragraph, but the gist is to understand you've handed over your property once and for all.

14. **"Insurances"**: There's always an Insurance policy protecting someone along the line. . . . But here, it'll be the Purchasing party with the policy. This clause essentially grants Purchasing Production Company to include both Jessica Screenwriter *and* Jessica's script on their General Liability coverage and/or Errors and Omissions insurances. This way, if any claim were to be brought against the Company, they have a policy to payout the damages caused either by Jessica's negligence (or the plagiarism/theft/non-cleared matters of her script). This is just a standard language block; no one is accusing Jessica of wrongdoing, it's just clearly stating a plan of action to protect the Purchasing Party.

15. **"Assignment"**: Assignment refers to the act of "assigning" a property's rights from one party to another. . . . This very Agreement is assigning the rights of Jessica's script to Purchasing Production Company. But could Jessica sell this Agreement to someone else or transfer the responsibilities to another entity? No. . . . However, the Purchaser can. In fact, that's the very nature of a distribution agreement or option agreement; Jessica is signing the rights of her script to Purchasing Production Company, specifically allowing them the right to shop her script—or possibly even sell it—to third parties if necessary, all in an attempt to get her script Produced into a motion picture. Generally, at least in entertainment contacts, whoever the initial ownership source is who's signing their content over to a third party, is rarely allowed to assign their agreement responsibilities to another party. . . . However, the party who is inheriting your rights generally can.

16. **"Re-Acquisition of Rights"**: If the Option in this Agreement is exercised and Jessica's script is officially Purchased by Purchasing Production Company, *but* after an extended period of time (usually well over ten years), no motion picture ever moves into Production based upon her script, she might have the ability to "re-acquire" the rights to her script. Do understand that the Purchasing party has (in the eyes of the law) fully Purchased

all rights to Jessica's script, so it would not be a simple "hand-over" of the rights back to her. . . . She would have to *buy* them back. How much? Who knows. In ten (or more) years, Purchasing Production Company might be in financial trouble and simply want to take in any excess cash they can, *or* maybe Jessica has become a hot-shot Oscar winning writing talent and her new manager wants to buy them back on her behalf to prevent a flunky film crew from taking one of her old scripts and tarnishing her reputation (which they'll see as an opportunity to play hard ball). Nevertheless, in most "Option/Purchase Agreements" there will be a clause addressing this issue.

17. **"Passive Payments"**: When referencing money, the word "passive" refers to income that is generated without doing any direct work with which to earn it. . . . Think about an investor buying a company's stock, when the stock increases in value, the investor is earning money without having to do any real effort (which is why earnings on a stock are classified as a form of "passive income"). For Jessica, as a screenwriter, passive payments would refer to any prequels or sequels (theatrical or straight-to-home entertainment) derived or associated with her intellectual property (her script). If a deal is struck with a third party and this contract is assigned to them, they might be able to move forward with prequels, sequels, or remakes. If such a work is ever produced, Jessica will receive a small bonus (generally equivalent to 50 percent or less of the Purchasing Price or Commission payment plan to the new writer). However, when your feet are kicked back and passive income arrives, who's really complaining? Passive income for Jessica would not constitute royalties or commissions directly related to *"SELLABLE FEATURE-LENGTH SCRIPT"* in that she did the actual work that generated those earnings.

18. **"Miscellaneous"**: Yep, everything else they can squeeze in. Let's highlight a few simple terms, but go ahead and assume they've thought of every contingency here:

    (a) *Condition Precedent*: This is a phrase used to essentially state that *all* the terms in this agreement are contingent upon the following elements (it's used to protect the buying party—or in this case, the Purchaser):

        (i) *Execution of the Agreement*: Both parties must sign the Agreement. . . . Seems straightforward, but you'd be surprised how many times one party signs an Agreement, then sends it out for countersignature but never receives the other party's John Hancock. Until you have both parties' signatures affixed (next to one another), you don't have a deal.

        (ii) *Chain of Title*: The Chain of Title is a series of legal documents that trace "ownership" and "right" back to a single source. For Jessica, as a newbie writer, she would have a copyright, a WGA registration form, and might have to present a written statement that she (and only she) produced the script (based upon an original idea derived from her own imagination), and that if any other party claims the work it is by pure coincidence. . . . Again, this is all to protect the party with the money (Purchaser) so that they can guarantee they're investing their money into something that no other entity might actually own (or litigate against) later on.

(b) *Entire Agreement*: Just because one sentence on page three could mean one thing, but another sentence on page four means the opposite, an arbitrator or lawyer will only be reading both sentences in context within the "entire Agreement," or how they related to the whole Agreement.

(c) *Notices*: All notices, statements, announcements, or any other form of correspondence must be in writing for it to be properly considered "received" in the legal world. . . . Therefore, here each party will be clearly required and responsible to keep the other party aware of any updates to their contact information. For instance, if Jessica moves apartments, she must inform Purchasing Production Company, and if Purchasing Production Company changes offices, they must notify not just Jessica, but all clients they're in business with. Although it's now assumed, there is usually a statement explaining that email notices are perfectly valid. (It's also important to keep the other party aware of any changes in address so that there's no hold-up with future payments either.)

(d) *Arbitration*: Things don't always go according to plan, and even the very best Agreements (that seemingly cover every conceivable issue) can occasionally be too vague or allow "open to interpretation" language. Rather than each party "lawyering up" and heading into a courtroom—which is extremely expensive across all fronts—they can simply arbitrate. In such instances, both parties would schedule an arbitration hearing, overseen by a single arbitrator, under the rules and regulations of the American Arbitration Association. Generally, it's stated that there will be only one hearing and that the determination of the Arbitrator (whichever side they deem to be "correct") will be final in the eyes of the law and on behalf of both parties.

(e) *Governing Law*: There will always be a listed location whereby the laws of this Agreement will be filtered through in the event of a dispute. Generally, these will be the State and City of the Purchasing party: "in accordance of the laws of the State of California, city of Los Angeles."

(f) *Relationship of the Parties*: In these Agreements, there will usually be a clause explaining that both parties are not forming any type of legal partnership. They are engaging in business on this particular occasion (with signatures affixed), but that does not in any way constitute nor guarantee continued business down the line. (In short, just because Jessica keeps writing scripts doesn't mean Purchasing Production Company will continue [or be obligated] to buy them). This protects both parties.

(g) *Publicity/Press Release(s)*: People like attention. . . . And in today's media-heavy world, just about any time anyone sneezes, they want to issue a press release or a public statement. In this case, it's a positive thing: "Purchasing Production Company Inks Deal with Newbie Jessica Screenwriter." Same for Jessica—she might have a following for previous works she's done (or she might turn into a well-known name in the future). Or, perhaps the movie is a runaway success. In any possible scenario, and for any possible reason, *if* either party wishes to mention this Agreement, the relationship, or the script, they must clear it with the other party. Nothing too formal, you just send over a copy of the announcement to the other party and allow them to proofread it and make any necessary changes.

(h) *Confidentiality*: Consider all the detailed terms in any Agreement like this completely confidential. Just like any job you take on, you shouldn't go around boasting how much you earned or how the financial structures are orchestrated. This clause is here to protect both parties. Maybe Purchasing Production Company is offering Jessica much more than they normally would for an "Option/Purchase Agreement." If so, they don't want that information leaked and have to deal with previous clients coming back to complain. Same with Jessica, maybe she'll take less money here and know she can hold out for more cash on a later deal with another company, after she's built a track record; meaning, if the financial terms of this deal were disclosed to other parties behind her back, she would lose some leverage. When in doubt, trust the classic saying: "Loose lips sink ships." Keep your mouth shut.

(i) *Force Majeure*: A French phrase found in all contracts describing things that are out of our control, like a flood, war, political protest, or any other unforeseen and unstoppable event.

(j) *Severability*: Jessica won't be able to escape this deal since there is no formal Exit Clause after a "Purchase." However, if a dispute were to ever lead to a formal Arbitration hearing and within that hearing the Arbitrator deemed any single portion of this Agreement to be "illegal" or otherwise "unenforceable," then that determination (due to the "Entire Agreement" clause above) would mean that the *entire* Agreement would be seen as illegal and unenforceable—which would essentially make this Agreement moot and worthless. This is rare, but nevertheless you'll see the language.

19. **<u>Agency</u>**: If Jessica has an agency representing her, this is where they'll wedge in their information so that it's clear any possible dollar (whether from Option Payments, Purchase Price, or even future Passive Payments, via Purchasing Production Company or any future entity it Assigns the rights of this deal over to), this agency will be entitled to its pre-negotiated cut. Jessica certainly doesn't need an agent to negotiate this Agreement. Even if she's unsure of how to approach it on her own, she can hire a lawyer for a one-time fee and have a professional handle the bulk of it . . . and if she chooses that route, the lawyer won't wedge in an ongoing cut. Nevertheless, there will usually be a statement addressing the agent or any third party representing Jessica's talents and Ownership. Also, if Jessica were to have entered this deal while under agency representation and later dissolved that relationship (even the day after this Agreement's signature date), her agent would still have his or her 10 percent claim on all future earnings.

And then both parties sign. . . .

AGREED AND ACCEPTED:	PURCHASING PRODUCTION
OWNER	COMPANY, LLC

By: _____

Name: Jessica Screenwriter
SSN: 123-45-6789

Its:

(Occasionally, this Agreement will be accompanied by what's referred to as a "Short Form Assignment" or "Instrument of Transfer." This is essentially a one-page document (that's notarized) stating clearly that the Owner (Jessica) is hereby and forever "Assigning" or "Transferring" the aforementioned rights to the Purchaser (Purchasing Production Company). Although this Agreement serves that purpose and even outlines all procedures, some companies who start this Agreement as an "Option" that then transitions into a "Purchase" (by any agreeable means), might therefore request the Assignment or Transfer at that time—to be exercised or requested by means of "Additional Deliverables.")

GLOSSARY

All the fancy (and confusing) phrases that get tossed around—and what they *really* mean.

AFM—Acronym for the American Film Market, an annual film market held each November in Santa Monica, CA.

Agent—Offers a service of writer representation in exchange for a 10 percent fee; brokers deals between the writer and producers/production companies for either commissioning their talents to write or negotiating the acquisition of their intellectual property. See also "Manager."

Arbitration—Arbitration is the process whereby two parties with a disagreement formally seek out a pre-vetted (and licensed) arbitrator to hear out both sides of their argument and grant him or her the authority to make a formal (and final) decision settling the disagreement. Organizations within the independent film world, such as the non-profit organization Independent Film & Television Alliance (IFTA), offer these services for reasonable rates.

Attachments—Actors, director(s), or other "elements" (e.g., composers, political organizations) who legally commit themselves to work on a project prior to, or during the process of, funding. This process is called "packaging" and is used to increase the value of a script (or property) in order to presell and/or raise funds for productions, therefore increasing the potential for a green light.

Backdoor Pilot—A gimmick used to introduce a new series or concept by making the series premiere or pilot feature-length, therefore making it capable of existing as a stand-alone TV movie if that pilot never transitions into a full-fledged series.

Backstory—The biography of each of your script's characters, which has helped shaped their (a) personal opinions and perspectives, (b) approach towards problem solving and decision making, and (c) has brought them into your story in the unique and interesting manner in which they arrive (and dictated how they can either help *or* hinder your protagonist). Backstories can also detail locations or other abstract aspects of your story. . . . But it essentially covers everything that's already happened that has led us to your page one.

Beat—A definitive moment of transition within a story (either for the overall story/plotline, or simply with a character during a given scene). It can be a moment conveying (verbally or non) a revelation or realization, or simply a character drawing a conclusion on what action he or she knows they must take.

Beat Sheet—A handy tool for screenwriters of any level, a beat sheet is a breakdown of the most common feature-film story beats needed to keep a strong character arch, a solid B-story, and a flowing plotline in motion—all while ensuring the action, risk, and intensity of whatever your protagonist is experiencing climaxes at all the right points for maximum audience (and reader) appeal. Some beat sheets offer as few as five to six beats, while others climb near twenty-five . . . regardless of your preferred style, it's a great way to keep your story on track.

Bible (or Series Bible)—A massive document, similar to a business plan or proposal, used to present the complete breakdown of a scripted television program; they generally flesh out all details regarding character, location, theme, concept, and tone. Most include at least the first season's full episode slate (with a detailed synopsis for each episode); many offer clear direction where the series will lead in future seasons. The bible is the filter that keeps all associated parties (i.e., showrunners, writers, and producers) on target.

Budget—The cost of a film production; the budget can be heavily inflated (or deflated) depending on who's asking (and who's telling). Regarding payouts, screenwriters generally receive the equivalent of 5 percent of the total (actual, out-of-pocket expenses) of the entire production's budget.

Cannes—Generally refers to the Cannes Film Festival (held each May in the small port city of Cannes, France); the city also hosts two international TV markets: the Marché Internationale de Programmes des Television, translated simply into Market of International Programs of Television, but generally referred to as MIPTV (April) and the Marché Internationale de Programmes des Communications, translated simply into Market of International Programs of Communications, but generally referred to as MIPCOM (October). I would argue that 90% of those attending these "MIP" markets have never heard the formal names, they only use the acronyms to describe them.

Cliché—The obvious, the dull, and the predictable. A cliché is the script, plot, or scene that offers nothing unique or interesting. There was a time when its idea or concept was groundbreaking, but it has become overused to the point where it has lost its spark and/or original meaning. A good rule of thumb is knowing that generally your first idea for a scene is also everyone else's first idea (making it clichéd and predictable), therefore a good approach is to do the exact opposite of the clichéd idea to shake things up a bit and keep them interesting.

Colored Pages—With each revision, a script (or sometimes just revised pages) is printed on different colored paper so that production teams can easily know if they have the latest version. The colors follow this order: White, blue, pink, yellow, green, gold, then back to white.

Consider—The second most powerful word, before "recommend," that a reader or assistant development team member can use to rank either your writing talents or your spec script. Even if your script is not recommended, your talents as a writer can be (see "Coverage").

Coverage—A simple two to three-page breakdown or synopsis of a submitted screenplay, which is drafted by a reader, specifically with the goal of summarizing not just the story, but also the worthiness of the submission (and of its writer) for the upper-level development executives. Both the script and writer are given one of three rankings: pass, consider, or recommend. The important thing for newbie writers to remember is that it's very hard to sell a spec script, but that even if a script submission receives a "pass," the writer can still be given a ranking of "consider" (which is sometimes more important when building a career).

Credit—Refers to how a writer's name is listed (if at all) during the credits of a film. The Writers Guild of America (WGA) has very specific rules as to how a writer's name is treated with regards to being given credit for writing or cowriting the script (or if considered only responsible for the story), and so on. These rules also dictate situations where two writers collaborated together on a script (where their names are unified with an ampersand, as in "Written by Writer One & Writer Two"), or when a script is acquired by a production team and a new writer is assigned for a rewrite, but both the original and new writer deserve equal credit (where their names are unified, only with the word "and" to signify a separation of responsibilities, as in "Written by Writer One and Writer Two"). Even non-WGA signatory companies follow these general guidelines when assigning screenwriting credit.

Development Hell—A joking expression used to describe the (sometimes endless) process of getting a spec script of interest from initial acquisition to green light. Sometimes these scripts are constantly revised during their development periods in order to satisfy different investors, other times the company keeps the script as is, but must take a long period of time in order to secure proper funding for the films eventual production. Some films never get out of development hell; others float through very easily.

Direct to [blank]—A phrase used to describe an independent film or production specifically designed *not* to exhibit in theatres. Films or productions can be produced as "direct to video," "direct to TV," and now, "direct to VOD." These are targeted, middle-zone productions, generally with limited budgets and heavy on genre appeal. . . . These are also excellent starting places as a newbie writer! Most "direct-to-[blank]" films are produced from gold-mine genre types.

Driver—A high-level film or project (either completed or in development) that gives a seller or distributor leverage to lace additional titles (usually of lesser quality) into the package. Sometimes called a "locomotive."

Domestic—The word used to describe the territory (or geographic market-place) of the United States of America and *English-speaking* Canada (also called "North America"). In the film industry, anything outside of this above definition would refer to the international marketplace (even geographically North American places like French-speaking Canada or Mexico). For more information, see also "International" and "Territory" below.

Dubs—Verbalized translations of spoken dialogue taking place within a film for purposes of adapting a film for a foreign-speaking audience.

Elements—See "Attachments" above.

Episodic—The word used in contracts to classify a program as composed of multiple episodes in total duration, as opposed to a single one-off feature film. The exact running time of each episode differs on genre and platform (from ninety-minute episodes in a long-running episodic mini-series, forty-two-minute episodes for a dramatic series with ad breaks, down to five to ten-minute episodes for an online Web series). The total number of episodes will also depend on genre, platform, and longevity. (Compare to "Feature").

Extension—When an option agreement is extended by the person or company optioning the script—generally for an additional fee, most commonly because the project is packaged and very close to being green-lit but just needs more time. Extension periods vary, but six months would be an average.

Feature—The word used in contracts to classify the length of a film or program as a one-off production that is movie length. The exact running time of a feature differs by genre (and depending on whom you ask), so the word 'feature' is often used to simply indicate movie length. (Compare to "Episodic").

First Draft—After general storylines and treatments are approved, a screenwriter will apply these scattered ideas into a rough draft, which is then cleaned up into a full-on first draft of the script, which stands as the first fully realized version of a screenplay encompassing all involved parties' ideas and criticisms.

Green Light—The coined phrase signifying the official moment when the party representing necessary financial resources agrees to produce (invest in) a project. When a project is green-lit can vary wildly—projects can be green-lit with or without a completed script, a locked cast, or even an attached production crew.

Gross Points (or "Gross Royalties")—A point is equal to 1 percent; "gross" refers to all monies (in total) earned *before* expenses or outside costs are incurred against that figure. Therefore, a single gross point is 1 percent of all monies earned, which is a far contrast from the commonly distributed "Net Point" (see below).

High-Concept—An overly thrown-around phrase that essentially describes a film or TV concept that is extremely straightforward and easy to describe (does not mean big budget, but rather that within a few words of pitching your audience will have a very clear understanding of your project).

Home Entertainment—A generic phrase used to describe the various rights (or various methods) by which a customer can view a film or TV program in any conceivable personal manner (whether purchased or rented) outside of viewership in theatres, paid public exhibitions, or on commercial airplanes, hotels, or commercial cruise liners.

Hook—The unique—and often simple—aspect of a story that makes it stand out from another. It's the glue that transforms a dull idea into an extraordinary one, that gives it competitive edge to distributors and "sell-ability" to audiences.

Independent—Refers to any company or film production that exists outside of the major studios. Can range from tiny micro-budget operations to major Hollywood entities (e.g., Lionsgate or Relativity).

International—The word used to describe any country or region outside of the United States of America and *English-speaking* Canada when defining geographical rights definitions in film-industry contracts. Divisions between domestic and international markets are vital in the presales process, which has major influence on which scripts receive green lights. For more information, see also "Domestic" and "Territory."

Letter of Intent (LOI)—A formal means for one entity to express a (generally) legally binding interest in working with another party. It essentially functions as a "proof of commitment" in moving forward with a formal agreement *if* all the elements required to enforce a functional deal come together. Example: To presell a movie, a distributor might secure a name actor with a letter of intent; if the distributor moves forward with the production, that actor will be required to take on their agreed to role, however if the pieces don't come together and no film is green-lit, the actor is not required to perform (and the distributor is not required to pay them).

Locomotive—A high-level film or project (either completed or in development) that gives a seller or distributor leverage to lace additional titles (usually of lesser quality) into the package. Sometimes called a "Driver."

Logline—A short descriptive sentence (less than 100 words); it quickly summarizes a script's (or story's) concept, while clearly defining its genre type and overall hook.

Manager—The objective of a manager is to shape the longer-term direction of a writer's overall career. Unlike an agent—whose objective is on the more immediate, easy to close deals—a manager aids a writer in mapping out a course of action and helps build their portfolio to max out success. They are harder to obtain than an agent, but offer more time and guidance—recommendations via friends is the best approach to find one. Some work on a retainer basis, others work on commission. See also "Agent."

Net Points (or Net Royalties)—A point is equal to 1 percent; "net" refers to the monies left over after all other parties owed money (and after all expenses incurred) have been paid out or recouped—essentially all the leftover cash. Therefore, a single net point is 1 percent of all the leftover money, which is a fraction of a gross point.

Non-Union—Refers to a production or a potential project that is being produced independent of any unions. For an actor, the project would be independent of SAG (meaning any SAG actors could not perform). For a writer, the project would be independent of the WGA (meaning any WGA member could not write). Crew-related unions, such as IATSE, do allow their members to work on both union and non-union productions—an IATSE member joining a production he or she knew to be non-union would be doing so on the understanding that his or her day rate might be less than on union productions and that standard working hours might be different.

One-Sheet—A small sales sheet, generally an 8½″ x 11″ mini-poster, that is handed to clients to provide insight to the cast, genre, and budget level of a film. It would look almost like DVD cover art (front and back), only on a sheet of paper for easy filing and reference.

Option (or Option Purchase)—An option is when all rights to a script are leased by a producer, generally for an upfront fee and for a period between six to eighteen months. During this option period, the producer will pitch the film to investors or attempt to package the script in order to get a green light from a production company. If the script is green-lit and the film is produced, the writer will generally receive a production bonus—pre-negotiated in the initial option agreement. If the script is not green-lit, upon expiration of the option period, all rights will revert back to the writer.

Output Deal—An agreement between two parties where one entity agrees to take on all (or a confirmed minimum number) of produced content (finished films, scripts, etc.) for a pre-negotiated price. Example: I'm a producer and I've just secured an output deal with a client in Japan. . . . Because I have proof that this Japanese client will buy any film I produce for a fixed (pre-negotiated) price, I can use this as collateral when raising funds with investors (so that I can hire writers and produce the new films).

Packaging—The process of making a script a more attractive property by "attaching" actors, directors, or other elements who contractually commit themselves to work on the project if it were to be funded or green-lit.

Pass—The ranking that readers or creative executives give to a script (or writer) they feel does not meet minimum criteria worthy of "consider."

Pitch—The presentation of your script's story; can be verbalized or written (as in a pitch email), but it's generally a short, concise explanation identifying genre type and concept.

Pilot—A fully produced sample episode of a proposed TV series, generally made as a one-off example to present to studio executives or international clients to gauge interest. If the series is green-lit, the pilot is generally broadcast as the first episode. See also "Backdoor Pilot."

Polish—At first glance, this would be a simple clean-up job requested of a screenwriter, but a polish can at times walk a fine line to that of a full-on rewrite! The idea of a polish is for the initial author of the script (or a commissioned third party) to tighten, fine tune, and tweak key sequences to really make the script flow. . . . But sometimes the instructions they're given are lengthier than the screenplay itself; as a novice writer, be mentally prepared to tackle a rewrite if offered a "simple polish."

Production Bonus—A predetermined amount of money guaranteed to the screenwriter if their script is green-lit and production commences. This amount is calculated in advance within the writer's initial option agreement or contract.

Purchase (or a Preemptive Purchase)—When a producer or production company purchases all rights to a script, in advance of packaging or financing. Though rarely done, the purchase is generally a one-time lump sum payment, and the writer revokes all rights to the script into perpetuity. Studios and large media companies sometimes employ this technique to weed out potential competition.

Readers—The individuals hired to actually read all those unsolicited spec script submissions so that the higher-ups in the company don't have to. Their real objective is to summarize each script into a two to three page synopsis called "coverage," in which they'll also list out their general impressions (or criticisms) of the submission, then assign both the script and its writer with a ranking of "pass," "consider," or "recommend." Readers come from all kinds of backgrounds, some hold masters degrees and are looking to transition their professional careers into creative development, others are still in school and are looking for an "easy" internship that gives them class credit instead of money. As a screenwriter, you never know what type of reader will be assigned your script.

Recommend—The most powerful ranking a reader can bestow upon a spec script (or its writer). It essentially places a submission into a production company's "fast lane" of review. Very few writers (and even fewer scripts) ever receive this coveted ranking. For more details, check out "Coverage."

Rewrites—Usually paid, but sometimes not, rewrites are formal changes or revisions to a screenplay requested by a development executive or producer of the screenwriter. Generally, these are labor intensive (to the point of starting from scratch) otherwise they would be considered "polishes." On some occasions the original writer is commissioned for the job of rewrites, other times the job can be handed to a third-party writer.

Schlock—Extremely low-quality product, generally ultra-low budget films with very poor image and sound quality (sometimes purposefully, other times due to a filmmaker's lack of resources).

Screener—A non-commercial copy of a completed (or near finished) film, intended only for the purposes of a professional to evaluate. Screeners can be handed out as physical DVDs (with a "burn-in" on screen to prevent piracy) or as online screening links (with password protection).

Screening(s)—Scheduled premieres or private showings of a finished (or near finished) film; can be used to (a) present a completed film for potential distributor representation, (b) for a distributor to present a film to international clients, (c) to seek out additional funds, or (d) any other conceivable business motivation.

Services (Writing Services)—The process of writing is considered a "service," much like that of any independent contractor. In agreements dealing with the acquisition or option of a completed script, or during the commission of a writer to create a script-made-to-order, the word "services" is associated with the writer's job responsibilities.

Showrunner—The true king of the television world, a showrunner outranks even the director! Part executive producer, story doctor, and visionary, the showrunner is a jack-of-all trades that is generally waist-deep in a series' writing process, its scheduling, and its overall conceptual flow. They represent the single voice that guarantees the studio or production company financially responsible for the program gets exactly what they're expecting.

Sizzle Reel—A condensed version of a feature-length film, specifically used to entice a buyer or consumer to transact upon the film (either for pre-sale purposes at the development level or for pre-sale purposes at the consumer level). A trailer or 'preview' is a sales tool, where as a Sizzle Reel readily gives away themes, plots, reveals, etc.

Spec Script—A screenplay—either for feature-length content or episodic content—which is voluntarily written without any upfront payment, client request, or contractual obligation. A writer conceives of an original idea and writes a script from scratch with the hope of selling it later, upon completion. (A writer may also voluntarily acquire the rights to a story or book and write an adapted screenplay on spec based upon that material.)

Step Deal—A layered screenwriting agreement in which the hiring entity (producer or production company) either (1) acquires a writer's script with the intention of keeping the writer on board to furnish new drafts, or (2) commissions the writer's talents with the express purpose of shaping and developing a project together. The overall agreement is for a pre-negotiated amount of money, but the pay-outs of that lump sum are divided by the writer's completion of each step in the deal. The total number of steps equals the number of permissible drafts or materials to be commissioned:

One Step Deal—The writer is hired to produce a workable treatment or initial first draft.

Two Step Deal—The writer is hired to produce a workable first draft and will stay on board to rework the script into a workable second draft.

Three Step Deal—The same process as above, only additional drafts or materials are tacked on. There is no limit to the number of steps. And once each step is accomplished, the writer receives a portion of their overall payment . . . On that note, the writer's duties can also be terminated at any point in the process. (For more explanation, see "Appendix II: The Non-Union Writer-for-Hire Agreement.")

Subtitles—Written text detailing dialogue and descriptive text indicating audio sounds (crucial to the storyline), or translations of foreign written visual text applied on screen as a burn-in, running parrellel with the dialogue, sounds, and actions taking place within the film. Some international territories utilize Subtitles rather than Dubs (China's Mandarin is written the same throughout the country, however the spoken dialect varies greatly from one region to another; the Middle East is made of over twenty countries, all use the same written Arabic, but each has a radically different verbal use of the language).

Territory—"Territory" is a distribution term, used to describe a country (or often a group of countries) that are commonly accepted to represent a geographical region where the rights to a film can be licensed. On one hand, the individual nations of Poland or Japan represent a territory, but so does the Middle East, which is made up of over twenty individual countries. For more information, see also "Domestic" and "International."

Treatment—A double-spaced outline of a story concept (ranging from a few pages to dozens, lacking any dialogue) that is used by a writer to present his/her ideas to a production team to ensure it meets their needs prior to attempting a first draft of a screenplay.

Turn-Around—The process after a script is purchased, where the writer attempts to re-acquire (purchase back) the rights previously signed away.

WGA—Acronym for the Writers Guild of America, a labor union that sets industry ground rules on writer credits, fees, and royalties; members can use the WGA for arbitration. Non-members can submit treatments and/or drafts of writings to be "registered" (for a fee). For detailed information (including boilerplates of many writer-related contracts and forms), check out their website: www.wga.org.

WGAe—Writers Guild of America East (offices located in New York).

WGAw—Writers Guild of America West (offices located in Los Angeles).

WGA Signatory—A production company, or other similar entity, that has signed an agreement with the Writers Guild of America (WGA) and is therefore required to hire only writers who are current Guild members. Under such an agreement, working with or commissioning works from any non-Guild member would be a breach of contract worthy of a stiff fine.

INDEX

acquisitions agents 8, 25, 98
acquisitions assistants 106
acquisitions executives 6, 17, 91, 106
acquisitions process 6–8
acting classes 101
action films: budget issues 47; guidelines for 44–7; introduction to 41–2; real-world examples 47; storylines related to 42–3; unbalancing element of 43–4
adventure films: budget issues 48; guidelines for 50–1; introduction to 48; producers and distributors and 48; real-world examples 52; storylines related to 48–50
agents: commission and fees and 120–1; defined 175; introduction to 115; myths about signing with 115–19; networking and 107; producers and distributors and 117–18; screenwriters and 115–21; television writing and 116; when to hire 119
agreements: option 158–73; types of 126–8; writer-for-hire 145–57
Alien (1979) 37, 38, 61
alternative television *see* non-scripted tv
Amazing Race, The (tv show) 77
American Film Market (AFM) 103, 175
American Pavilion program 103
analysis paralysis syndrome 12
animation writing 82
Arachnoquake (2012) 41
arbitration 154, 171, 173, 175, 183
attachments, defined 175

Bachelor, The (tv show) 77
backdoor pilot 92–3, 175, 181
backstory 59, 175–6
bad dialogue 63
Band of Brothers (2001) 71, 84
beat 62, 65, 176
beat sheet 98, 176
bible (business plan) 82, 93, 176
Big Bang Theory, The (tv show) 79
Black Dog (1998) 43
Blob, The (1958) 41
Blood of Redemption (2013) 47
Border Run (2012) 47
Bork, Erik 71, 84, 90
Breaking Bad (tv show) 80, 81
Bring It On (2000) 62
budgets: action films 47; adventure films 48; announced and actual 18–19; defined 176; for indie titles 133

call-out clauses 134
Cannes Film Festival 11, 103, 104, 176
Christmas Colt, The (2013) 31
cliché 61, 63, 66, 176–7
colored pages, defined 177
comedies 24–7, 78
commission and fees 120–1
commissioned script 125, 129
consider ranking 56, 58, 61, 177
contract negotiations 11, 115, 117–18
coverage, defined 177
Creative Mind Group 103–4

creature features: description of 37; guidelines for 38–41; real-world examples 41; subtext and 37–8
credits of a film, defined 177
crime stoppers, storylines related to 49–50

deal structures 126, 128
Delta Force 2: The Colombian Connection (1990) 42
descriptive blocks 66
development hell, defined 177
dialogue blocks 63, 67, 141
digital realm 132–4
directors of development, making first contact with 106–7
"Direct-to" entertainment 6, 13, 19, 177–8
distribution executives *see* producers and distributors
District 9 (2009) 37
documents *see* forms and documents
"dog films" 28, 31
domestic territory, defined 178
don't take my baby thriller 32
Double Jeopardy (1999) 32
draft date 141, 142
Dragon Wasps (2012) 41
drama: format and structure of 82; as a genre 24; real-world examples 34; spec script for 78
driver, defined 178
dubs, defined 178, 183
DVD/VOD distribution 16, 27, 29, 31

elements, defined 175
email communication, making first contact with 108
entry points: description of 86; gag writing 86–8; office assistant 89–91; showrunner hand-off and 93; staff writing assistant 88–9
episodic program 178, 182
Escape from New York (1981) 43, 45
European Film Market 104
everyday hero, storylines related to 43
Expendables 2, The (2012) 42
extension, defined 178
extra, working as an 104–5

face-to-face communication 108–9
family Christmas dog adventure: demand for 28; guidelines for 29–31; producers and distributors and 29; real-world examples 31
family-safe tween romance: description of 34; guidelines for 35–7; producers and distributors and 34–5; real-world examples 37
f-bombs 40, 47
feature, defined 178
Ferris Bueller's Day Off (1986) 62
filler movie 7
film commissions, volunteering for 104
film making *see* movie production and distribution
film markets, volunteering for 102–4
films, drafting posters for 17
financing issues: green-light project 13; independent film makers and 12–14; presales and 17–19
finished movie, pitching of 15
first draft 126, 154, 178
Forced Vengeance (1982) 42
forms and documents: introduction to 139; script coverage 140–4
Friends (tv show) 79, 81
From the Earth to the Moon (1998) 71, 90

Gabe the Cupid Dog (2012) 31
gag writing 86–8
genre: choosing the right 23–4; comedy 24–6; drama 24; the good, the bad, and the ugly 24–7; scripts with mixed 60; *see also* gold-mine genre types
gold-mine demographics 79–81
gold-mine genre types: action film 41–7; adventure film 48–52; backdoor pilot and 92–3; continuing writing 91–2; creature feature 37–41; family Christmas dog adventure 28–31; as high-concept films 52–3; as safest go-to genres 134; tween romance 34–7; universal appeal for 53–4; woman-in-peril thriller 31–4
green-light project: defined 178; before final script 14; financing of 13
Grey, The (2011) 39
Grey's Anatomy (tv show) 81

gross points, defined 179
guaranteed placement concept: output deals and 10–11; presales and 11–12

hedging system: Hollywood system and 9–10; independent film makers and 13
high-concept films 52–3, 179
Hollywood pitch fests 101–2
Hollywood schmooze game *see* networking
Hollywood system: acquisitions process and 6–8; analysis paralysis syndrome and 12; biggest secret of 14–15; budgets and 18–19; catch-22 of 20–1; guaranteed placement concept and 10–12; hedge effect and 9–10; Hollywood hierarchy and 6; independent film makers and 12–14; pitching finished movie in 15; presales and 15–18; spec scripts and 8–9; writers and 21–2
Home Alone (1991) 50
home entertainment market 13, 41, 48, 133, 179
hook, defined 179
horror scripts 52
hostage-taking, storylines related to 42–3
House of Cards (tv show) 81
How I Met Your Mother (tv show) 77, 80, 86
How Not To Write A Screenplay: 101 Common Mistakes Most Screenwriters Make (Flinn) 66
Hulu 14, 15, 34, 76

idiot dialogue 63–4, 101
improv groups 100–1
Independent Film & Television Alliance (IFTA) 103
Independent Hollywood/independents: acquisitions process and 6–8; defined 179; digital realm and 133–4; financing issues 12–14; introduction to 6; *see also* producers and distributors
"insider info" approach 3
international market, defined 179
intern-level readers *see* readers
Invasion U.S.A. (1985) 42
Invictus (2009) 54
It Came From Outer Space (1953) 41

Jaws (1975) 37
Jinxed (2013) 37
joke writers 86–8
Junior High Spy (2011) 52

kidnapping, storylines related to 42–3
kids programming 81

Law and Order: SVU (tv show) 81
letter of intent (LOI) 127, 179
line producers, role of 68–70
literary purchase 127
locomotive project, defined 179
logline, defined 179

managers: defined 180; screenwriters and 120
marketing trends, innovative 133–4
message boards, finding opportunities through 123–4
middle-aged Americans demographics 80–1
Monster Mutt (2011) 52
movie production and distribution: budget issues 18–19; hedge effect and 9–10

Nelson, Donie 71–2, 99
Netflix 6–7, 14, 25–6, 65
net points, defined 180
networking: delivering fresh content and 98; having target portfolio for 98–100; honing skills for 100–2; importance of image during 111–12; introduction to 94–5; meeting needs of the industry and 97–8; meeting right people for 112; myth of going to the top for 105–6; navigating reception's desk for 108; preparing for 96–100; principles for 95–6; self-confidence issues 100; soft pitches for 96–7; timing the marketplace for 109; voluntary 102–5
newbie writers: agents and 116, 119; digital realm and 134; non-scripted tv and 86; spec scripts and 77; *see also* screenwriter/screenwriting

Nielsen ratings 79
Nightmare Nanny, The (2013) 34
non-scripted tv: description of 76–7;
    entry points for 86–92
non-union option agreements: defined
    125, 180; introduction to 158–9;
    section-by-section description of
    160–73; story theft and 130
non-union projects 129, 180
non-union writer-for-hire agreement:
    agents and 119; certificate of
    authorship 156; deal structures and
    128; introduction to 139, 145; net
    profits definitions 157; section-by-
    section description of 145–50; terms
    and conditions 151–5
Notes on a Scandal (2006) 32

Office, The (tv show) 79
office assistant position 89–91
one-sheet, defined 180
one step deal, defined 183
option agreements *see* non-union option
    agreements
"other movies" 6, 7, 8
Outbreak (1995) 37, 38, 39
output deals 10, 180

packaging, defined 180
parallel lines 68
pass ranking 56, 58, 181
personal assistant, Hollywood decision
    makers and 89–91
PG-13 scripts 40
pilot episodes 78, 80, 82–5, 92
pitch meeting: asking for 109–10;
    following up after 111; as an informal
    meeting 110–11; *see also* networking
point system 129
polish job 63, 90, 148, 181
Pop Star (2013) 37
preemptive purchase, defined 181
presales: financing issues and 17–19;
    guaranteed placement concept and
    11–12; reverse engineering and 15–18
producers and distributors: adventure
    films and 48; agents and 117–18;
    family Christmas dog adventure
    and 28–9; making first contact with
    106–8; presales and 11–12; script

coverage form and 143–4; tween
    romance and 34–5; woman-in-peril
    thriller and 31
production bonus, defined 181
Puncture Wounds (2014) 47
purchase agreement 158–73, 181

query letter 108–9

Rambo (2008) 44, 46
readers: defined 181; making their job
    easier 58; script coverage form and
    140–4; scripts reading and ranking by
    56–7
reality TV 76, 89
reboots and remakes 6, 10, 12, 149–50
recommend ranking 56, 58, 181
reverse engineering, presales and 15–18
rewrites, defined 181–2
romantic comedies 25
R-rated scripts and films 40, 47

sales teams, making first contact with
    107
Sam Steele and the Junior Detective Agency
    (2009) 52
*Save the Cat: The Last Screenwriting Book
    You'll Ever Need* (Snyder) 63, 65
schlock, defined 182
Scoot & Kassie's Christmas Adventure
    (2013) 31
screener, defined 182
screening(s), defined 182
*Screenplay: The Foundations of
    Screenwriting* (Field) 63
screenwriter/screenwriting: agents
    and 115–21; agreements for 126–8;
    being branded as a 99; catch-22 of
    Hollywood and 20–1; commission
    and fees and 120–1; contract
    negotiations and 11, 115; demand
    for 135; entrepreneurial aspect of
    121–2; evaluating strengths and
    weaknesses of 56; getting paid for
    124–6, 128; getting started for 135–7;
    hardest part about 55; having L.A.
    experience for 131; hedge effect and
    9–10; introduction to 1–4; inventing
    your own opportunities for 122–3;
    managers and 120; message board

123–4; movie budget issues and 19; non-union productions and 129; persistence for 136–7; script coverage form for 140–4; self-motivation for 137–8; story theft and 130–1; success of being a 5; *see also* networking; spec scripts

script consultants 70–1

script coverage form: introduction to 140–1; section-by-section description of 141–4

Secret World of Alex Mack, The (1994–1998) 36

self-motivation 137–8

series bible 82, 93, 176

series idea, developing your own 78–9

Sexting in Suburbia (2012) 34

Sharknado (2013) 41

Shooter (2007) 44, 45

showrunner, defined 182

sitcoms: comic writers for 78; format and structure of 82; storylines related to 79

6 Bullets (2012) 47

sizzle reel, defined 182

slap-stick humor 26

Sleeping with the Enemy (1991) 32

Snakes on a Plane (2006) 61

spec scripts: for action films 41–7; for adventure films 48–52; blessing and curse of writing 83; character names' issues 59; conclusion about 73–4; consistent point of view 62; convincing producers by 22; for creature features 37–41; defined 182; for family Christmas dog adventure 28–31; finalizing 66–8; getting feedback for 70–2; having a gut instinct about 72–3; having fun with 66; Hollywood system and 8–9; with idiot dialogue 63–4; keeping facts straight 59–60; length of 58–9; line producers and 68–70; with mixed genres 60; with no hook 61–2; parallel lining 68; with poor structure 62–3; purpose of 8, 9; quick turnaround for 20; reading and ranking of 56–7; risk of too many ideas for 81–2; sample 77–83; scenes with dilemmas and decisions and 67; screening

festivals and 113; things readers hate about 58–65; to-the-point writing style for 60–1; tween romance 34–7; with typos and errors 64–5; for woman-in-peril thriller 31–4; writing clear-cut 57

Spy Kids (2001) 48

staff writers: description of 75; joke writers and 86–7; writing assistant for 88–9

stalker ex thriller 31–2

step deal 120, 121, 125, 126, 182–3

Stolen Child (2012) 34

storylines: related to action films 42–3; related to adventure films 48–50; related to crime stoppers 49–50; related to everyday hero concept 43; related to hostage-taking concept 42–3; related to kidnapping concept 42–3; related to sitcoms 79

story theft 130–1

studio movies 7, 10, 11

studios: analysis paralysis syndrome and 12; financing issues for 13–14

submission release agreement 127, 130

subtext, creature features and 37–8

subtitles 24, 25, 183

talent agents 115–16

target portfolio 98–100

Teach Yourself Screenwriting (Frensham) 63

television and VOD platforms 25, 27, 34, 76, 77

television writing: agents and 116; backdoor pilot and 92–3; breaking in to 75–6; catch-22 of 85–6; entry points into 86–92; getting feedback about 83–4; gold-mine demographics for 79–81; holding onto 84–5; judgment of 83; spec script for 77–83; type of 78; where to begin 76–7

territory, defined 183

terrorism, storylines related to 42

That 70's Show (tv show) 77

3 Holiday Tails (2011) 31

three step deal 126, 183

3 Times a Charm (2011) 37

top secret spy adventure, storylines related to 48–9

transactional video on demand (TVOD) 34, 133
treasure hunters, storylines related to 50
treatment, defined 183
Tremors (1990) 38, 39
turn-around process, defined 183
TV series 82, 84, 89, 92
TV spec script *see* television writing
tween-themed programming 81
Two and a Half Men (tv show) 80, 81
two step deal, defined 183

UCLA Extension classes 84

VOD platforms 25, 27, 34, 76, 77
Voice, The (tv show) 77

Walking Tall (2004) 43
WGA signatory, defined 184
Wheel of Fortune (tv show) 77

woman-in-peril thriller: description of 31; guidelines for 33–4; producers and distributors and 31; real-world examples 34; types of 31–3
writer-for-hire agreement 119, 128, 139, 145–57
writers *see* screenwriter/screenwriting
writer's employment agreements 127–8
writers' groups 72
Writers Guild of America 85, 128–9, 183–4
Writer's Store classes 84
writing assistant 88–9
writing coverage process 56
writing services, defined 182

Xtinction: Predator X (2010) 41

Your Script Sucks!: 100 Ways to Make it Better (Akers) 66

ABOUT THE AUTHOR

Scott Kirkpatrick is a film and television distribution and development executive. He lives in Los Angeles with his wife and daughter.